LIVE
FOR THE DAY

ROD NEWBOLT-YOUNG

ryelands

First published in Great Britain in 2017

British Library Cataloguing-in-Publication Data
A CIP record for this title is available from the British Library

ISBN 978 1 906551 44 5

RYELANDS
Halsgrove House,
Ryelands Industrial Estate,
Bagley Road, Wellington, Somerset TA21 9PZ
Tel: 01823 653777   Fax: 01823 216796
email: sales@halsgrove.com

Part of the Halsgrove group of companies
Information on all Halsgrove titles is available at: www.halsgrove.com

Printed and bound by Parksons Graphics, India

Contents

Foreword

As his younger brother, I was delighted when asked to write this Foreword about the author. Ironically, having served 38 years in HM Forces I feel that by comparison I have led a more sheltered life than him; indeed, I have to say I've benefited from the various experiences that have shaped his life and have often thought 'Whatever happens I'm not going down that route' or 'I'll have a go at that, it's very appealing'. Yes, for me at least, truth does lie behind the thought that the younger sibling has it easier than the elder one. Having read through these 50 'episodes' or chapters, not only did I find out more about my brother, but I also now appreciate that a number of 'his events' have helped to influence my own path, but that's another story.

Suffice it to say from toddler to senior citizen the author does not roll over easily and is always ready to make a challenge when he senses injustice; I suspect that most who read this book will come to the same conclusion. Of more relevance is that where he has taken up an issue he has nearly, if not always won, and that's an incredible record. It characterises someone whose radar for right or wrong is well tuned, a man with integrity, patience and energy to the point where he could be accused of being tiresome! But following this approach has enabled him to manage a successful family farming business, become a skilful single-handed yachtsman for over 45 years and got involved with a number of extreme pursuits in his youth.

These personality traits have carried the writer through life in such an extraordinary, exciting and some might argue, hap-hazard way. No matter how it's viewed, he has a story to tell and he does so here in a very open and, when appropriate, humorous way. Above all, behind the tough veneer is a thoughtful and loving family man, whose commitment sets a fine example to those who follow in his wake.

Whether family, friend or simply curious this is a good read.

Simon, the younger brother.

Acknowledgements

Motivation for writing this autobiography has stemmed from medical disorders that have 'clipped my wings' requiring me to change my way of life and becoming more desk bound.

I have also been faced with the real possibility of death at any time as was made quite clear to me by one of the support nurses that care for me.

I started telling my stories to friends who listened with interest and some reckoned that they were actually inspiring at times. I was asked to write my book as my life was quite a story with the question always being asked: 'Why'?

It was often joked that the reason for my survival to date was so that I could get my biography published so I started writing along with researching which I found fascinating.

My brother Simon and a great friend of the family, Lyndy, were a tremendous support reading through all 50 of the chapters as they emerged. There were times however when my proof readers strongly suggested that perhaps I should not think of putting certain facts in print. So be it

I would also wish to thank my wife, Elizabeth and my five 'daughters' for all the backing they have offered not only in assistance for producing this book but at times for the physical help they offered such as driving me into hospital with a severed artery and so on. Without exception there was not at any time panic, and following admissions to hospital there were countless visits. I have been unbelievably supported.

Rod Newbolt-Young
June 2017

Introduction

It is hoped that the reader may come to their own conclusion on 'why' and that they enjoy this account of my exploits. One thing for sure is the fact that one should never give up physically or mentally as it is an important part of survival and this is the story of my survival journey since 1956.

I now live on Dartmoor in Devon, U.K. where the family have been farming and operating a tourist business since 1962 from our lovely old property. I am married to Elizabeth and have five daughters. My youngest daughter has now taken on the business with her husband so I presently have time being semi retired to write. My main hobby is sailing, mainly single handed, in an old 28 ft yacht that is featured within this biography.

I was named after an uncle who was a tea planter in Burma. He died whilst fighting the Japanese in 1944 aged twenty-eight.

Mother and father had been married before as was often typical of wartime marriages. From photos obtained it looked an austere wedding. However this resulted in my birth in 1948 in Germany where mother and father were stationed at the time. Three years later in 1951 my younger brother Simon was born. He went on to become a prominent soldier reaching the rank of brigadier.

I never met my paternal grandmother as she died of septicemia in 1936 following a wasp sting to her upper lip. My grandfather was a tall man with long swept back grey hair and striking blue eyes. He was a distinguished soldier reaching the rank of an Army brigadier.

Mother had two sisters who I remember as being elegant and attractive. Elsa lived in Spain and Marcella, who was married to a wealthy successful South African businessman, lived in Johannesburg, South Africa. She also had one brother, Desmond, who served in the Special Boat Service during the war.

My maternal grandmother was an elegant beautiful woman even during her final years. She had a good sense of humour and lived her later life with Desmond in Hampshire. I did not know my mother's father who I believe owned a plantation in Jamaica.

It is interesting to note that my paternal grandfather, father and younger brother were brigadiers in the British Army. I once proudly explained this to an American lady and she replied that I was obviously from a family of warriors. This was an interesting observation although I did point out the fact that I only reached the rank of Lieutenant, the lowest Army officer rank, to be informed that I was obviously a brave young warrior.

This book is based on true facts and incidents that did actually occur. However imagination has been used in places to cover 'The Fog of Time' and to make it more interesting for the reader.

The question 'why' I have survived is often asked and the response is diffi-cult to explain if at all possible. I have always enjoyed 'sailing close to the wind' with life-taking risks that many would not contemplate. Was it foolhardiness, Sod's Law, bad luck, being in the wrong place at the wrong time? Could it have been possible that the events contained in these pages were simply unavoidable, an act of God, that was managed correctly resulting in the survival of the author?

I have been dealt my fair share of challenges, being now diagnosed with an 'unusually aggressive cancer', severe heart failure and further cardiac complications. This is not to mention the fact that my left ankle has collapsed due to previous injuries, which has partially immobilized me.

Despite all this, I am content with life, taking this and whatever comes next as a challenge to be defeated. I have always been grateful for what I have and do not complain for what I have not got.

It has been stated a number of times that perhaps there is a reason for this survival and maybe that reason could be this book. I am a believer that a negative will always produce a positive and the positive in this case is my writing as undoubtedly my wings have now been clipped. Perhaps this story could even be an inspiration to others facing challenges in their lives.

The author would like to thank the Good Lord and all those who have saved and supported him with particular gratitude to his family and friends who have at times made an extensive effort to assist.

Chapter 1

Fastnet Sailing Race - 1979 The Start

The Rolex Fastnet Race covers a distance of some 608 miles from Cowes on The Isle of Wight to The Fastnet Rock off Southern Ireland finishing in Plymouth. It is normally held very other year in August.

Little did I know what I was about to experience with this race that was my third Fastnet event. The following account was written shortly after the rescue so as such is accurate and in my opinion holds fresh emotion.

It was in June 1979, after a Channel Week series of races in the new 34 ft OOD yacht *Charioteer*. We had done rather well being placed in the top five boats and had qualified for the famous Fastnet Race. After such enjoyable sailing with John the skipper, who was great to crew for, I mentioned to him that I had done two Fastnet Races, in 1971 and 1973 and would not mind doing another.

I then related some of the stories on my experiences on the races, one of which included how on my last race in 1973, we had come across this large tanker off the Lizard in thick fog. I had been posted on the front of the yacht to act as lookout. Suddenly I heard voices above me and relayed this fact to the skipper who was in the cockpit at the back of the boat. I was told to behave myself and just as he said that the massive form of the bow of a large marine fuel tanker appeared. I could clearly see the two lookouts, whose voices I had heard, looking over the forward section of the ship. Chaos ensued as the helmsman took immediate action to avoid a collision. Fortunately we somehow managed this although I thought that at one stage we were going to collide with the huge thrashing propellers. This did not happen and we were left in a state of disarray as this vast vessel 'thumped' (we could now hear the engines), away from us. The remainder of that race was incident free and we did not do too well but it had been enjoyable.

John was very interested in my tales and said he would give the 1979 Fastnet some thought. Shortly after this I got a telephone call from him stating that he was going to enter the Fastnet Race, as well as the races in Cowes Week preceding the Fastnet, and he was looking for crew. Would I be interested? I did not hesitate to accept although I questioned the fact that crews normally had time to work and 'rehearse' together as a team before the race and would this be possible? John responded that every crew member would be 'person-ally selected' by him and would be experienced although time was short.

The 11th August 1979 approached fast and again we performed well in the races during Cowes Week, including The Round The Island Race where many boats compete against each other in very close proximity sailing around the Isle of Wight. This is one of my favorite yacht races as there is constant 'jostling' for position with the helmsmen and crew being continuously tested. To my concern, however, four of our crew for the Fastnet changed after Cowes Week and as I saw it there were some seven strangers of differing sailing and life experience being thrown together, some of whom had not even set foot on *Charioteer* before and in my opinion this could cause problems.

The day before was set for preparation in The Hamble Point Marina on a pontoon, which had been reserved especially for the Fastnet Race yachts. The atmosphere was full of excitement with the crews talking and joking with each other whilst carrying out their preparations on their respective yachts. This was also a chance to get to know my new crew members and it seemed good on this lovely sunny day with us all 'bonding' well. The seven of us on board consisted of the skipper, John, who was an experienced and competitive sailor and was doing well in his new boat, Aubry, Philip and Gerry all of whom were experienced helmsmen, big Steve who had done some sailing, Robin who had done very little sailing and wanted to do the Fastnet for the experience, and myself who had crewed in a number of races including two previous Fastnet Races.

So, on the face of it we were a well found crew apart from Robin, an accountant, who did seem a bit nervous over what he had let himself in for. I did confidentially approach John on my concern about Robin but as John pointed out he had been let down. This was the best he could do and he wanted a full crew and it was too late to change things now.

John had carefully worked out the watch system so that we all had a structured role on board. We were to work in pairs for three hours at a time with the skipper being free. I was paired up with Gerry and as he was a newly made young Royal Marine officer, an experienced sailor and full of enthusiasm, I was very happy with that choice. With my former military experience we would most probably know how each other would be thinking.

The skipper had spent a considerable sum of money purchasing the required equipment demanded by the strict rules of the Royal Ocean Racing Club before a race of this nature. We were all shown exactly where everything was stowed and at the end of the day I felt that we were well equipped and organized for the venture ahead of us, little knowing exactly what horrors that we were going to be confronted with and how important it was to know where the flares and bolt crops were.

We were up early on the morning of Saturday the 11th August and it was a warm sunny day. After a good 'fat boy' breakfast onshore we slipped in the morning making our way under motor down the River Hamble to the start at Cowes, which was due at 13.20hrs. Starting in the Fastnet Race is always an exciting and wondrous experience due to the number of yachts competing, mixed with the official and media launches. This year there were some 303 starters all jostling for the best position to start. It was great and complemented by wonderful weather.

We started well in the front and quickly got the sails set and boat balanced. The crew worked well and spirits were high. We were way up in the front concentrating on many short tacks that were required to reach the entrance buoy to the Solent, which would free us to The Channel. By the evening we were sailing well and started to settle down to our respective watches. The wind started to decrease during the night but we still had a reasonable speed especially when Gerry and I were on the helm chasing and catching up larger yachts. The Dorset and Devon coast glided past on our starboard (right hand side), however on the Monday morning we seemed to have lost any form of wind and were becalmed and then the dreaded fog descended.

Fog at sea is not pleasant as one can get totally disorientated and of course the risk of collision is increased. There were many yachts out there not to mention large ships and even if you were aware of their presence it did not mean that they were aware of yours, especially with ships, as sometimes they cannot pick up your radar reflector and need room to manoeuvre even if they do detect you. It is always damp and noises become weirdly muffled and sometimes it feels very restrictive especially when there is no movement. Occasionally we could hear voices from another invisible boat in the distance and then silence. Every now and again we heard the thumping of a ship's engine along with the fog horn but they were some distance away and of no real concern.

Incessant heavy rain then started followed by an increase in the wind speed. We were sailing again even it was in a wet thick grey soup, at least we were moving through the rippled flat sea

According to the lunchtime forecast the wind was due to change direction to the West and increase and it was not long before the fog cleared and we could set a course for the Fastnet Rock. We did in fact manage to fly the spinnaker (a large colorful sail flown from the front of the yacht), and started to speed along. Gerry and myself were on the helm late afternoon and it was so exhilarating, despite the rain, pushing this racing boat to its extremes and sometimes getting 10 to 12 knots out of her when surfing down the waves that were now building rather alarmingly along with the wind.

However all good things come to an end and the next watch, Phillip and Steve, were keen to take on in the evening so Gerry and I reluctantly handed over and went below to feed and rest. The weather forecast was now predicting the wind backing to the South and increasing up to gale 8. This was not too disturbing as we had raced in a gale 8 before without incident, although the sea was increasing and there was a fair amount of movement in the cabin now.

Gerry and I awoke when I heard movement above and it sounded as if there was a sail change going on. I clambered back into my very damp wet weather gear, struggling with the rather lively movement of the boat. Suddenly the feared shout of 'Man Overboard' was heard. We both had finished togging up and raced for the hatch.

As I was clambering out, a very wet Steve stumbled past us collapsing in a heap on the floor of the cabin. He quickly stripped off and John calmly instructed Gerry and me to stay below as everything was in order with the sail change. I asked what had happened and apparently Steve was carrying out the sail change on the foredeck and was washed overboard as he was not strapped on. Unbelievably he was washed back on board landing in the cockpit where he was grabbed by John and Phillip and all this happened in a fraction of a minute. We just could not believe how lucky Steve was. Once stripped off Steve disappeared to the front of the cabin in the bow and collapsed on the sails where he remained.

The sea was now building but *Charioteer* was creaming along even under reduced sail. I stated to Gerry that I was going to keep my kit on as things were getting a little lively and he responded that he was going to do the same. John came down below mentioning that he was just slightly concerned over the conditions out there as there was something not quite right as the weather and sea appeared to be changing very fast.

Shortly after there was a strange forecast anticipating winds of between force 8 to storm 10 in the Fastnet and Lundy area. This was repeated and John got us together to ask whether we should withdraw now and return to the mainland or continue. The vote was to continue as even if we returned we would be caught by the storm on a lee shore and as we had passed the Scilly Isles we had plenty of sea room. I joked that this was a new boat with a good crew so we had nothing to worry about even if it was a storm 10 forecast and then realized what I had just said.

The VHF radio suddenly came alive with a boat (against the rules), querying the last weather forecast of storm 10 winds with a coast guard station. It was confirmed that the last weather forecast as issued by the BBC at 17.50 was correct being a Southerly gale 8, which was very comforting, although we all felt something was not right as the conditions were now rapidly getting worse not to mention the rate the barograph was dropping.

Having secured everything in the cabin and checked on Steve, who would not speak to me, I tried to get some rest by lying on a bunk to windward, securing myself with a lee cloth (a strong piece of fabric that is tied to strong points in the cabin), reinforced with some spare cord. Gerry clambered into the pilot berth above me and did the same. John was at the chart table, Robin in the lower side bunk and Steve in the fore cabin amongst the sails. Aubry and Philip were on watch. Apart from the noise and what now seemed extreme movements at times all seemed in order down in the cosy cabin lit with a single red light. Surprisingly despite still being clothed in our wet weather gear and boots, both Gerry and I slept, probably due to sheer exhaustion.

I was awoken around midnight by a sudden very severe movement. The noise of the sea and the screaming wind was deafening but all still seemed in order. I noticed John was still sitting at the chart table and he saw that I had awakened. 'I just don't believe it' he said, 'how can you sleep when its blowing a hurricane out there' I replied that 'I was very tired and I am now starving so how about a sandwich?' He shook his head in disbelief as I started making a peanut butter sandwich which was quite a challenge.

Suddenly it seemed that there was a pressure change in the cabin and then a tremendous jolt that seemed to lay the boat on her beam end that threw me onto the galley stove despite the fact that I was well wedged in. Some cans of food came loose in the cabin so I quickly concentrated on catching them and securing them. It was then that I realized how quickly objects like that can turn into missiles that would inflict injury to those in the cabin with conditions like this. I found part of my sandwich stuck peanut butter side up to the roof of the cabin!

Gerry was now awake and time was coming for our watch, John asked us to ensure that we were well strapped on and informed us that he had taken all sails off. At 01.00 hrs Gerry and I opened the wash boards and I was amazed at the conditions out there. It was dark and the sea was a boiling mass of fluo-rescent green with huge waves that every now and again would crash down with a sound similar to a large gun. There was a continuous screaming of the wind in the rigging, the sea sounded like an artillery barrage as waves broke and communication by voice was practically impossible.

I handed my harness strap clip to Aubry, who was acting as relief for Steve, to clip onto the cockpit strongpoint and Gerry closely followed. I noticed that all the sails had been taken down and that we were running under bare poles as informed by John. I was concerned about this as we were at the total mercy of the sea broadside on which was not good. After a few minutes, having taken the helm, Aubry and Phillip handed over the torch, wished us luck, I think, as we could not hear with the noise of the storm and disappeared below replac-ing the wash boards behind them leaving us feeling strangely isolated and exposed.

Whilst Gerry was sitting next to me it was almost impossible to communi-cate although he let it be known that he wanted a pee. I could not believe the situation so I shouted to him in his ear that he would have to do it in his pants just sitting there. This was followed by a nasty little wave that broke over the stern and filled the cockpit so that we were sitting in water up to our chests. By standing up the water came up to our waists but it soon drained leaving us soaked and cold.

We settled down as best as we could and I was aft on the helm and Gerry sitting next to me. I did wonder why I was 'on the helm' as we were not moving forward and if anything we were being blown through the water beam on or drifting sideways. I noticed our class pennant (a small triangular flag), that was secured to the backstay being shredded by the tremendous force of the wind that was now registering over 65 knots on the anemometer (the wind meter).

Suddenly I saw something drifting past in the water very close to us. I shined the torch onto this object and it was a body. It was a man with brown curly hair wearing an inflated lifejacket. His head was tilted back with mouth and eyes open staring lifelessly up to the sky. I pointed this out to Gerry who suggested that perhaps we should try and recover him. I did not think that was a good idea in these conditions not to mention the fact that space on the boat was short with seven live bodies not to mention one additional dead one.

Our conversation was then interrupted by our first of many knockdowns which sent us both, without any warning, flying into the lower lifelines and into the sea. It was very unpleasant and I could feel bruises and pain everywhere. *Charioteer* quickly righted herself and again we were left standing up to the waist in a cockpit full of water. Gerry, in addition to his safety harness, then tied himself on with some free rope. I did not like the idea of this so I was only attached by my harness that was secured to the backstay.

We settled down again and then a large steady intensive bright white light could be seen in front of us some distance away on the horizon. Gerry could see this light as well and it was very firm not moving in any way. We were intrigued at this spectacle and then it suddenly disappeared. Gerry reckoned that perhaps it was an oil rig and I stated that there were no oil rigs around here. We both saw this intensive light on a number of occasions and to this day have no idea what it was although there have been a number of suggestions from angels to overactive pituitary glands.

Chapter 2
Fastnet Sailing Race - 1979
The Storm

I decided that time had come to say my final prayers and to prepare myself for the end as the weather and sea conditions were steadily getting quite horrendous. I told Gerry, who was on watch with me in the cockpit of our yacht, what I was doing and spent a few peaceful moments locked in prayer thinking of my three year old daughter, my wife and family.

Following this I felt remarkably relaxed and what would be would be. It was then I realized the sheer scale of the waves that were far higher than the mast and seemed extraordinarily steep. The anemometer seemed frozen on the maximum reading of 70 knots or it was broken. I was then transfixed on 'wave watching' and it was not long before we experienced a number of knock downs. I shouted a warning as I could see these monster steep waves rushing towards us from behind. This was better and more masculine than just screaming but it had the same effect. Again and again the boat righted herself although as time went on it seemed to take longer. It was obvious the yacht could only take so much punishment before breaking up.

The waves were now an unbelievable height and seemed almost cavernous with white water at the top of them that cascaded down the face with tremendous force. It was now getting lighter as dawn was approaching and I noticed what seemed like another ship on the horizon although there appeared to be no other vessels about which seemed strange.

I then saw a massive wave building by us seemingly staying static and just rapidly increasing in size with a curling white water top. I knew that we could not survive this one and shouted my usual warning with all the strength I could muster feeling that this was going to be my last physical action. It hit with tremendous force throwing us into the sea. I was being pulled by my harness through the water being bashed about at a frightful speed. I thought that I was being dragged to the bottom by the sinking boat and was preparing myself to take a deep breath of as much water as I could ingest so that I could drown as quickly as possible.

As I did so it was not water but air. I was on the surface amongst the rigging and mast that was floating in sea. Confusion set in as I was not sure where I was and what was happening, until I felt pressure against my chest as bits of the mast were crushing me with the movement of the waves. I was alive and breathing air, but now what was going to happen as I did not wish to die a slow cold death having survived a 360 degree roll like that and where was everyone else?

It was then I thought that I heard a voice behind me. I looked back as best

15

as I could and there was *Charioteer* not far away lying low in the water with no mast and John standing in the cockpit in his white Arran pullover that seemed to be rapidly turning purple from the top down. It was then that I realized that I could only see out of my left eye and there was a lot of blood coming from my mouth and face.

There was a possibility of survival here if I could get back to the boat and I was now beginning to feel very cold but it was so peaceful with no screaming of the wind in the rigging. I shouted and tried to raise an arm but I was well entangled in the rigging. This was the first challenge and I had to forget about the cold and get myself sorted to live. I started slowly moving my arms underwater and managed to free one arm and then the other. However I was still crushed up between two sections of the mast that had broken in three places.

Much to my surprise Gerry swam out to me and helped free me from the mast which entailed going under the floating mast and out. I was free and Gerry helped me back to the boat, he climbed back on board and then pulled me up onto the deck. It was fortunate that *Charioteer* was low in the water as in normal circumstances I would not have had the strength to do this.

Gerry got me back to the cockpit where he strapped me in and then went on to treat John who was badly injured by the galley stove that had broken free and was flying around in the cabin. It was thought that he was suffering from a broken neck and a deep cut to the head where there was considerable loss of blood. This was why his pullover was seen to be changing from white to mauve as it was blood seeping down from his head through the white wool. As a doctor he gave instructions on how to administer treatment but he was badly dazed and shocked.

It all seemed rather peaceful without the screaming rigging although the sea was very noisy still. Gerry seemed in control and suggested that we should inflate the life raft. Steve made an appearance with the life raft and it was thrown overboard to inflate which it did. However the painter, (the line that secures the raft to the boat), parted and we watched the raft fly away in the wind.

I then remembered that I had seen a vessel on the horizon just before we had been rolled and shouted for some flares. A para-illuminating flare was produced and I just could not set it off as I was so cold. Gerry grabbed it and launched it unfortunately into the cockpit.

This was actually an amusing incident at the time although highly dangerous and fortunately nobody was injured. I shouted for another flare and gave it to Gerry asking him politely to launch it skywards rather than seawards! Gerry responded by stating it was great to have me back and then up went the flare.

It was not long before it was obvious that the vessel on the horizon had changed course and was responding to our distress signal. Life was once again a possibility and spirits on board rose.

I went below into the cabin to recover my wallet from my blazer that was in the hanging locker amidships. I was astounded at the chaos in the cabin that

CUSTOMER RECEIPT
THE CAFE ON THE GREEN
THE CAFE ON THE GREEN WIDECOMBE IN
THE MOOR NEWTON ABBOT, DEVON , TQ13
7TA
25/10/2017 11:06:16
RECEIPT NO. 54207
MID:XXX12923   TID:XXXX8773
AID:A0000000031010
VISADEBIT
XXXX XXXX XXXX 0425
PAN SEQ NO. : 00
ICC
SALE   GBP17.00

TOTAL   GBP17.00

PLEASE DEBIT MY ACCOUNT
PIN VERIFIED
PLEASE KEEP THIS RECEIPT FOR YOUR
RECORDS
AUTH CODE: 251253

was now waist deep in water. There was a stench of diesel, gin and blood below, a hideous concoction and I am not sure where the gin came from!

I waded to the hanging locker and there was my blazer, which my mother had given to me some years ago, still in its cover bone dry. I tried to put it on but it just would not fit over everything so I took my wallet out and made my way back to the cockpit noticing a strange loud hissing noise that was coming from somewhere.

Chapter 3
The Rescue - 1979

It was not long before the large French trawler, *The Masigny*, that had been fishing langoustine on The Laberdie Bank, arrived on the scene. The skipper of this trawler had to manoeuvre with some care as he could broach or capsize in these huge seas himself very easily. He got the trawler up wind of us facing the sea and wind and rubbed up against us. Two lines were thrown for us to attach the bow and stern of the yacht alongside. We watched as the pulpit (the stainless steel guard rail found on the front of yachts), was ripped off along with what was left of the life lines and some fibreglass.

Many years ago I had read about how lifeboats used to do this with floundering ships and survivors had to jump onto the lifeboat. I decided that I was going to do this and calmly made my way amidships of our floundering yacht and at the right time launched myself into the trawler to be caught by two French fishermen. It had worked perfectly but with this sea one false move would have meant I would have been crushed between the two vessels; at one moment the trawler was some 30 ft above us and then 30 ft below us, it was not easy.

Miraculously all seven of us including John with the help of Gerry managed this and a small glass of whisky for each survivor was produced by the French crew and we drank a toast to our lives on the oily and fishy stern of the trawler in the sun that was just beginning to rise, it was really quite surreal.

The stern rope of *Charioteer* had been cut so she was now attached to the trawler by the bow at a distance. The French skipper appeared with a knife and quickly cut the tow line tied to the stern of the trawler. I heard John exclaim that 'Oh well there goes £75,000' as *Charioteer* gradually disappeared from sight and looked as if she was settling into the sea by the stern (the back of the boat).

We were then shown into the crew's mess room that had six 'rabbit hutch' bunks around it. John was given the largest bunk after first aid was administered by a French crew member, who seemed very proficient as well as being guided by John. It was all rather comfortable, dry and warm despite the violent motions of the trawler. However the problem was that there were only six bunks for seven of us. I stated that I would take a bunk later as I wished to make a VHF call back home to inform everybody that we were safe and was shown to the wheelhouse where I found the skipper and the helmsman.

None of the crew could speak English, but I could speak some French, enough to be understood which was adequate. I asked the skipper whether I could make a call home to inform them that we were safe and he directed me to the radio. I called Falmouth and much to my surprise there was a response. I informed them of the fact that all seven crew from *Charioteer* had been rescued by the French trawler, *Massigny*, and that we were now riding out the storm.

This information was much appreciated and then I asked to make a 'one link call'. This was when you could be connected on marine VHF to the telephone network of the UK, in other words you could make a telephone call through your vessel's radio. Everybody could of course be listening into your conversation so I was careful what I said to Elizabeth, my wife, who had just heard on the news that there was a problem and that *Charioteer* was one of the boats that had been posted as 'missing', so it was a tremendous relief to hear that we were safe.

I sent my love to everybody and told her I was really looking forward to seeing her and the family in three-four days time as we were riding the storm out at present. With that I signed off and much to my surprise I was then asked by the telephone operator if I was a Fastnet survivor. I replied that I was and he then informed me that the call would be free and wished me luck.

I then went into the wheelhouse and watched the helmsman coping expertly with the mountainous seas using throttle and the wheel to ride up and down head on into the waves. It was obvious that one mistake could easily broach this large trawler with instant catastrophic results. The skipper offered me his seat and I observed and reflected, noticing that I was still in my soaking clothing and barefooted, as I had lost my sea boots during the roll.

For some unknown reason I asked if I could take the helm and the skipper agreed with the helmsman standing close in case he had to take over. It was very similar to the film 'The Perfect Storm' with the vessel being powered straight up the waves and then essentially keeping her on course whilst descending down the waves. One mistake here could be fatal resulting in a broach and capsize. After some fifteen minutes I began to feel very tired so handed back to the helmsman who congratulated me along with the skipper. I then returned to the galley where breakfast of coffee, croissant and langoustine was being prepared for the trawler crew as all my lot were asleep in their bunks.

I then just happened to see myself in a mirror and was shocked at what I saw. Caked blood was still attached to my nose and the right hand side of my face that was badly grazed and swollen completely covering my right eye. I had a bad cut on my upper lip where my teeth had broken through and this was still oozing. My upper front teeth had been broken. One of the Frenchmen saw me gawping at the apparition and offered to clean me up and this was done very gently despite the trawler's abrupt motions. Everything was moving so violently but there was such an air of normality about this boat as if this could have happened everyday.

After the cleanup I was offered a place at the galley table where another glass of whisky was produced with the coffee. After breakfast I fell asleep strapped in a chair to wake an hour later covered in a blanket but feeling very cold, wet and sick. This was noticed by a Frenchman, Eugene, who produced his smart shore clothes for me to change into.

I was touched by his kindness and it was bliss to be wearing warm dry clothes again. Eugene then showed me to Gerry's bunk as Gerry had insisted that I should take it. I did not argue and fell into a deep sleep for many hours.

I awoke in the afternoon and some of my crew were up and talking. I tried to remember which day it was, Monday or Tuesday and decided that it was Monday 14th August. Robin confirmed that and reminded me that it was still blowing a hurricane out there. Lying in my bunk I could see that we were rolling to extremes and that every now and again I could see huge waves through a window. We were as much at risk as before, the only difference being that if this vessel sank six French fishermen and the seven of us would most probably die.

It was surprisingly warm and snug in my bunk so I rolled over and went back to sleep. The next big event was an evening meal of langoustine, steak (horse) and chips along with bottles of red wine. The weather was beginning to improve with the wind and sea decreasing. We all sat together apart from the skipper and helmsman and had an enjoyable meal, relating our tales to the fishermen in our scant French. It was a very interesting repast and there was also an atmosphere of relief with the improving weather.

The following day we learnt of a dilemma that was facing the skipper of the trawler. He was concerned that he was running low on fuel and was fearful that he would not have enough to return to his home port of Perros Guirec in Brittany. John was insistent that he should return via the most direct route and not worry about dropping us off in the U.K. However it was suggested that perhaps he could sail to Newlyn, drop us off and refuel at the same time.

John offered to pay for this and it was decided that was what we would do, so we set course for Newlyn in Cornwall on the Tuesday morning in a rough sea, which seemed positively calm after what we had witnessed, and a rapidly decreasing wind.

I began to feel quite excited now as it seemed that we were going to survive and was really looking forward to getting home to my family. At 02.00 hrs we docked at Newlyn and said our farewells to our rescuers who were actually quite emotional with lots of hugs! The Seaman's Mission was there to welcome us to Newlyn, as well, and to ask if we would like something to eat or a bed for the night. I was astounded at their effort and felt a little guilty in not accepting their kindness and support.

Gerry had organized his father, Phillip, to meet us and to very kindly drive us home. It was at 05.00 as the sun was rising on a beautiful warm morning that I was dropped off outside my gate. I padded barefoot and still wearing my 'shipwreck' clothes over the lawn that was wet with dew and it smelt so good along with the sound of the birds singing. So good in fact I knelt on the wet grass running my hands through it and offered a prayer of thanks.

I then walked into the kitchen and up to the bedroom of my three-year-old daughter Alona. She was so thrilled to see me, jumping up and down in her cot. I hugged her and then started to weep uncontrollably as Elizabeth appeared and we had a big warm and rather wet hug. It was great.

The Outcome

I suffered nightmares, especially when the wind was blowing at night, despite the fact that I was wrapped up in bed with Elizabeth. Even worse was the fact that I would suddenly have weeping fits anywhere at any time. Often it used to happen in a public place and if I was talking to someone I used to have to quickly escape, trying to laugh it off by stating they should not worry as they just have that effect on me. I did get some very strange looks and can well imagine the gossip.

On one occasion Gerry insisted on visiting me shortly after. Having carried out some Ragwort pulling on the farm he suggested that as he was so thirsty he would really appreciate a lunchtime drink in our neighboring pub, The Rugglestone. We walked there and the two of us stood by the bar ordering our drinks. Audrey the landlady welcomed me and asked who Gerry was. I introduced him as my 'blood brother' as he had just saved my life. Gerry was embarrassed over this and tried to wave it off, but Audrey was intrigued and I started to tell the shortened tale and she insisted on giving us our drinks, on the house.

I detected that Gerry really was feeling uncomfortable so I then declared that drinks were on me as we were going to celebrate. After all there were only few people there. However it only took a short period of time before The Rugglestone was filled with neighbours and locals. I am not sure how this happened so quickly but a good party was had and we did celebrate with Elizabeth collecting Gerry and me later that evening.

We saw quite a lot of Gerry and his young Royal Marine friends during the next six months and then they got posted to various parts of the world so their numbers dropped until they had all gone, rather like the swallows.

I gradually recovered although I had nasal problems over the next two years that could have been due to the sea water being flushed through my respiratory system. A few weeks after the storm we all received a Brittany doll from the crew of the trawler to celebrate our lives. I found this touching as I had got to know these fishermen well during my stay on board *The Massigny* and I think they felt close to us having been through such an experience together.

It was not long before John was in communication with his crew asking for a suggested financial donation that would be put towards a personal gift to each member of the French crew, such as an inscribed tankard and a sum of money that would be presented to the skipper of *The Massigny* to cover the cost of the fuel used in our rescue.

The following summer Elizabeth and I were invited by John to accompany him and his wife Sheila for a sail to Santander in Spain in their new boat, a Carter 34. I was flattered to have been asked and accepted without hesitation.

It was a wonderful sail although there were some incidents. On one of our overnight stays on the French coast a student fell off the quayside to become impaled on a stanchion of the neighboring boat having fallen some 25 feet. It was awful with the casualty twitching and blood pouring out of his mouth just in front of us. I looked at John for advice on what first aid I should administer. His reply was ' just take a blanket and cover him up as he will not survive that fall'. The casualty's friends were screaming and wailing on the quay above us; it was a nightmare. The young lad was taken to hospital by ambulance where he was pronounced dead on arrival.

My mind started working overtime and I began to wonder why we were here, considering a year ago on another yacht it was touch and go whether we were going to survive and now we had just witnessed, at close quarters, the death of a young man. Elizabeth and Sheila were wonderful and I think John was also affected as he went very quiet. However, we somehow managed to put this awful accident behind us and enjoyed the rest of the holiday making a perfect landfall on Santander where we met the joint owners of this new Carter 34 yacht, John and Pat, who were going to sail the boat back to UK, with my step-daughter Claire.

Following this trip I purchased a Hurley 22ft yacht which I initially moored in the River Yealm and then moved to the Tamar where I kept this little boat on a picturesque mooring at Hole's Hole, just up river from Weir Quay.

I still have that mooring, but I have upsized to a 28ft yacht, named *Wild Oat*. I have sailed in her to France, Channel Islands, Scilly Islands and the South Coast with one or two incidents, but there lie other stories as described later. For some unknown reason I really enjoy sailing on my own. It has been suggested that perhaps nobody will sail with me!

There were some 303 starters in the Fastnet Race of 1979, split into 5 classes, class 0 being the bigger boats up to 79ft and class 5 being the smaller from 28ft. Not surprisingly it was the smaller boats in classes 3, 4 and 5 that got badly hit by the storm with only 13 finishing including one class 5 boat, *Assent*. Overall 194 yachts retired and there were 19 vessels actually abandoned but recovered later. 5 boats were never recovered, presumed sunk. *Charioteer* was one of those 5.

With sadness it must be remembered that 15 competitors lost their lives in this race all from classes 3, 4 and 5.

Following this, lifetime catastrophe memories then started to flood my mind resulting in clearly embedded memoirs. In the following chapters I have described them as from 1956.

Chapter 4

Memories with my First Flight and Pneumonia Aged Eight - 1956

The two engines of the British Airways DC 3 were started with a roar and we taxied out to the runway. Lisa, the 'Air Hostess', sat next to me and we took off and settled down to the flight above the clouds. It was such an exciting and exhilarating experience. It was not long before I was led up to the cockpit where the co-pilot offered me his seat muttering 'I am going to get a drink, here you take over'. I was rather surprised and Lisa strapped me in next to the Captain. A pair of headphones was placed on my head drowning out the constant noise and vibration of the two engines. It was rather annoying as my legs stuck out in front of the seat and I could not see over the instrument panel. Despite this it was explained to me on how the control column operated along with a few instruments. I did actually fly the aeroplane pulling the control column up and pushing it down and was instructed how to carry out a slight turn. 'Not bad for a seven year old' the Captain retorted, 'just keep an eye on your instruments as after all you are flying by them anyway. Maybe when you are older you will be able to see out of the front and that will simplify matters a bit as you will be able to see the horizon'.

The co-pilot returned and Lisa took me back to my seat when suddenly the aircraft lurched.

She hurriedly strapped me in and then quickly checked the other passengers returning to sit next to me. I was surprised to see that she strapped herself in as well. 'I think we are about to experience some turbulence and there is nothing to worry about'. Just after she had said that suddenly it felt as if I was hanging by my straps as we dropped out of the sky. A woman in front of us started to scream and a large man sitting the opposite side of the aisle started to be sick in a brown paper bag.

On one of our rapid descents Lisa pointed out a tray she had dropped that appeared to be stuck to the ceiling of the cabin and quietly stated that this was quite normal. It was not long before we suddenly started going up and I was pushed with force into my seat. The Captain then announced in a calm voice that we were experiencing clear air turbulence and that there was nothing to be concerned about and we would soon be through it.

I pointed out to Lisa how much the wing was moving as it seemed that at one stage to be almost bent double. She explained that wings were designed to do that. Some ten minutes later everything calmed down and the woman stopped screaming. There was a stench of vomit in the cabin now as a number of passengers had been sick and not into the brown paper bag but mainly over themselves.

All this was actually quite exciting to me probably due to the calm behavior of Lisa despite the screaming that I did find upsetting. The rest of the flight went without incident and we landed at Blackbushe Airport near Camberley. I was invited up to the cockpit for the landing where I sat in the small ' Jockey Seat' just behind the two pilots. It was a landing in bad visibility and we were being 'talked down'. This was fascinating listening to communications and watching how the pilots reacted to the instructions calmly relying on their instruments and experience as there was nothing to see ahead of us apart from grey. Suddenly the runway appeared in front of us through the mist and murk 'just where it should be' as the Captain said. The Captain landed explaining to me what he was doing and the landing was so gentle it was hard to think that we were back on the ground, we taxied to the airport buildings, parked and closed the engines down following the laid down sequence. The passengers disembarked, some looking a bit worse for wear in their stained and smelly clothing.

This was my first flight in an aeroplane and it was all rather confusing as whilst being booked into this new school in Hampshire we had moved from Bovey Tracey, in Devon, to Celle in Germany, where my father, an Army officer, had been posted with The Devonshire Regiment as the Commanding Officer. He held this appointment for two years and supervised the amalgamation of The Devonshire Regiment and Dorsetshire Regiment in 1958.

On arrival at the school I was shown my bed in the stark, damp and cold dormitory with no heating, which I was sharing with some seven other boys and then guided around the school with other 'new boys' who had just arrived. We were shown our 'common room' class rooms, toilets, the gym etc. I soon made friends with two other boys, Neal and Alan and this seemed to help the situation. We had tea that consisted of fried spam, boiled potatoes and cabbage, enough to turn the stomach, and various rules were explained to us. One rule was that we do not talk after lights out in the dormitory and if we were caught so doing we were to be beaten.

After tea we unpacked and then it was time for bed. We washed and were inspected in silence by Matron and her attractive young assistant, Miss Rowntree, and retired to our respective beds and I had a lovely rug on mine that my grandmother had given me. We chatted away although some were tearful and unfolded the story of my flight and how I flew the aeroplane not forgetting how the air hostess got stuck on the ceiling when we were falling 5000 ft. This was listened to by my neighbours with some interest until it was 'Lights Out'. Matron turned the lights out and that was it. We were left in darkness in our own little worlds and that bed suddenly became 'home'. Sobbing became louder from certain quarters and those next to my bed, Alan and Neal quietly asked questions on my story.

Whilst answering these questions the door suddenly burst open, the lights were flicked on and there stood the headmaster holding a cane. He was a large man and seemed to be shaking with rage. 'Who was talking?' he demanded. I nervously held my hand up along with Neal and Alan and we were instructed to get out of bed and stand at the foot of our bed.

'As you were honest to own up that you were talking on this occasion I am not going to beat you so get back into bed and no more talking'. With that he switched the lights out and left the room slamming the door. It was time to reflect in my little home so I pulled the blankets over my head and wept myself to sleep longing to be in my loving home again with mother, father and little brother Simon.

The next morning we got up at 7 a.m., washed and dressed ready for breakfast at 8 a.m. Following breakfast we assembled where we were counted and had to answer our names and then split into various classes. The routine and food were not pleasant and I made good friends with two other boys, Humphrey and Charles that helped and together we seemed to get through this rather draconian life.

I started to suffer asthma attacks. I was taken to see Matron who gave me a little white pill, that I was told was Ephedrine, which seemed to free my breathing up but I could feel my heart beating overtime and it was weird. I continued with life as normal as was possible and after a few days started to develop a chest cough. This got worse until blood appeared in the phlegm. I was now feeling awful so once again I went to see Matron who took my temperature and put me to bed in the 'sick room'. She informed me that she was calling a doctor to see me. The doctor arrived told me that he thought that I had pleural pneumonia and that he would prescribe some Penicillin. I had to rest and he would visit me the next day. I was in a dark place and despite sleeping I was so cold and then hot with sweat streaming off me. The doctor arrived the next day and he seemed concerned over my condition and started talking about admitting me to hospital as I would need a drip. It was all rather frightening and I seemed to be in a different, horrible and painful dark world.

The following day I seemed to feel more relaxed and it was as if there was light at the end of that black tunnel in my troubled slumbers. I awoke to find my mother sitting next to me, knitting and talking as if there was no problem and as if I was awake. She suddenly realized that I had opened my eyes and started to stroke my hair. I just could not believe that she was there and seemed to get immediate strength and comfort from this. I started to eat and drink again and it was a matter of days before I was well on the route to recovery. It was then a question of whether I should return early to Germany with mother missing some two weeks that were left of term or to stay and end the term trying to catch up the two weeks I had missed whilst being sick. The latter was decided and mother said her farewells and I started counting the days when I would be flying back home at the end of term. Before she left she informed me that I was extremely lucky as I had been very sick and that is why she had flown over to be with me.

The days flew by and it was not long before the final night of that dreaded term had arrived. I was to be collected by taxi and then to be taken to Blackbushe Airport to catch my plane. I just could not sleep and spent most of the night watching a big clock that was hanging in the passageway outside the dormitory. Six 'o' clock arrived and the lovely Miss Rowntree appeared to wake me up. I was already dressed and excitedly followed her downstairs to the waiting taxi. Surprisingly she gave me a hug and bid me a safe journey stating that she looked forward to seeing me again next term. I jumped into the taxi and off we sped for Blackbushe Airport.

It all seemed very quiet at the airport and as before I was met by an air hostess who seemed more formal than Lisa and insisted on tying a label that had my name and destination, onto my coat. She then led me to the plane, a Douglas DC3 again, and showed me to my seat that was by a window over the wing. I asked if I could fly the aeroplane and she gave a smile and said she would see what she could organize.

That was the last I saw of her on this flight. No checking the aircraft with the Captain, no cockpit and no company or food. It did not seem to matter as I was longing to land at Hanover Airport and see my family. Mother, father and Simon were there and after the excited greetings we made our way to the family car, a Ford Popular. We drove to Celle and the house was as welcoming as ever. After a huge supper I went to bed early and slept very well.

Chapter 5
Paralysis Aged Eight - 1957

I awoke fresh and ready to go after such a good night. Mother had got breakfast ready and Simon and I gulped the boiled eggs and toast down and said farewell to father for the day as he left in uniform for his office in the barracks. He was the first Commanding Officer of The Devonshire and Dorset Regiment.

I then planned with Simon to go for a walk on the heath with Kim, the yellow Labrador that had grown so big having purchased him as a little bundle of yellow fluff last year. He was a lovely dog and adored us boys. Mother gave us consent to go and ordered that we should be back within two hours. Kim was on a lead and it was not long before he got scent of a rabbit and off he went. I jumped on his back and clung on as we galloped over the sand dunes, branches smacking me in the face, it was really exhilarating. In the end I just could not hold on any longer so I slid off and rolled to a halt unharmed.

I now had a problem as I had parted company with Simon, aged six, not to mention the dog. I decided that I must find Simon and was soon reunited. Thankfully shortly after this Kim trotted back to us and we continued our walk, with Simon threatening to tell on me unless I was nice to him.

I well remember one particular day when it rained with gale force winds. I loved watching the trees swaying in the wind and had a strong desire to climb to the top of a tree so that I could sway with it! I chose a tall larch tree and climbed to the top. It was great swinging from side to side looking out at the view.

Suddenly I felt the top of the tree bending right over on a particular very strong gust of wind and there was a resounding crack as the top of the tree broke. I fell heavily though the branches and landed on my back in the grass below. A severe shooting pain went through my back and with horror I realized that I could not move my arms or legs or even feel them. I lay on my back unable to move and screamed in terror and pain.

It was not long before a large German gentleman arrived. He looked very alarmed and shouted at me in German and then ran off. I continued to scream and I was now having problems in breathing; I thought my time had come to die. It was not long before mother and her two neighbours, Elizabeth and Veronica, arrived with blankets and bandages. Mother calmly informed me, as she gently placed a blanket over me, that an ambulance was on its way and that everything would be alright.

I noticed the large German gentleman had reappeared, babbling at mother, looking very alarmed and again he dashed off somewhere. 'Thank God for that, he was driving me crazy,' said Elizabeth. 'I think he said that he was going to guide the medics over to us' replied Veronica. She then informed me that she was a former nurse and that it was very important for me to stay very still and not to move.

Mother gently stroked my hair and then two uniformed medics ran up with the German gentleman leading the way. The medics gave me some what they called 'laughing gas' to alleviate the pain in my back. After that they started to get me ready for a transfer onto a special stretcher. I was gently slid onto the stretcher and seemed to be strapped head and foot onto it. The pain was not so bad now but I could tell that those around me were concerned over my injury and I still had no feeling in my legs or arms. It was very frightening and mother was desperately trying to remain calm talking to me all the time being supported by Elizabeth and Veronica.

I was carried some distance to the ambulance and then taken to the nearest large military hospital. Two doctors carefully examined me and I was informed that I had to have an x-ray to see what injury I had sustained. I was also told that there was every possibility that I had just bruised my spinal cord in which case I would get the feeling and use of my limbs back probably very soon.

Father appeared and we then had to wait for the results of the x-ray. After a while one of the doctors appeared with a smile stating that he had good news and that it would seem that I had just bruised my spinal cord and that everything should be fine after a short while. I was to remain in hospital until I had made the recovery. Mother and father hugged each other and then me. I noticed mother had tears streaming down her cheeks and father stating that women do this type of thing and not to worry.

The relief all around including with the medical staff was noticeable and I felt excited although still in pain. Some three days later I was able to walk out of that hospital without any ill effects and had regained the use of all my limbs.

I soon fully recovered and one day father suddenly announced that we were going to visit a former German Jewish concentration camp known as Bergen-Belsen that was nearby. I had overheard him talking to a friendly elderly German neighbour who had lived in this area for many years. Father asked the direct question 'had this German known about what was happening at Belsen as the stench of burning hair and flesh must have been overcoming?' This poor man burst into tears and wringing his hands stated that if he or his family had even mentioned anything about this to the authorities they would have joined those that went through those gates never to be seen again. This apparently had happened to some of his friends.

Actually we soon learnt that there were no furnaces in this camp and it is reported that some 50,000 inmates that had died here did so through sickness malnourishment and abuse from the guards.

I was and have since been affected by this overheard conversation all confirmed by the visit to Belsen. Mother was also overcome bursting into tears when we arrived stating how quiet it all was. I remember Mother, Father Simon and I looking at a large grassy mound with a wooden plaque in front simply stating 'Here lie 5000 Jews' and so on. There were many of these mounds and I remember asking Father, 'who were the Nazis?' as they had murdered so many of these Jews. This appears to be a question that often repeats itself within my mind and indeed the minds of my family today.

Chapter 6

Machette Attack Aged Ten and Arterial Cut to Wrist - 1958

Time soon came to return to school this time with Simon, and we were taken by mother and father, to Hanover Airport where we boarded another old aircraft. Flying to me was exciting and I reassured Simon that everything would be OK and that I could fly anyway. This did seem to fill him with a certain amount of confidence and we soon completed the flight, landing at Blackbushe Airport and then onto St Neots School by taxi. Simon was separated as he was a junior and I soon met up with my friends with excited chatter over what had happened over the holidays and so on.

It was back to the grindstone but we did have some escape in as much as that we were allowed out having obtained permission, onto the grounds and woodlands at certain times. We were encouraged and shown how to build dens or small shelters in the woods. This was great fun and we were organized into some 10 sections of six boys who were interested in doing this. There was then a competition over the quality our huts within the sections, with the assistant head master, Mr Hooper, being the judge.

On one occasion there were three of us, Nelly [Neal], Alan and myself within the section building our den. Suddenly a large strange looking man appeared.

'Do you want to see my panga'? he asked.

Much to my horror Alan showed an interest and walked over to this weird looking fellow from the relative perceived safety of our den.

'Yes please, how long is it and can I hold it'?

I asked Nelly to join me in approaching this chap and Alan which he did. Having got within grabbing distance of Alan, I stated

'Alan its time to go back now', and grabbed his left arm to pull him away but he resisted.

It was then that this weird character suddenly growled and with horror I noticed that he had raised his knife with both arms and was running at me shouting,

'I am going to chop your head off.'

I seemed fixed to the ground and just could not move until the last moment when I side stepped and my attacker whilst swinging his knife at my neck tripped and fell heavily to the ground. That dreaded lethal looking knife had just missed me and I am sure I felt the disturbance of the air on my face as it flashed past.

That was it and in terror I realized that this was our chance to escape so without hesitation I shouted to Nelly and Alan to join me in the escape run back to school. I ran as fast as I could and hearing Nelly panting behind me filled me with reassurance. After some 200 meters, asthma started to affect me so I stopped and Nelly ran into me knocking me down.

'Where's Alan' I asked Nelly when I got my breath back.

'I don't know, he didn't start running with us, he must still be with that man'

There was nothing for it we had to go back and try to rescue him.

So we ran back to our den and approached very carefully with me puffing away with asthma. Alan was not there so Nelly suddenly turned tail and started to run back to school. I followed as best as I could and on arrival at the school burst into the Master's Common Room. There were four teachers sitting in arm chairs reading newspapers.

'It's Jones, a man with a big knife has taken him,' I exclaimed with some difficulty as I could hardly breathe.

This got immediate attention and the teachers got up from their chairs and one asked me to sit down and relax and to get my breath back. This I did and then explained what had happened. One teacher telephoned the police and the other three asked if I could direct them to our den.

This we did and the teachers carried out a check of the area and asked me where all this had happened. There were actually some scuff marks on the ground where my attacker had fallen. We were soon joined by the police and a further search was organized. I was taken back to school by a teacher and was informed that it was all fine and that Alan would be all right and that he would be found very shortly. Nelly suddenly appeared from somewhere and we went into tea together trying to forget what had happened.

Alan did not appear for tea. In fact he was missing for some five days and then it was announced by the Headmaster that he had been found alive and well. He was to go home for a while and perhaps start again next term. I never saw Alan again. Apparently I was informed some time later that he had been abducted by this man, who had escaped from a nearby mental home, Broadmoor. Apparently, Alan had been found strapped to a bed in a remote hut in the woods. His mother committed suicide by gassing herself in the family cooker not long after this incident and it was all very sad.

Following the Alan incident the term raced by and Simon and I were once again on the aeroplane winging our way home to Germany. It was all so exciting with the situation enhanced by attractive air hostesses not to mention the fact that I was once again flying. Our parents were at the airport to meet us and to drive us home to Celle.

Simon was growing up fast now and made plenty of friends and on one occasion he and another young lad whilst doing things in our garage were interrupted by a rather bossy young girl, Caroline, who lived next door. Caroline tried to stop them doing whatever they were doing claiming that it was wrong. It was not long before she found herself tied to a chair and was then painted green by the two boys. Not unnaturally mother was not too amused when she found the poor girl in a state of distress in the garage and then had the task of returning her to her parents. Fortunately Caroline's parents were good over the matter and Simon plus his friend had to write a letter of apology to Caroline and deliver it by hand. All was forgiven and Caroline is very much about today and we are all good friends.

I carried on with the walks on the heath with our now large yellow Labrador, Kim, and Simon. I tried to teach Simon on how to ride Kim but he never quite managed to get onto his back when he was after a rabbit. In the end I gave up this riding pastime as it got very painful being bashed in the face by branches, thistles and so on.

However for a bit of extra entertainment I then started jumping from heights. To begin with I jumped from the garage roof, which was some 20 odd feet. I discovered that if I rolled as soon as I hit the ground I would not feel anything. The top of the garage progressed to my bedroom window that was a little higher. This time, whilst my jump went according to plan I bit my tongue rather badly. I asked mother for assistance and she was shocked at the injury as apparently I had actually bitten through my tongue. It was very painful and then I was asked how I did it. 'Jumping' I replied and mother did not seem too concerned about that, thank goodness.

Some weeks later, after I had recovered from my injury I had this driving desire to carry out the highest jump possible around the home and that was from the top of the roof. I climbed through the attic skylight and crawled along the ridge of the roof to the gable end. This put me in an ideal position with some good height being approximately 30 feet. I felt the adrenaline pumping and whilst everything was telling me not to do it I stood up to get ready for the jump. I was just about to launch myself into space when suddenly my mother appeared beneath me asking in a concerned voice 'what the hell do you think you are doing'.

I was rather taken aback by this as mother never normally swore and she did look very troubled. 'Jumping Mum, look I will show you', I replied. Mother stood firmly under me commanding me in a calm voice not to do it. Well I did not jump and mother was joined by father in his uniform, who then climbed onto the roof to retrieve me.

I was taken down to the kitchen where over a cup of tea I was closely questioned by my parents. 'Do you realize what you were doing and the fact that people do this to kill themselves?' my father asked. 'Yes I do realize what I am doing and that I can survive jumps from a fantastic height' I indignantly replied. My mother then made me promise that I would not do this any more as she was terrified that I would kill or badly injure myself rather like I nearly did when I fell out of the tree bruising my spinal cord. I suddenly realized what I was actually doing and this was confirmed by father stating 'you are not immortal you know, if you carry on like this you will kill yourself do you understand'? Yes I did understand and I never jumped like that again at least not without a parachute.

The holidays went by only too fast and it was time to fly to the United Kingdom with Simon. This time it was different because we were starting a new school known as Wellington House at Westgate-on-Sea in Kent. This school was established in 1886 by two clergymen whose intention it was to prepare young boys as British Empire builders. The school, when we attended in 1959 to 1962, consisted of some 80 boys.

This was a challenging time because on our first visit with our parents Simon and I were introduced to the headmaster Hubert Riley, commonly known as 'HR'. It was obvious that he was a strict disciplinarian and he explained to us the routine of the school. For a start the school was required to go on an early morning run every day down to the main beach and back where a cold shower would be waiting on return. Boys could only be excused this run if the formidable Matron, who was known as 'Kite' because of her uniform headwear, had excused them due to illness and this was a very rare occasion. I was assured that asthma would not be considered as an excuse not to participate on this run.

Furthermore following the run and breakfast the day would start at 09.00hrs and would not finish until 18.00 hrs and then we would have tea. After tea there would be an hour and a half spent doing a supervised 'prep'. It was a long and arduous day but Simon and I had our own cubicle and all boys were given a bottle of stout with every lunch. To cross the discipline line would be enforced with a beating on a naked rear end with a birch that would leave some unsightly weals which became obvious during the cold shower after the run.

This was a real challenge and I was strangely looking forward to this new school and was not disappointed. To my surprise I did not suffer much from my asthma and could partake in these jogs without problem. Even better my studies had improved and I found that I was actually learning a lot to such a degree that I was singled out for special tuition in Latin and Greek by HR as, apparently, I had a flair for these classic languages.

I found myself in the first eleven cricket team and became a 'fearful' bowler being able to deliver a fast ball with accuracy. Even better I really enjoyed playing Rugby and again was chosen for the first fifteen where I played as a wing forward. Life had changed for me very much for the better due to the challenge of the disciplined routine of this school.

One day after the run whilst undergoing the cold shower, HR asked me to open a window which I tried to do but failed as it was jammed. I then pushed with force on the window pane resulting in my right hand breaking through the glass causing a deep gash to the inside of my right wrist.

The amount of blood that was pumping out of my wrist was unbelievable and the boy next to me fainted at the sight, collapsing in a naked heap with a thud onto the concrete floor. HR immediately took control of the situation by coming over and holding up my injured arm and held the upper artery with some force thus controlling the blood flow to a degree. At the same time he commanded another boy to wrap my wrist in two towels and another to get Matron immediately and to inform her that there was an arterial cut to a wrist in the shower room that required immediate and urgent attention.

HR, who was covered in my blood, was calm and those around responded to his orders. It was a good example of how to control a tense situation. He informed me that I had cut my artery but as he was there I would not be dying. However he stated that it would be probable that I would not be attending any lessons today or runs and cold showers for the next few days. I would be going to hospital although it would be possible that I would be back by the evening as it was only a cut wrist.

'Kite' arrived and we were all amazed to see her without her matron's kite and she was also in a long pink dressing gown with a full length white apron. She had amazing thick auburn hair that flowed down to below her shoulders and she looked totally different. It was such a distraction to me that I forgot my predicament and just stared at her as did other boys. She was clutching a tourniquet and a bag of bandages.

'So what have you been doing' she asked me calmly as she applied the tourniquet. 'I was trying to open the window and my hand went through it, I can't feel any pain' I replied.

'Thank you Matron, perhaps I can let go of this young man's arm now you have the tourniquet in place,' stated the blood-soaked HR. Matron gave him leave to let go of my arm and he immediately went to the assistance of the boy that had collapsed who was now regaining consciousness. I noticed that the floor was covered in my blood but the bleeding had just about stopped with the tourniquet doing its job.

Matron asked if I would be capable of walking to her surgery with her so that she could treat the wound. I said that I could and HR asked two boys to accompany us both just in case. We arrived at the surgery and our escort was thanked by Matron who sat me down in a chair and got out from a cupboard a rather unpleasant looking bottle of liquid. 'I am afraid that this is going to be a bit painful but I have to do it as I want to ensure that you have not picked up any infection' said Matron and with that she started to pour the liquid onto my wound. I was amazed to see it bubbling away and yes it did sting a lot but I was determined not show any discomfort.

Shortly after this the doctor arrived with two ambulance men. The doctor put on an apron and asked Matron to release the tourniquet which she did and sure enough blood pumped out of my wrist. The doctor asked Matron to reapply it and confirmed that this was indeed an arterial cut that would require immediate surgery.

I was taken to hospital in an ambulance and soon made a recovery. Holidays in our new Army quarter at Bushey in Hertfordshire were fast approaching. I was very proud of my scar although my parents constantly reminded me how fortunate I was to have received such good medical treatment at the time.

Chapter 7
Allhallows School - My Health and a Facial Explosion - 1962

Bushey was not the most exciting of places as we were living in a typical military married quarter. However Simon and I did have our bicycles and we were allowed to go exploring on them. It was not long before we found a fascinating stagnant pond of quite some size complete with a home-made raft moored on the bank. Simon and I had great fun on the raft and it was not long before Simon fell into the stinking water. We cycled home hoping that mother was out but of course she was not and some explaining had to be done over how Simon had got himself into that state complete with the slime in his hair. Mother was surprisingly tolerant, I think, mainly because I had chosen to tell the truth as Simon had already launched into a detailed description on how we had paddled around this huge lake on our homemade raft.

As always holidays came to an end and I was starting a new school. It was Allhallows public school, at Rousdon, situated between Lyme Regis and Seaton. The school was based on a lovely old mansion built in the late 1800s by Mr Peek of Peek Frean biscuit fame. The school overlooked the sea and was situated in idyllic grounds consisting mainly of a wild landslip cliff area. The boys were permitted to roam freely throughout the grounds although we had to sign out and in.

Unfortunately my asthma started up again and I suffered. Unable to sleep properly at night, my academic studies suffered similar to the time I had at St Neots if not worse. I found that I was so tired during the day I spent a lot of the time in a warm class room dozing off normally to be awoken in no uncertain terms by an irate teacher who would normally clip me over the head with an open hand. I was eventually given the affectionate nickname 'Dopey' by my class mates who I knew understood my problem and this seemed to make light of the problem facing me.

One day I was enjoying a quiet snooze in a science lesson. 'Herby' (his first name was Herbert), the teacher came up behind me, when I was participating in a snooze, and clipped me over the head. I instinctively rose to my feet, grabbed Herby by the throat and pushed him against the wall where I had every intention of flattening him. He was a small man who wore glasses and I noticed that he had gone ashen white and was trembling with his glasses broken and askew. My right fist was raised and ready for the blows whilst I was holding him against the wall with my left hand. Fortunately I was actually being held back by two of my class mates and I suddenly came to my senses wondering what I had done to this poor man and was also surprised at my strength.

I was pulled away by the two boys holding me back and Herby tried to regain his composure with difficulty as his glasses were now broken. He apologised for hitting me and I expressed regret for attacking him. With that he closed the lesson early and asked me to come with him to the Master's Common Room where perhaps we could discuss the matter. I did not know it at the time but this incident changed the course of my life very much for the better.

I was now nervous of what would happen as this had never happened before in the school. Herby made us a cup of tea and we sat down to talk about the situation. He asked me about my health as I was looking very tired and I blurted out that I was not sleeping due to asthma attacks at night. He asked whether I was seeking medical advice to which I replied that I was not. He then arranged for me to go and see my House Matron, Barbara, who may be able to help.

Then much to my surprise Herby asked if I was interested in rifle shooting as this would not cause problems with my asthma as it was not very physical but challenging. I replied that I would be and he announced that the next shooting practice would be at the indoor shooting range that afternoon and that if I did come he would personally coach me, although he would have to find another pair of glasses before that!

I left the meeting wondering how a man I had just tried to beat up was so caring; I attended the shooting session that afternoon and was surprised by the number of boys who were actually shooting. Herby did coach me and I was amazed at how technical and mind-controlling target shooting was. I was hooked and soon started to produce some excellent results to such a degree that I was chosen for the first eight shooting team. I participated in a number of shooting matches against other clubs and schools gaining my 'small-bore' shooting colours. This meant that I was entitled to wear a black tie with rifles emblazoned on it.

I also joined the School Army Cadet Force and proudly wore my uniform. We were instructed on how to shoot the Lee Enfield .303 bolt action rifle at Colyton Ranges and this was similar to the small bore .22 rifle shooting. It was not long before I was selected for the 'full bore' shooting team earning my colours which meant that I could wear another black and silver tie. I also attended the cadet training camps once a year with the most enjoyable being with The Royal Engineers at Wyke Regis. We learnt, at the age of fourteen, how to lay and detonate explosive charges along with having fun in the assault boats; it was great.

One day my House Matron, Barbara, spoke to me whilst passing and insisted that on my next asthma attack I should go and see her any time day or night. I was not quite sure what to make of this as in the past I had suffered quietly without complaint. However the time soon came, one cold morning at about 03.00 hours. I was huffing and puffing trying to control my breathing as quietly as I could so as not to wake the others in my dormitory which had happened so many times before. In the end I put my dressing gown and slippers on and padded down the dimly lit marble corridor flanked by the amazing Peake collection of preserved national wild birds, to her room. I quietly knocked and after a short while she opened the door, wearing a negligee and her hair was disheveled. She invited me into her room and sat me down on a sofa next to an open fire. She then went to a medicine cupboard and produced the little white pill that I was informed was Ephedrine.

Barbara then quietly talked to me asking how I felt and what was upsetting me to cause this asthma attack. Much to my surprise I suddenly burst into tears exclaiming that everything was getting on top of me and that I wished to do so much but couldn't. With that she tenderly hugged me stating 'My poor little one, we are going to do something about this' and gently stroked my hair. I was suddenly in a warm and loving world and above all the Ephedrine was taking effect so I could once again breathe normally although my heart was pounding as was often the case with this drug.

Barbara settled me down on the sofa next to the fire under a blanket and I slept soundly until she awoke me at around 05.00 hours and asked if I would mind returning to my dormitory as she did not wish for certain people to get the wrong idea about me being in her room overnight. However once again she implored me to come and see her whenever I was not feeling well.

It was not long before my next asthma attack and once again I was treated by Barbara. This time after issuing the pill she started to lay out a programme for me. She had arranged for me to begin a course in gymnastics under the supervision of the Physical Training Instructor, Sergeant Major Hicks, and that I was to start doing press ups, ten press ups morning and evening. On top of all that I was to walk some 2 miles a day to the garage and Post Office at the top of the school drive. I was eager to carry out her instructions as I saw them as a challenge and a way forward.

My ten press ups soon became thirty, and I enjoyed the gymnastics, becoming a gymnast certified as 'third class'. Above all my walking turned into gentle runs although I was still suffering from the dreaded asthma attacks. Things were looking up and then I volunteered for early return on the next term for rugby training. Barbara was thrilled and the rugby captain, knowing that I was asthmatic, took the trouble and time to explain to me that this training would be very physical and tough. I replied that I was fully aware of this and that I was hoping to be selected for the first fifteen when the time came. He shook my hand, wished me luck and said he was looking forward to next term.

My life was now rapidly changing with the support of a number of people including my parents, who were praising me for the physical feats but were obviously concerned by my academic situation. Things were not looking good and my term's report suggested that I would be lucky to pass any forthcoming 'O' level examinations. I promised that I would try as hard as I could to listen and concentrate on the various subjects that were being taught.

I returned for that winter term a week early for the rugby training. I had been out running at home during the holidays and this paid off as there was a lot of physical activity involved. I flourished and was always at the front leading the enthusiastic group of ambitious rugby players numbering about thirty in total. I was actually soon noticed by the two coaches who remarked upon my fitness and endurance.

The term started along with lessons and I really did try hard although I realized that it was just too late. My rugby was improving every day and after one particular match in the second fifteen I was approached by the captain of the first fifteen who asked me if I would play for the first fifteen as hooker in the front row of the scrum. I had achieved my ambition and I was soon playing well in this position. I kept Barbara informed of my progress and she would always be there in the crowd watching on at the home matches. One day after I had played really well scoring a try twice I was awarded my first fifteen rugby colours. The school was cheering and I noticed that Barbara was quietly weeping into a handkerchief as I passed her whilst running through the applauding tunnel. I could now wear the coveted first fifteen rugby tie with otters on it along with the colour's purple blazer.

I went to see her later and she hugged me with such affection stating that she was so proud of me and that I had achieved my ambition against all odds. It was then that I realized what I had actually accomplished and above all my asthma was now non existent. She then produced a small blue device and explained that this was an inhaler and whenever I felt wheezy I should inhale a puff. I was not quite sure of this but it was shortly put to the test one night when I awoke with the normal breathlessness. It was wonderful and offered me immediate relief.

I started taking an interest in stage management for the school play that was always held at the end of the winter term. I was working with the 'props manager' Martin who was also a bit of an electrical wizard. One particular scene had to be ended by two loud explosions. Martin decided that these explosions could be achieved by using electrically detonated maroons that could be primed and dropped into a tin dustbin just outside the stage. There was only one problem, he could not find a volunteer to prime and drop these maroons into the dustbin as it involved disconnecting and then reconnecting the primers of the maroons in the dark within some ten seconds.

I bravely volunteered and we carried out two night rehearsals away from the school and the noise of the explosions were tremendous, although I managed the change over no problem. However despite wearing ear defenders I was still deafened. The big night arrived and the performance was going well. The time came for the explosions and I took up my position by the bin and maroons. I was to be warned before the first explosion by a flashing torch and this went to plan and then I had ten seconds to change the primer over to the live maroon.

However I knocked my torch over and had to carry out the task by feel which meant that I was slightly delayed. There was a tremendous flash in my face and I remember being blown back against a wall by the maroon that had exploded in my face. I regained consciousness with Jane, the Sanatorium Matron, giving me first aid as I had a deep cut above my eye not to mention a number of smaller splinter wounds on my face. I was totally dazed shocked and deafened and spent the next day in the Sanatorium recovering, which I quickly did as the term was ending and holidays were approaching. Fortunately my sight or hearing were not affected by this accident.

Chapter 8
Allhallows School - Cliff Fall - 1964

The summer term arrived and this term I was due to take some six 'O' level exams. Mother, father and indeed my teachers were concerned over my academic performance. I blamed my asthma for this although other distractions, such as girls who I was meeting, were also cited as reasons. I promised that I would work as hard as I could to try and achieve at least two or three 'O' levels.

At the same time I was selected for the first eleven cricket team as wicket keeper. I really enjoyed my cricket as well as tennis. At this time of year we also could participate in 'full bore' rifle shooting where we would carry out target shooting at Colyton Rifle Range using the old .303 rifles similar to the ones used during the Second World War. This was great fun and a natural progression from the 'small bore' shooting that would take place in an indoor range. We would do this once sometimes twice a week with the ultimate aim of shooting a match between other clubs and schools at the Ashburton Range.

So life was rather active during this term and then I won my first eleven colours that entitled me, as with the other colour awards, to wear the purple blazer. I also performed rather well at The Ashburton Cup rifle shooting competition and won my first eight shooting colours. This now gave me the right to wear a silver and black striped tie along with a black blazer so my wardrobe was rapidly expanding!

Time came for the dreaded exams. I took comfort over the fact that I was not the only one struggling to answer the questions let alone being able to understand them. It was obvious that I had not done well apart from maybe in Art and English. I was honest with my parents over the matter who mentioned the fact that they were now seriously considering sending me to an educational crammer to concentrate my mind on the various subjects. This all sounded very plausible although I would be sad to leave Allhallows and my friends.

After the exams a small group of six of us, (all labeled as hopeless academic failures), went 'down the cliffs'. It was a lovely day and we were relaxing after the intensity of the exams and waiting for the term to end, it was a good time even if most of us were not expecting to pass our exams. One of my friends, nick-named 'Chile' (as he came from there), started to practice his Judo on me to which I responded. We were on the cliff top and suddenly we started to slide down the wet grass towards the edge of the cliff over which there was a sheer drop of some 120 feet. I desperately tried to catch hold of the grass as it slid past but the speed of my slide got faster as I was approaching the edge and probable death.

Suddenly I managed to grab a small sapling that practically ripped my arms off but I had stopped my fall. I was now hanging by my arms onto this small tree with only inches to go. However my friend 'Chile' had gone, obviously over the edge, and I had survived. I felt awful and quickly started to dig my feet into the ground to try and support some of my weight as my arms were beginning to feel the strain.

I was successful in doing this and it was with relief as I was now almost standing on the steep slope on the edge of this cliff. I saw my friends at the top running around and one shouted down to me that 'Chile' was still alive as he had landed in thick brambles. I was also informed that help would soon be on its way.

So there I was too petrified to move as one slip or movement could send me over that cliff edge and I might not be as lucky as 'Chile'. It was not long before I noticed two Land Rovers and a number of men above me dressed in orange boiler suits and white helmets securing ropes to the vehicles. Two rescuers lowered themselves down to me and one got under me. They explained that they were going to secure me into a harness and then winch me back up to the cliff top. This happened without incident and in fact 'Chile' was pointed out to me on my way up. I could clearly see him on his back buried deep in brambles with his legs above him his white shirt turning red with blood from cuts on his back. It looked ominously odd but I saw his head move in response to a shout from me so it appeared that he was alright. My rescuers pointed out that it was going to be a complicated retrieval with the height of those brambles but that just added to the challenge!

First aid was administered to my hand that was quite badly cut and we waited for 'Chile' to be hoisted up the cliff. It took some time but eventually a stretcher appeared with 'Chile' strapped on lying on his stomach with his back bare showing some horrible lacerations and scratches. He was on good form, though, only too happy to be alive and together we were taken to hospital where we received treatment. 'Chile' remained in hospital for a number of days and I was discharged the same day.

The school investigated the incident resulting in a ruling that before any boys went down the cliffs in future their footwear would have to be appropriate, inspected by a member of staff and approved accordingly. Also a strict ruling was made that there was to be no fooling around on cliff tops. Failing to observe this ruling would result in a term time gating on the area: in other words you would not be permitted to 'go down the cliffs'.

Chapter 9
Sailing - Me Overboard at Night -1964

Idid not return to Allhallows School after that term. Mother and father informed me that they had decided to send me to a crammer known as Foys situated in the heart of the Dorset countryside near a beautiful and remote village known as Chetnole. However my friends and I were determined to keep in contact and one friend, Derek, asked if I would like to come with him on a friends' 34 ft yacht sailing probably across the Channel to the Channel Islands and maybe France for five or six days with three or four other people. This sounded great and it was arranged that we would travel together to the Hamble River where the vessel was moored and board in the afternoon with the intention of sailing overnight, weather permitting.

As planned we arrived and were met by the skipper, John, who was an experienced yachtsman and we were invited aboard his yacht that he had brought alongside a pontoon. It was all so exciting and Derek and I were allocated the 'Focsle' or the front bit of the boat as our sleeping accommodation. We were then introduced to a sailing friend of the skipper, Malcolm, who was also an experienced sailor and together they had done a lot sailing. They both understood that Derek and I had not really sailed properly before and this filled us with confidence as we were now beginning to understand how daunting all this was becoming. We were fitted with lifejackets, harnesses and shown the emergency equipment on board along with how it all worked.

We completed the safety briefing and were just enjoying a cup of tea when the final member of the crew arrived. She was introduced to us as Sue (the cook), and I remember she was wearing a skirt, high heels and her white peroxide hair was beautifully back combed. She also had a rather high pitched voice and Derek seemed to know that she was a croupier from a local casino. In fact Derek quietly informed us under strictest confidence that John had 'employed' her for the trip. I assumed from that Sue was actually very experienced at sailing until Derek calmly put me right by explaining that she was very experienced in other channels of life and it was not sailing or indeed gambling but prostitution. I was intrigued as I had never met a prostitute before and I noticed that she had gone very white after she had climbed down into the cabin. John showed her to her bunk which was the quarter birth and suggested that she could start unpacking after which Malcolm would give her the safety brief and fit her with a lifejacket and harness.

With that John had to go and get some charts with Malcolm and Derek leaving me with Sue. After they had left I heard Sue being sick. The boat was very calm alongside and I thought that this was not a good start to our trip. To make things worse I soon discovered that Sue had been sick into the skipper's sleeping bag and was very upset. I suggested that she should come up on deck, which she did and then set about cleaning the mess up as best as I could. I found some seasick pills and gave her one along with water and comfort. Much to my surprise she quickly started to recover and we were shortly discussing on what to tell John when he arrived back. It was decided that the truth should be told and that she just could not stop herself from filling John's sleeping bag. She was so grateful for all my assistance and I was rather impressed at how she had handled the situation.

It turned out that John had a sense of humour and, fortunately, a spare sleeping bag. Final preparations were made for our night trip across the Channel to Guernsey. The weather forecast was good with a fresh wind on the beam so it was arranged that we would have supper at the local pub before slipping.

At about 22.00 hrs we slipped and motored out of the Hamble. It was a magic warm September evening. The river was like a mill pond and with the shore lights reflected on the mirror water surface it was a wonderful sight as we chugged our way out to sea.

It was not long before John asked Malcolm to get the sails up. Derek and I were asked to go up with him to get the feel of the boat and the equipment and maybe learn how to handle the sails. He would stay at the helm with Sue. The main sail went up first followed by the foresail and then the boat started keeling over in the wind and we started to heave up and down in the waves. It was great and we were well attached to the boat by our harnesses. Every now and again some spray would fly past but Derek and I were getting our sea legs with Derek repeating the fact that we should always have one hand for the boat and one for ourselves. Malcolm patiently and calmly instructed us on what to do and it was not long before we were well under sail with skipper shouting out in exhilaration that we had at least 6 knots and that we would soon be in the Channel Islands.

A watch system was organized with Derek on watch with the skipper and Sue with me on watch with Malcolm. It was decided for the skipper to take first watch so Malcolm and I went below to get some sleep. I soon realized that the only lighting was a dim red light in the cabin so as not to dazzle the deck crew and Malcolm told me to get my head down. I did not sleep at all and I was soon soaking wet as the front hatch above my bunk leaked. However it was not long before there was a shout from the skipper to reduce sail as the wind had increased.

Malcolm instructed me to put on my waterproofs, lifejacket and harness as this could be a little rough. I followed Malcolm onto the deck making sure that I was strapped on and we clambered up to the bow as we were going to put on a smaller foresail. Now the boat was really moving and was keeled over. It was difficult to move about and work the sails all in the dark. Malcolm gave me calm instructions and then I used both my hands to try and pull the sail down.

I lost my footing and fell onto the deck and slowly slid under the lower lifeline into the sea. The shock of the cold sea made it difficult to breathe and then I was being towed along beside the side of the boat being attached by my harness. Fortunately I was in the water on my back with my shoulders and head acting as a 'breakwater' so I could actually gulp air but it was so cold. I heard shouts of 'Man Overboard' and very quickly John managed to slow the yacht so I was not being pulled through the sea at what seemed a tremendous speed.

Malcolm was kneeling on deck close to me and in fact had hold of my harness shoulder strap to hold me up as far as he could. The vessel then became upright and Derek appeared helping Malcolm to pull me back on board. I was soon lying on the deck shivering and being sick as I had swallowed a lot of seawater. I was assisted into the cabin where Sue, who seemed to have completely recovered, helped me out of my wet clothing. She then got me into dry warm attire and into a sleeping bag where she joined me, fully clothed, to help keep me warm. It was wonderful being embraced by this warm sweet smelling woman and it was not long before my violent shivering ceased. John sent Derek down into the cabin to keep an eye on us both in the sleeping bag and Sue was given strict instructions to behave herself.

Sue and I remained in that sleeping bag for the rest of the crossing although we could not get any sleep we certainly kept warm. A perfect landfall being made at first light with John deciding to anchor off Sark as it was such a lovely morning.

Having dropped anchor in a lovely calm spot, it was decided to go ashore after breakfast. Sue did not wish to do so nor did I as I really felt tired and wanted to sleep. It was decided that Sue and I would stay on board and the others would 'walk the steps of Sark'. They departed in the inflatable dinghy and I then enjoyed a deep sleep on my own in my sleeping bag. It was the first time I had experienced that type of heavy sleep caused by exhaustion. However I was suddenly awakened and there sitting on my bunk was Sue, naked, gently stroking my hair. She instructed me to move over and started to undress me. I resisted stating that I was in love with another girl and she backed off stating that I had missed the point. After that she left me alone and the rest of the trip went well without incident.

Chapter 10
Motorbike Accident - 1964

Istarted at Foys Crammer in Dorset in the autumn term. It was a remote country house in the middle of nowhere, with a bit of land that had been dedicated as a sports field. There were some twelve boys attending this crammer and we were all in the same situation in as much as that we had failed our 'O' level exams and were in need of extra academic attention. The accommodation was comfortable, the food good and we had almost one to one tuition with some excellent tutors.

Sports were played in the form of hockey, football and cricket, although competing for a position for a place in the team was not exactly arduous. We also were free to cycle around the countryside and to various villages, towns and of course Sherbourne that was about 14 miles away.

The day started at 06.30 hrs with a hearty breakfast and we then worked through to lunchtime. After lunch we were free to play sports or go for a cycle ride to be back for tea at 16.30 hrs after which we would work until 22.00 hrs. It was a gruelling six-day routine although we had Sunday off. I enjoyed this hard schedule and started to understand the subjects that I was being coached in to such a degree that I carried out extensive research gaining much more knowledge. I was to take another six 'O' levels at the end of the following term and that should end my cramming session. If successful I would have passed 8 'O' levels which in mother and father's opinion was acceptable and with those qualifications may just get a job.

The two terms passed rapidly and I took my exams with confidence and was rewarded with six good passes much to the relief of my parents who made it quite clear to me that this was an expensive education. I was sorry to leave Foys as I had enjoyed my stay and came away feeling that I had accomplished the impossible and was not academically hopeless, as was made out to me at my previous school.

The next problem was to decide what I was to do now that I had finished schooling. Father had just started a new posting as Chairman of the Army Regular Commissions Board at Westbury in Wiltshire and we were now living in a lovely large country residence known as Hawkeswell House. It had been converted into four flats and was surrounded by extensive garden and woodland. Mother was concerned as she had visions of me languishing at home, doing nothing apart from maybe getting up to no good. However within a week I had found myself a job as a forester with the Ministry of Defence working the Erlestoke wood area near Westbury. Father was so impressed with my action he went out and purchased a James 150cc motorbike for me. It was all rather exciting and he taught me how to ride the motorbike and with the 'L' plates in place, I was now mobile and able to travel the 6 miles on the quiet narrow country roads to work.

I was assisting two mature men, Lyn who once operated an extensive rabbit eradication business on Salisbury Plain, and Reginald who used to drive lorries. They had both 'retired' into this job and enjoyed it, especially as I had been drafted in to help them with the aim of decreasing their work load. The day started at 08.00 hrs and we would be clearing, maintaining and planting woodland being assisted by a tractor and trailer, chainsaws etc. We would have half an hour off for lunch and continue in the afternoon finishing at 17.00hrs. It was surprisingly pleasant work. I got on well with my senior peers who sometimes used to ask me to work a little slower especially in the morning, often using the expression 'first load light boy'.

I was getting more experienced with my motorbike now and the quest for speed was there. However being only an old 150cc motorbike the only way to build speed up, I learnt, would be down the hills. I could get up 65 mph going down one hill and it was exhilarating.

One morning it was raining, the roads were wet and there were leaves on the road. I was not fully aware of the added hazard of these road conditions, despite my father's warnings. I was doing the normal 60 mph down the hill when there in front of me blocking the road was a small fuel tanker coming in the opposite direction. I hit the brakes and within an instant I felt the bike skid over onto to its side and I was now sliding on the road on my back towards the tanker.

It all happened so fast. The next thing I knew was that I had slid under the vehicle and rolled into a large blackberry bush on the side of the road. It was uncomfortably prickly but I was alive and appeared uninjured although my back felt numb and cold. I could not move because of my thorny situation which was aggravating as I wanted to see if I was uninjured.

The driver of the road tanker came running up to me asking if I was alright. I informed him that I was fine and would appreciate assistance in getting out of the blackberry bush. He gently pulled me out and I stood on my feet a bit dazed but apparently uninjured. He exclaimed that he just could not get over how lucky I was as I had passed under his moving vehicle and it was incredible that I had not been crushed by one of the wheels. He then checked my back as he noticed that I was not wearing leather motor bike clothing. He informed me that I had lost all the clothing on my back and that there was a fair amount of blood about. This was not to mention gravel stuck in my back, commonly known as 'gravel rash'.

The driver gave me a lift home in his road tanker and although sore I assisted my father repairing the damage to the motorbike. We soon got it going again and after this incident I was a little more cautious especially on wet roads.

Chapter 11

Army Recruit Training/Exposure on Salisbury Plain - 1966

L ife was good with me working as a forester with Lyn and Reg. Sometimes I would walk the 6 miles to work across the fields or use my motor bike to get to work. All day would be spent outside and I would return home at Hawkeswell to a hot bath and supper with mother and father and then bed.

However, the time had come to make that decision on whether or not I was to join the Army and to start with my driving lessons. Father suggested that I should begin with my driving now and that he would drive me into Salisbury at the next opportunity for my first driving lesson. I had already acquired my provisional driving licence and purchased my 'L' plates and was waiting for the invitation from mother to start driving her small Fiat under her instruction.

To my surprise that invitation came during this discussion and it was decided that father would book my first driving lesson and it was suggested that perhaps I could attach my 'L' plates to mother's car now. Father also suggested that he would drive me to the Army Recruit Office in Salisbury so that I could sign up. This happened on the 23rd February 1966 and I was presented with The Soldiers Prayer Book, although no start date for my recruit training, with The Royal Green Jackets (RGJ), in Winchester could be given as they were fully subscribed at that time. Things were now moving and it was all very exciting.

I continued my job as a forester with the Ministry Of Defence for another four months and during this time I passed my driving test. Following this I was then called to join the RGJ at Winchester to start my recruit training as a rifleman.

Father drove me to Peninsula Barracks in Winchester. I entered the gate where I was shown into the guard room and I was checked off. There waiting as well were some six other individuals from all over the country joining this recruit training course. It quickly became clear that one of my problems was going to be able to understand the different accents of my fellow recruits. Many came from the North, particularly Liverpool. We soon completed the first six weeks of basic training although two of our section 'resigned'.

The basics of marching, weapon handling and fitness had been accomplished and now we were being instructed in subjects such as map reading, first aid along with completing the assault course fully equipped, living in the field and shooting our weapons. It was strangely enjoyable.

We had to undergo a map reading test at night on Salisbury Plain in early January. Groups of three of us would be dispatched onto the Plain to follow a course where we would sign into various checkpoints. The Corporal organizing the exercise came across a problem as he seemed unable to split us into the correctly numbered groups due to the number he was working with. I was not quite sure what his problem actually was but confidently suggested that as I had previous map reading experience in Brecon with the cadets I would be happy to go on my own around this course that would only take two hours at the most. To my surprise he agreed to this, as I was a potential officer.

I was issued with map, torch and radio and was instructed not to get lost. I was the last to start on the route, that was based on one of the remote artillery range impact areas of Salisbury Plain and by that time the weather had got bad with wind and rain.

The Corporal was assured by me that I was fine and that I would be back within the hour. I was dressed in my working uniform with the idea of running around the course that would not only keep me warm but may just set a record!

There were no problems to start with, checking into various points well in time and knowing exactly where I was. The map reading was simple and I took an un-authorized short cut across the course that would half my time. However whilst jogging along a tank track I 'turned' my right ankle and tripped into a large 'tank puddle'. I crawled out gasping for breath as it was so cold. I was soaked and in the wind it was bitter. Furthermore I could not put any weight on my damaged ankle so I began to realize that I could be in bit if a situation as I was some distance from any road and even if they did come looking for me I was not anywhere near where I should be. I was on my own!

I fumbled for my torch but it seemed that this had been lost in the puddle. I had no means of illumination and it was a dark stormy night. I knew roughly where I was and then tried to switch my radio on to summons assistance, but it was dead, probably damaged by the water. It was then that I realized the gravity of my situation and I was fully aware of the hazards of exposure.

I decided first to try and get out of the bitter rain and wind as I was soon shivering uncontrollably. However I could only crawl but remembered that shortly before my fall I had passed a wood. I crawled to that wood through the soaking grass and puddles and arrived after some thirty minutes of painful struggle. I crawled into the wood and found a depression in the ground that was full of water, over which there was a large tree. I found that by lying on the side of the depression under the trunk of the tree I could get out of the wind that was cutting through me. I checked my Army issued luminous watch, it was 23.15hrs and I realized that first light would not be until 07.30hrs so it was going to be a long cold night.

A wood at night at the best of times is a dark place and in a storm it is also very noisy. I was out of that wind but I was so cold it was painful. I tried standing up but my ankle was now throbbing. Every five minutes I would beat myself with my arms to keep the blood circulating. I tried covering my head with my army combat jacket but this exposed my waist and that was even colder. I shivered quite uncontrollably and kept moving.

Somehow I kept the five minute routine of moving about going and discovered how to think laterally which seemed to alleviate the pain of the cold and my ankle. Those good times I had experienced (those girls I had met and so on). At 07.15hrs it started getting lighter and my spirits began to rise. It had stopped raining now, the wind had decreased and it looked as if the sun was coming out. My goal of reaching daylight had been met and that would mean I would survive, although I was not quite clear how as I was incapacitated.

Then I heard it; the sound of helicopters. I crawled out of my shelter onto a bank where I could see down onto part of the Plain. There were four helicopters that seemed to be flying in a low hover formation not far away. I just could not believe it, was I to be rescued by helicopter? Were they looking for me?

I wondered how I could attract their attention as I could not move far. Perhaps if I took my jacket off and waved that about they might see me. I started to take my jacket off and the sodden remains of my map fell out. I grabbed it and started waving it above my head but it fell to bits.

However one of the helicopters stopped and then turned and flew directly towards me landing a short distance away. I fell onto my knees and offered a prayer of thanks to The Good Lord, I had been saved. The helmeted observer got out and ran over to asking if I was O.K. and if I was the only one I could not answer that question but just nodded my head. With that he grabbed my arm and then realized that I was injured. He half lifted and dragged me to the helicopter and I was strapped into a seat with a blanket placed over me and headphones placed on my head.

The pilot verified the fact that I was the only one to be rescued and that I was Recruit Young. I nodded and was shivering so hard now that it felt as if the aircraft was vibrating with me. I then burst into tears and the pilot instructed me to 'hang in there and that it would only be another ten minutes before I was in Tidworth Hospital' as he took off.

It was warm in that blanket with the observer hugging me and the next thing I remember is waking in a hospital bed feeling very hungry. My painful ankle brought me back to reality as to what had happened. I was informed that I had suffered exposure and that my ankle was not broken but badly sprained. I was advised that it would be a good six weeks before I would be using it again fully.

Later I was visited by my Platoon Commander and Platoon Sergeant who were in good form giving me a bunch of grapes! They wanted to know if I had been on my own, what clothing I had been wearing and what equipment I was carrying. I informed them that I had volunteered to go on my own, that I had been wearing light weather gear as I was running the course and had been issued with all the equipment that had failed me after total immersion in the tank puddle. The Platoon Commander then informed me that I would have to be back squadded to join the next platoon when I had fully recovered and that in the meantime I would go on sick leave for at least four weeks. My parents had been informed and they were going to collect me shortly after I had been discharged from hospital.

I accepted this without problem and looked forward to my luxury four week break with mother and father before I would be completing my final phase of recruit training.

Chapter 12
Skydiving Hangup - 1966

Irejoined the Royal Green Jacket depot at Winchester after four weeks and continued the final phase of my recruit training without incident. The new recruit training platoon that I had joined seemed more mature and capable than my previous one with no recruits dropping out.

Following the pass out parade I was informed by the Platoon Commander that I had been recognized as a 'potential officer' and that a place would be reserved for me at Mons Officer Cadet School at Aldershot. I had to seek at least two sponsors and in the meantime was to be promoted to Lance Corporal and would be assisting in supporting the administration of the recruit training here at Winchester.

This was great news as my main task was to deliver tea and food to the training platoons out in the field wherever they were anytime day or night, and every now and again prepare their accommodation in the old type of Nissan huts found on Salisbury Plain. I took this duty seriously as I realized how important it was to get the support there in the correct place at the right time in any weather. I was on my own driving a Land Rover most of the time. It was enjoyable and satisfying seeing tired recruits enjoying their food or tea having battled through blizzards, floods and mud.

I managed to get myself on a three-day climbing course with three other soldiers and the four of us had two experienced climbing instructors. We travelled up to North Wales for the climbing and were accommodated in a climbing hut complete with 'fresh rations' all sponsored by The Royal Green Jackets apart from a contribution of £20 per student. It was a chance not to be missed especially as we had been given the time to do this as well.

Our instructors were good and it was made quite clear that discipline was essential for this activity and it was not just a case of deciding to climb a rock face and then going for it! We started well tethered on a 'difficult climb' progressing to a 'very difficult' and were introduced to abseiling. It was great.

At the same time I was being invited to interviews by my potential sponsors, those being the Parachute Regiment and The Royal Green Jackets. I had decided not to join the family regiment, the Devon and Dorsets as I felt uncomfortable with father being the first Commanding Officer, and as I explained to him I always had this yearning to jump from heights. Both of my sponsors agreed to support me as long as I passed all the necessary selection and training so I was home and dry.

I was given two weeks leave and this was taken up with an Army Parachute Centre skydiving course held at Netheravon Airfield. My dream to parachute was about to come true.

After five days ground training we carried out our first jumps from an old

De Haviland Rapide aircraft early on a calm and sunny September morning in 1966. In those days the first jumps were carried out with the assistance of a static line. This is a cord that is attached to the aircraft and to your parachute in the absence of a ripcord. It was designed so that the student parachutist did not have to worry about pulling the ripcord as the parachute was opened by the static line once the student had jumped. We were warned during ground training that it had been known on very rare occasions for the static line to wrap around the parachute pack after jumping and then the unfortunate student would be dragged behind the aircraft until being cut free by the instructor when the emergency parachute could then be deployed by the student.

On my second jump I suffered a hang up. There was a tremendous jolt and I realized that I was not falling but flying through the air behind the aircraft which I could hear clearly above me. I carefully looked up and sure enough there was my instructor leaning out of the door above the wing, showing me his knife. The drill here was to place your right hand on your helmet and the instructor would then cut you free and I would then pull my reserve parachute.

I slowly placed my hand on my head and was then flicked over by the slip-stream and this deployed my main parachute as it should have been. The only problem I had now was that I was miles away from Netheravon Airfield some-where over Salisbury Plain. I landed safely and waited hoping for a lift from a tank or another type of military vehicle. It was not long before the centre's Land Rover arrived to collect me.

This was the start of a varied and successful military and civilian parachut-ing experience completing over 800 jumps not without further incidents.

Chapter 13

Mons Officer Cadet School - Knife Attack - 1966

I had just returned from a delivery of tea and food to a location on the Plain. I was told to report to the Orderly Room as soon as possible as the Chief Clerk wished to speak to me. He informed me that there had been a last minute cancellation on the Mons Officer Cadet course and if I could get there within the next two hours they would accept me. He apologised for the short notice but felt that I was capable of dealing with it and wished me luck adding that 'he would look after the admin this end as long as I could hand in everything that I should.'

Without hesitation I started sorting my kit out as I had to sign off certain items etc. A quick farewell was said to those I saw and then I drove as fast as I dared to Mons Officer Cadet School, in Aldershot, arriving just in time. It was the normal recruit reception with uniform bedding etc. being issued whilst being guided around the premises. However I noticed as with the other officer cadets we were addressed as 'Sir' by the soldiers and Non Commissioned Officers (NCOs), who were supervising our entry administration.

We were shown to our accommodation block, which was a wooden Nissen Hut and our names were on the respective beds. It all seemed very organized and there were eight of us in one room with four beds either side. I immediately gelled with my next door neighbours, Charlie and Tony. Charlie was keen to emphasis that he was 'An Honourable' and Tony a 'Man Of God'. The other five room mates consisted of two old soldiers, Phil and Andy, who had just returned from being mercenaries in The Congo, Martin who was a broad Cockney, Joseph who came from Jamaica, Zulu from Africa (who claimed to be a prince), and what appeared to be an intellectual from Libya, Muammar, sent by his country to Mons to be commissioned. This started the interesting, amusing and challenging flavour of this fourteen week course that lay ahead us.

Our instructor, a Corporal Of Horse (COH), made an appearance and informed us that he would be responsible for the daily discipline etc of this section and that there were some three other sections within this training platoon. To start we were shown how to present our bed blocks every morning. This consisted of our sheets and blankets being folded neatly into a precisely measured box and that this inspection would take place at 08.00 followed by a drill parade at 08.30 and so the day would progress. We were also instructed to pack our civilian clothes away in our suitcases that would then be handed into the guardroom and kept there for the next six weeks. After which following completion of the basic military training we would be allowed out for our first weekend leave.

We met the other officer cadets during our evening meal and there were 32 of us on this course all from varying countries and backgrounds and it was very interesting. After the meal having talked to a number of other officer cadets we settled down for the night. At 06.00 hrs the guard woke us up and following breakfast we had our first room inspection. We were warned about mis-shaped and wrongly sized bed blocks, dirt and dust in the room etc and instructed to put it right by tomorrow morning. We all had to have the standard army haircut whether we needed it or not and then there was the first parade when we marched around the drill square as a platoon.

This is where the first problems were accounted with one or two officer cadets finding it difficult to march due to lack of co-ordination. They were unable to swing their arms in time to their opposite leg which apparently is quite common. Much to my surprise I was given the task of sorting out Zulu's lack of co-ordination and told to report back to the square within forty-five minutes having succeeded in this task.

Zulu and I found a quiet corner of the drill square where we concentrated on marching. Zulu was very upset as he informed me Princes don't normally have this problem but after some fifteen minutes of perseverance suddenly it came. Zulu could proudly march about with his long arms flying through the air in the correct sequence along with a broad grin with the white of his teeth and eyes seemingly flashing in the sunlight. It was a sight to behold!

Zulu was very grateful for my effort to such a degree that he invited me to London with him and his family on our next weekend when we were permitted out in some five weeks time. Whilst I was tempted I refused the kind invitation as I would be keen to see my own family. A point he appreciated.

Having rejoined the platoon the marching session for the morning was completed. We were then introduced to our Platoon Commander, John, who was a Parachute Regiment Captain. He informed us that he would be instructing on tactics and other such matters. He did actually approach me and two other cadets, Martin, the broad cockney, and Colin, who was a university entrant, informing us that he had noticed that we had been provisionally selected for the Parachute Regiment and that he would be keeping a careful eye on us!

The six-weeks military training completed without too much problem. There were plenty of personal and room inspections, marching, weapon and fitness training. There were some late nights scrubbing our accommodation block floor and painting the room's stove coal white until the early hours of the morning, but all this was almost amusing with Charlie about. Charlie did many extra guard duties as he always seemed to be late or turned up in the wrong uniform at the wrong time despite all our efforts. However he had a smile on his face most of the time and nothing got him down and we were able to laugh with him wondering what would happen next. This was a good lesson in life as there is normally always one in a situation like this and 'The Honorable' Charlie was that one.

Our first weekend when we could go out arrived. A smart Rolls Royce pulled up in front of our accommodation block and we all wondered who it was. Much to our surprise it was Zulu's transport so we then realized that Zulu was indeed most probably a Prince and perhaps I should have accepted his London invitation!

It was at this stage that the three prospective candidates for the Parachute Regiment, Colin, Martin and I, were approached by Captain 'John'. He announced that he was keen to find a crew of two to man a canoe that would be competing in The Devizes to Westminster Canoe Race during the next Easter weekend. He stressed that it was a 'tough race' being 125 mile non stop that required physical and mental stamina not forgetting the planning. John was keen to represent Mons Officer Cadet School in this race and it would be ideal for 'Special Force Candidates' to show what they were made of. Colin immediately stated that he could not participate as he had a lot of university work to complete in the next eight weeks, which left Martin and self. We made the point that we had not canoed before and John emphasised that we would be given proper training over the next eight weeks so that we would be competent.

It all suddenly looked rather exciting so Martin and I volunteered, to be told that our first training session in the local swimming pool would be on the evening on our return from the weekend. The description of the training and the race itself follows in the next chapter.

The weekend soon passed and it was good to drive my old Vauxhall Victor again along with staying with mother and father sleeping in a comfortable bed in my own room and not having to rise at 06.00. I returned to Mons and immediately we had to get our uniform and kit ready for the next day. Whilst there was still the rigid military training everyday we were now being instructed in a classroom on subjects such as tactics, social etiquette etc. It was interesting and at times amusing especially with Charlie about.

We eventually had our final 5-day test exercise in the Brecon Beacons. Certain officer cadets would be chosen to fulfill positions such as Platoon Commander, Platoon Sergeant etc. to show their capability, or lack of it. Sure enough I was selected to be the Platoon Commander on the first stage of this exercise to include commanding an ambush patrol.

I was confident and it all went well apart from one incident in the command post. I was finalizing the initial position briefing and commanded a black officer cadet, who seemed to be doing not a lot in the command post to dig a latrine. Having issued my order I turned my back on him and then there was a tremendous commotion and I noticed that this black officer cadet who I had just given an order to dig a latrine, was lying on the ground face down with Phil, the former mercenary, standing over him. It was obvious that Phil had knocked him down and out with his rifle butt and was muttering the fact that 'you can never trust them,' and that perhaps I should not have turned my back on him having issued my instructions.

I and our instructor John, who was also present, having called for a medic, asked Phil why he had done this. He pointed out that if we looked at the victim's right hand we would notice that he was still holding a bayonet which was correct and then stated that having issued my order to dig a latrine this officer cadet had drawn his bayonet and was apparently about to stab me in the back. This was confirmed by two other witnesses.

The unconscious attacker was carried out of the command post and taken to hospital where he made a full recovery. I was asked if I would wish to press charges and I decided that this was not the course to take as we were all tired and some act differently to others in situations like this. This was a good decision and the ambush and the rest of the exercise went well although we never saw my assailant again.

The passing out parade was a success and we all went our respective ways. Martin decided not to join the Parachute Regiment following The Devizes to Westminster Canoe Race, going for the Royal Corps Of Transport, (RCT) instead, stating that he wished for an easier life. That left Colin and me as prospective candidates for the Parachute Regiment.

Chapter 14

The Devizes to Westminster Canoe Race - The Capsize

Our Devizes to Westminster canoe training was now in full swing. We had ventured out from the swimming pool now, having completed capsize and safety drills, onto rivers. Our next training session was to be on the River Wye, starting south of Monmouth and paddling downstream with the tide towards Tintern Abbey with the aim of covering as much distance as possible within twelve hours.

We travelled up in a 3-ton Army truck with our K2 canoe. It had been a stormy night with heavy rain and there were floods everywhere and we also encountered plenty more rain on the journey up there. The rivers were in full spate and Martin was showing concern about canoeing in these conditions. I stressed the fact that we would be wearing manual gas operated lifejackets that had been borrowed from the Parachute Training Centre at Abingdon and that John would be following us by road, so we had nothing to worry about.

We launched as planned and started downstream at some speed; it was quite exhilarating although Martin was constantly asking 'what if', which I found annoying. However this was not for long as we rounded a bend in the river and there before us was a fallen tree across the river which we ran into, capsizing our canoe. We both surfaced and found that whilst the river at this point was wide we were actually standing up to our waists in surging water on a sand bank mid stream.

Having coughed the foul smelling and tasting brown water from our lungs Martin asked, 'I can't swim so now what do we do?' 'Simple' I replied, just pull your inflation cord on the right of your lifejacket and it will inflate and we can then swim for the bank', that was some 30 meters away.

We both tried inflating our lifejackets and there were resounding clicks from the gas bottles but no inflation with either of our lifejackets. So there we were in the middle of a river in full flood, up to our waists in strong surging water with no protective clothing such as dry suits etc. It did not take long before we started to feel the cold. My legs were going numb and there was a bitter wind that was cutting through the top halves of our bodies. We were beginning to feel weak and it was obvious that we had to swim for the nearest bank or we would soon be collapsing and would be swept under the tree that had caused this capsize.

Without further hesitation I shouted to Martin to hold onto me and that I would swim with him on my back to the bank. I was not the strongest of swimmers but somehow I managed to swim that distance. We lay on the river bank, wet, cold, weak and exhausted not really caring about what would happen next as we had survived.

A man walking his dog stumbled upon us, and after leaving his coat with us, for warmth, went to summon assistance that shortly came in the form of a police Land Rover, closely followed by John in the truck.

We were in a state of shock at this stage and hypothermia was setting in but with warm clothing, hot water bottles and a warm lorry cab we soon recovered enough to explain what had happened.

John was not too happy about the lifejackets and the very fact that he had set us off on the trip to start with. We were soon back at Mons Officer Cadet School where a hot bath and bed was very welcome.

We continued our canoe training without incident and in fact completed that River Wye stretch shortly after, taking care to avoid that fallen tree that had been removed from across the river. We completed the Devizes to Westminster race but we were not placed. However John stressed that it was an achievement just to complete the course with our experience and was complimentary.

It certainly was the first time I had experienced such conditions of deep fatigue, pain in my hands, upper body and above all, once again, the cold especially at night, when we seemed to be out of sight of any other humans. It was a strange, lonely and very uncomfortable sensation but together Martin and I got through it, although Martin swore that he would never subject himself to this type of rigour again. However the memorable sense of achievement made up for everything and that deep sleep that rewards those that are deprived of sleep for long periods was something else. I would not wish to do the race again!

Chapter 15

The Parachute Regiment Induction and 'P' Company - 1967

Following our passing out parade at Mons Officer Cadet School in April, Colin and I received our joining instructions. We were to report to the Parachute Regiment Depot in Aldershot where we had to undergo two more interviews and if successful would then start the selection process where it was made quite clear that this would be both mentally and physically demanding. We would be pushed to our limits and beyond. Those that are successful would be then entitled to wear 'the maroon beret' of the Parachute Regiment having completed the three week parachute training course at RAF Lynham. It was all very challenging.

On arrival I discovered that there were another four prospective Parachute Regiment young officers from Sandhurst so now there were six of us, which seemed to make it all less formidable. We were once again warned by the Adjutant, who had welcomed us on arrival, what lay ahead of us.

First we had to get through the two remaining interviews and then we would have to attend a two week 'build-up phase', when we would be trained by our own personal physical training instructors, (PTIs), who would aim to prepare us physically and mentally for the dreaded Pegasus Company ('P' Coy) test that would be held over a week. If at any time it was thought that we could not meet these demands, we would be suspended from this training and referred back to our second choice of Arm, in my case the Devon and Dorset Regiment, where once again we would face an induction process that would of course be far less rigorous. This was known as being RTU'd.

We were all successful in our interviews and the build up training followed. It consisted of load carrying marches where we had to carry a rifle, personal webbing and a bergen back pack weighing not less than 35 pounds, fast runs of anything up to 11 miles, circuit training, military skills that included map reading, first aid, field craft, bayonet fighting and the military swimming test. This was a strangely enjoyable course and none of us had any problems with it. In fact we were given a long weekend to rest before attempting 'P' Coy that was to start on the following Monday.

There were some 35 candidates starting 'P' Company with a 10 mile morning run carrying not less than 35 pounds plus water and weapon. We had One hour fifty minutes to complete this run. In the afternoon we were intro-duced to the Trainasium which was described to us as an 'aerial confidence course'. As this title might suggest it was an assault course that included high obstacles, anything up to 75 feet, with the objective of testing the candidate's ability to overcome fear at heights. A number of candidates failed on this and were RTU'd, but there were no injuries, just refusals.

The next day consisted of the Log Race where a team of eight of us carried a 60 kg log over wet and undulating ground as found in Long Valley, near Aldershot, over a distance of some 2 miles. More candidates dropped out on this test followed by a 2 mile forced march in full gear again over the same undulating boggy ground. It was becoming apparent that stamina was important now as we were all fit to participate in the various exercises but not all could meet the consistent physical challenge. The drop out rate began to rise.

In the afternoon we did a 2 mile speed march in full kit over hilly terrain and more candidates were RTU'd. Without physical relent the following morning we had to endure a steeplechase being completed with a 'water obstacle' assault course that was different. Spirits within the course were now high as it would seem that those that had survived thus far were here to stay.

The afternoon of this day (Wednesday), was completed with a bit of 'entertainment' in the form of an activity titled 'Milling'. The 24 surviving candidates were instructed to form a human ring and then two of us in turn would be selected to participate in a short period of 'controlled physical aggression' against each other. We were issued with boxing gloves for this task and were each supported by two PTI coaches in our respective corners. There were actually no rules and opponents were meant to be selected on similar height and weight, although we were warned that this was not always possible.

I well remember my opponent was a huge Fijian man about double my height and weight. This was met with a combination of mirth and booing from the assembled ring. My PTI coaches advised me 'to go in hard and fast' and that this character was actually a boxer of some success!

The bell was sounded and I noted that my giant aggressor was playing to the crowd a bit by waving his arms about and doing a foot dance. Without hesitation with the adrenaline flowing I ran towards him and launched myself in a form of a left hook catching him totally by surprise just under the nose. He collapsed onto the floor dazed with blood flowing from his mouth and nose. The fight was stopped and the referee held my hand up as the victor and there was loud cheering from all. I suddenly started to feel guilty as I had actually attacked this poor chap totally by surprise. I approached him as he was being treated by medics in his corner and he staggered to his feet stating that he should have known better and congratulated me on such a powerful and well aimed punch that had knocked him out. We shook hands and I felt a lot better now realizing that I had actually pulled off quite a feat that filled me with physical confidence.

Following a clean up after the milling, we boarded a coach and made our way up to Brecon in Wales, and arrived at a remote spot in the hills. It was a glorious evening and we were shown our harbour area where we were instructed to construct our bashers which would accommodate us for the next two nights. We were actually issued some clear plastic sheeting for this purpose.

We enjoyed a cooked evening meal having constructed our overnight accommodation, after which I escaped to a quiet spot just to admire the wonderful view and the tranquility of the Welsh Hills, as we had the evening off. Tomorrow we were competing in an individual timed map reading course of some 20 miles over severe terrain in full kit, consisting of a back pack weighing no less than 35 lbs plus a twenty-four hour ration pack, water and rifle. If we failed to complete the course in less than 4.5 hours we would fail the course. This would be followed the next day (Friday), by the final test of the course, the dreaded Stretcher Race. Teams of eight men would carry a 175 lbs stretcher over a distance of 5 miles. No more than four men would carry the stretcher at any given time. Individuals wear webbing and carry a weapon.

It was a warm grey June morning that greeted us and we cooked ourselves some porridge and made a brew from the twenty-four-hour ration over the small hexamine stove. First parade was at 08.00 hrs when we were inspected in full kit with random weighing of back packs. That completed we were then briefed on the 20 mile timed forced march. It became clear that the emphasis was not on completing the march within the stipulated time of 4.5 hours but that it should be of a competitive nature with accurate map reading and timing records to be broken. This filled me with excitement and the adrenaline began to flow.

We were started on five different routes with a fifteen minute break between each competitor. This was similar to orienteering which I had enjoyed in the past and was fully aware of the tricks that the checkpoint umpires could get up to. For instance if a bridge was a checkpoint they would probably position themselves under the bridge so you had to be confident in your map reading.

I started as number three in my group of five and decided to walk as fast as I could up the hills and then run down them. My map reading and speed was good and sure enough I soon came across a waypoint that was a bridge. I had caught up with my predecessor who I noted was looking for the waypoint judge who of course was under the bridge. I ran straight to the umpire under the bridge who was holding his finger to his lips instructing silence as he knew that there was a competitor searching above us. He quietly signed me off and let me drink some water from my water bottle before dispatching me to my next checkpoint.

On exiting this checkpoint I saw the lost candidate and pointed to beneath the bridge and he held his hand up in acknowledgement and made his way under the bridge. I knew that I was doing well as I soon was overtaking another runner and the checkpoint umpires were confirming that my time was excellent and if I continued at this pace I may be setting a record.

With relief the weather got worse with wind and rain as this was further encouragement to move faster. We were fearful of the fact that if it had been a hot sunny day this could cause problems with heat exhaustion which could strike anybody and I soon completed the course with encouragement from the supervising staff who congratulated me. I was directed into a large hut to wait for the transport back to our overnight accommodation along with others, including Colin, who had also finished. Spirits were high whilst we changed into dry clothing and a cooked meal whilst waiting for the transport. However it became apparent that those that were here now had all done well with good timings. It was then that I began to feel part of an elite team, it was a good feeling.

Eventually all members arrived and none seemed to have failed so it was onto the transport and back to our overnight accommodation. The weather was now improving until eventually it was a lovely June evening. We were then summoned to the top of a nearby 80ft cliff where we were informed that we would be abseiling down the cliff without top ropes. I had done quite a bit of abseiling before so this was no particular problem.

I had carried out two good abseils without incident and got rigged up for the final and third one. I casually launched myself off the top of the cliff, whilst talking to my friend, Colin, and for some unknown reason I attempted to slow or stop my descent by holding the rope with my left hand which was the 'guide hand' . I should have used my locking hand with the carabena on the right hand side. I plummeted earthwards desperately trying to stop myself by holding onto the rope with my left hand and crashed into the ground on my back.

There was no fear or pain just black on impact. I had been knocked unconscious. I came to shortly after and there were two medics, one supporting me and the other trying to release my bloodied left hand that was clamped onto the rope. They realized that I was coming to and politely asked if I could let go of the rope. Strangely I could not do this and my hand had to be forced open and then I was gently laid on the ground.

Whilst feeling dazed I got to my feet and immediately realized that my right knee was injured as I could not put weight on it and of course my left hand was beginning to get painful. The officer commanding (OC) came running over and asked who it was, to be informed that it was number six. I heard the OC exclaim, 'Oh no it's Rod' and then he realized that I was on my feet. He stopped in front of me and explained that I should not be standing up as I had just fallen some 80 feet down a cliff but I insisted that I was fine. I had every intention of completing this course although the concern was my knee.

He instructed me to get onto the stretcher that the medics had brought alongside me but I refused. I stated that I was fine although my hand perhaps needed attention and the medics had started to treat it. My knee was beginning to feel less painful now and with care I could put weight on it. The OC picked up my old First World War Lee Enfield rifle that had broken into two parts and my bergen back pack had disintegrated. He then stated that I was to be taken to hospital for a check up and I pleaded with him for this not to happen as I was really fine and would be running in the final test, the Stretcher Race, tomorrow.

Much to my relief he relented, instructing me to be ready for a medical assessment in his presence first thing tomorrow morning. I was then assisted back to my basher where I spent a painful and restless night but I was determined to attempt the Stretcher Race. The medical assessment took place the next morning with the doctor, and the OC was present. I was informed that I had been extremely lucky not to have broken my back or worse in that fall and that whilst I had a badly rope burnt left hand that could have possibly saved me, my right knee had water on it and was swollen. I could put my weight through it and I was instructed that if I used it excessively I may cause future problems and that I should only use it with caution.

The OC replied that he felt that he could not command me not to run the Stretcher Race but if I did it would solely be my decision and responsibility and that I should consider the implications if I did run. I confirmed that I would be competing and they left with the OC instructing me to hand the remnants of my rifle to one of the PTIs.

The race started with 24 of us and all were warned that whilst I would be running nobody was to assist me and that I would not be given any special treatment apart from the fact that I would not be carrying my rifle as it was broken. There was a loud cheer and I felt really good as if I was on a cloud, which may have been something to do with the painkillers I was taking. There was no pain to start with and I had no problem in doing my bit. A medic was running with me and another was carrying an empty collapsed stretcher nearby which was normal for this exercise.

Morale was high and the speed was fast and suddenly the finish came into view a half a mile away. It was pointed out to us and with a cheer the pace increased to a sprint. Suddenly my right knee gave way and I tumbled to the ground in excruciating pain. I found a stick to cling onto and hobbled the final stretch noticing that my 'brothers' having finished were running back towards me to encourage me in. This really helped me overcome the pain and I staggered over the finish line thinking that I had failed as I was probably out of time.

As I crossed the OC warmly congratulated me and shouted out that we had all passed and that it had been an exceptional Test Week. He then ordered me onto a stretcher and I was taken by ambulance back to the Royal Cambridge Hospital at Aldershot. The medics plied me with painkillers and treated my hand. It was a painful trip back but I felt on top of the world wondering how I had survived and managed to pass 'P' Company despite my injuries.

Chapter 16

Recovery and the Military Parachuting Course - 1967

After some days in hospital I was eventually discharged complete with a plaster on my right lower leg, with six weeks sick leave. There was concern over my right knee and whether I would now be crippled for life! I did not accept this and was positive that I would make a full recovery and pleaded to be booked onto the military parachuting course in some eight weeks time. Time as always would tell but the administration did book me on that course and that was a great support.

Mother and father collected me from hospital and once again I was back at home in my room being cared for by my parents, enjoying mum's cooking and their company. It was quite clear that they were very proud of me despite the damage I had done to myself.

After three weeks, time began to drag a bit as I could not walk or drive so I was in effect imprisoned to the house despite my parents efforts to alleviate my boredom by taking me out and about. I decided to take up art and purchased materials that all inspiring artists use including an easel. This was great as I could sit on a stool in the garden and paint. I soon recruited the assistance of a well known wealthy female artist in the area, who I had just met at a party and was coaching me. She was an attractive middle aged divorcee and it was not long before mother and others started to show concern over our 'relationship' that was totally innocent.

Father suggested that perhaps I could return to the Parachute Regiment Depot at Aldershot and carry out 'light duties', maybe under the supervision of the Adjutant. This sounded a good idea so I put the idea to the Adjutant who welcomed me in the role with open arms. This was the final two weeks of my sick leave and I had the plaster on my leg removed so I was now a little more mobile and was slowly building strength up again under the direction of the physiotherapists.

I was actually sent on a two week course on the role young officers can play in a Court Martial and indeed in Civil Courts. I found it fascinating and learnt a lot and of course this knowledge would be used later when I had to appear in the local courts representing 'the accused' (normally on minor charges of being drunk and disorderly), as 'the soldier's friend'. I made a lot of friends and seemed to spend many days at those Courts. It was a clever move by the Adjutant of the day.

After the six week sick leave period I was assessed as fit and received my joining instructions for the Military Parachuting course at Abingdon that was operated by the Royal Air Force. I was informed that this three week course was actually similar to a holiday camp, complete with excellent accommodation in the Officers' Mess. I really looked forward to it especially as I had previous parachuting experience and it was an activity that I enjoyed.

I booked into the Officers' Mess at RAF Abingdon on the Sunday evening to discover another two Army officers who were also on the same course. The mess was large and similar to a five star hotel. There were all types of characters here, mainly RAF, but also some from other countries who were something to do with flying. We three Army officers were very much treated as guests and at times, politely and lightheartedly referred to as 'Pongos'. At the social hub of the mess, the bar, I soon met flight crews who seemed keen to satisfy my enthusiasm for flying and I was promised flights sitting in the 'jockey' seat whenever I could get away.

There were 34 of us on the Military Parachuting course consisting of three officers and men all of whom had just passed 'P' Company. Whilst we were now entitled to wear the famous maroon beret of the Parachute Regiment, having passed 'P' Company selection, we were not as yet entitled to 'put our wings up' on our right shoulder.

The course started with the first week concentrating on 'ground training' where we learnt all about parachuting. Emphasis was placed on exiting the aircraft, drills on parachute opening and how to land, not forgetting on how to handle your open parachute on the ground that could be dragging you in the wind, perhaps towards the enemy who had somehow missed you with their rifle fire whilst being suspended under your canopy. It was enjoyable being supervised by 8 R.A.F. Parachute Jump Instructors, (PJI's), who were experienced and excellent at their job.

The PJI's proudly wore their insignia of the RAF Parachute Training School on their chests that read *'Knowledge dispels fear'*. I could not resist the temptation to challenge this motto by querying the fact that surely knowledge should instill fear not dispel it! I was told that it was not my position to question why… so I didn't.

Following ground training, the time had come for our first parachute jump from a balloon at 800 feet over another RAF airfield Weston-on-the Green. This was for some the most severe test as it was very quiet and when you jumped you descended straight down. There was actually one refusal here and the candidate was sent straight back to his unit without even a chance to bid us farewell.

After the successful balloon jump we then had to jump from an aircraft. The aircraft used at this stage was the Hastings with four engines. It was also classified as a tail dragger and one of the larger transport aircraft currently being used by the RAF at the time. (These aircraft are now on display in museums over the world.)

A number of jumps were made from this plane, including two night jumps, normally over Weston-on-the-Green. The course went well with high spirits and the thirty three of us passed out with a simple ceremony. We were now entitled to wear the maroon beret with wings upon our shoulders, which the

Parachute Regiment is famous for, to depict an elite force.

Having completed the military parachuting course I was posted to C Company the 3rd Battalion the Parachute Regiment based at Aldershot. I arrived at the Officers' Mess, one of four in an open garrison complex. It was here that the brigade HQ mess was actually bombed by the IRA in 1972 killing five female kitchen staff, an elderly gardener and the Roman Catholic Padre, Gerry Weston. Nineteen others were also injured in the blast that was claimed to be a revenge attack against the Parachute Regiment by the IRA following 'Bloody Sunday' earlier that year.

Fortunately when I joined and during my time serving in the Parachute Regiment, Northern Ireland was relatively peaceful although there was unrest in the region.

It was a Sunday evening and it had been organized for a 'friend', another young officer who lived in the mess, to meet me. This happened and we, along with other young officers who had joined us, had dinner together in the mess and they explained the various characters and the format. It was all a bit over-powering and at 08.00 the next morning I was to report to the Adjutant for, as my friend put it, 'an interview with coffee'. My newly acquired comrade would show me where to go and explained that this Adjutant, a Captain, who is responsible for the discipline within the junior officers and the battalion was best to keep the right side of to avoid 'extras'. These were extra Orderly Officer duties awarded for varying misdemeanors and it was explained that he was doing extras which was the reason for being in uniform. The others thought that this was amusing and thanked him for being their friend asking him to inform us what his misdemeanor was. He politely declined to do this, stating that it was all a bit complicated.

I reported as instructed and spent an hour with the Adjutant who explained the structure of the battalion and various matters to me. There were three rifle companies each with three platoons consisting of 27 – 30 men. There was also Support Company of about 80 soldiers who handled the mortars and anti-tank guns and a Patrol Company that specialized in deep penetration patrolling.

I was then introduced to my Commanding Officer (CO), a Lieutenant Colonel who was in command of the battalion and then to my Company Commander, a Major whose first appearance gave the impression of thorough-ness and exactness. He was very friendly and made it quite clear that he was 'Father' and that I should always approach him first on any actions I was intending to take with the platoon or indeed otherwise. He took me down to where my platoon was based and introduced me to my Platoon Sergeant, a small mature wiry man with a deep voice. It was instantly recognizable that he was experienced and I later discovered that in fact he had actually fought at the battle Arnhem during WW 2. My Sergeant in his turn introduced me to my three Corporals and some 20 soldiers. So this was my platoon and I organized a weapon cleaning session together until lunchtime as we were live firing on the local ranges that afternoon.

I felt confident on the ranges as I had done a fair amount of shooting although I had not done any range conduct courses apart from what we were taught at Mons Officer Cadet School. The aim of the live firing exercise in the afternoon was to 'zero' our personal weapons (mainly the Self Loading 7.62 mm Rifle, SLR), which is normally a straightforward exercise firing five rounds at a target 100 metres away. The targets would be checked and should show where the five rounds were hitting. They could be high, low or to either side and should be in a tight group at that range. The weapon's sights could then be adjusted so that the rounds would hit the target centrally.

In theory and normally in practice this is fine but on this occasion I soon noted that only about 50% of my platoon was actually hitting the targets even at this close range. I realized that most of the soldiers were not holding their weapons correctly let alone adopting the right firing procedure. This observation was confirmed by my Platoon Sergeant who quietly suggested that maybe I could coach them and show them on how to do it. It was obvious that he had done some research on me and was aware that I had done some competition shooting and as he pointed out this was a good way of introducing myself!

So I started coaching by adopting the prone position with my rifle to explain how a rifle should be held and how to use the correct aiming sequence. I then went on to inform the gathered platoon on how to squeeze the trigger and then to 'follow through'. I concluded the demonstration by firing five live rounds at my target to show them what a good group should look like!

Following this the soldiers eagerly went up to the target to find that in fact I had attained a tight group (much to my relief), the size of a tennis ball that was low left on the target. I could then explain that the sights of my weapon could now be adjusted so that the rounds would fall centrally on the target.

There was much joking going on over the fact that somehow I had planted the target and in fact I had not actually fired the rounds anywhere near it and that this was a clever move! The soldiers did of course realize that I was an experienced shot and took my coaching on board with good results, so much so we managed to zero nearly all the weapons that afternoon.

I felt satisfied over what I had accomplished on the ranges that first day and I was now keen to establish my position as Platoon Commander by leading from the front. I was fit, as indeed they were, and we were all in our early twenties apart from our Platoon Sergeant. (I was actually 19.) My Company Commander insisted that we should every day, complete a 5 mile road walk and run directly after the first parade which we did and this was similar to going for a walk.

With approval from 'Father' I thought that another method of testing character would be to run them over the Trainaisium that was on the route home on the road walk and run. Four PT instructors (PTIs) were booked and the company commander was present when we arrived for the event. A demonstration was given on each obstacle and then we had to complete the course. I led closely followed by the 'challenger' of the platoon who always seemed to know better and of course was the best.

He certainly challenged me on speed coming close up behind trying to overtake on the highest obstacle. This consisted of two boards upon which you would run along and then jump into a net and climb down to the ground. Suddenly I felt a blow from behind that made me lose my balance, fall forward and almost fell the 60 odd feet to the ground but somehow managed to cling on the plank that we were traversing.

Adrenaline kicked in and I managed to get my leg around the plank and get myself back on top. I then noticed my challenger was also clinging onto the board but was unable to right himself like I had done. I crawled back to him and grabbed him with both arms and at the same time shouted for assistance from the PTI's who I noticed were on their way up with a rope.

I noticed the fear in this lad's eyes and he was quietly pleading with me not to let go. It was not long before the PTI's had placed a rope around and under the casualty's shoulders and let him down slowly to the ground. I completed the course to be greeted by the platoon who had been gathered at the side of the course. I had made my mark although the 'wag' of the platoon loudly stated that he would not have done that and that this particular character had always been a pain.

With that I insisted that the platoon should complete the course with me once again in the front although 'the casualty' stood down on this occasion. It was good and my Platoon Sergeant stated to me that I had now made my mark and perhaps we could lead a normal life. However in the Parachute Regiment you could not live a 'normal life'.

Chapter 17

Night Time Parachuting
Accident -1967

Life was getting as 'normal' as could be expected over the coming months and it was not long before we were warned about a planned company night parachute drop that apparently happened about once a month thus earning our parachuting pay bonus. This was my first night parachute jump with my platoon and was destined to be over Salisbury Plain on one of the parachute drop zones (DZs).

I suddenly began to realise how terrified some of the soldiers were by the way they were looking and behaving. One or two of these poor men had not actually flown in an aircraft before volunteering to jump out of them and this was 'test time'. I was staggered at the courage they showed when the time came and not once in my parachuting career of over some twenty years completing 800 odd drops did I ever come across a refusal, apart from the one in the initial training on the balloon jump.

We were briefed accordingly and the drop was to be followed by a straight-forward patrolling exercise finishing the following evening so there was nothing too arduous to look forward to. I carefully studied the DZ on the map and aerial photos to ensure that I would know exactly where we were to be dropped. My briefing also included where we were to rendezvous (RV), having landed and that in an emergency we would go non tactical and the RV would be a red light on a prominent point manned by my Platoon Sergeant and/or myself. After a bit of a wait we were then transported up to RAF Lynham where in a hangar we were briefed once again in more detail complete with a Met Office report etc.

We were also issued with our twenty-four-hour ration packs, equipment and weapon containers, that are a square strapped piece of canvas with a rope and quick release catch attached and things looked good. Having packed our containers we were then fitted with our parachutes being checked out by the Parachute Jump Instructors (PJIs), some of whom I recognised from my recent parachuting course. Our Company Sergeant Major (CSM), who was not actu-ally jumping with us and seemed to be hovering about keeping 'an eye' on us suddenly approached and handed me a piece a paper upon which was printed the Court Martial warning that had to be issued to all that were about to jump vocally by an officer before boarding the aircraft. At first I thought that this was a joke but my Platoon Sergeant soon put me straight on this procedure.

A cooked evening meal was produced which only a few enjoyed and then we were led out to the waiting aircraft, an Argosy. I issued the Court Martial warning, *'The red light is the warning to jump, the green light is the order to jump, failure to comply with an order is a Court Martial offence'* (or words to that effect). The CSM seemed happy, wished us luck and departed. We boarded the aircraft under the supervision of the PJIs and were informed that we would be flying around the UK at low level first, and that would take some five hours. We would then drop onto Salisbury Plain, (some 30 miles away), at about 03.00 hrs so it was jokingly suggested by the PJIs, that perhaps we could try and get some sleep and were reminded that there would be no smoking!

The flight went as planned and at 02.30 we prepared ourselves for the jump in the dull red cabin light (used so that it did not ruin our night vision), with the PJIs checking us. Checks complete we were then ordered to stand up and to check each other once again and to attach our static line to the wire cable above us and to check our container rope attachment that was simply a special knot tied onto our parachute harness waist strap

Failure to tie this correctly would result in the loss of your container, weighing anything up to 55 lbs, once you were under your open parachute. That would not only be dangerous but you would also lose your weapon and equipment. This was another Court Martial offence and I was always paranoid about losing my container. That thankfully never did occur although every now and again it did happen to others although I was never witness to this.

After a wait, standing there holding your static line the red light would come on and the PJI's would shout 'red on' to the terrified soldiers some of whom crossed themselves. The smell at this stage within the aircraft was not good as some were spewing or worse and the look of fear in those faces seen in that dull red light is a sight I will never forget. Suddenly the light would go green and the PJIs would scream *'green on – go'* and off we went. In the middle of the 'stick' you would be forced along by the movement of the others and then you would suddenly be faced with dark open door with the flapping empty static lines and two PJIs 'assisting' us out into the night.

You are trained to 'kick out' into the slipstream, thus avoiding being spun down the side of the aircraft, which the PJIs termed carrying out a rivet inspection. This could also hinder your parachute opening as invariably it would result in twists in the parachute rigging lines which you would have to clear before reaching the ground.

A good exit into that cold pure night air was always bliss. This would be followed by hopefully a jerk that would be your parachute opening. Drills would then be 'check canopy', all correct. Then 'check around you' to ensure that you were not about to collide with another, all clear. You would then release your container by operating the quick release catch and with luck you would feel the tug of the line on your waist belt which meant that it was still attached to you.

Night jumps normally took place at about 1000 ft, which was slightly higher than the standard day time aircraft exit height of 800 ft. This gave us a bit more time under the parachute which of course meant that more could go wrong. You really could not see much at night, sometimes not even the other parachutes until you were about to collide with them. The ground was just a black morass although there was normally a horizon. You could make out the lights of towns and villages, along with large woods that were black blobs on the ground and sometimes make out rivers reflecting the moonlight if there was a moon. When you approached the ground you would feel your container rope go slack and then you would hit it praying that there were no obstacles such as trees, buildings, ploughs etc under you. There were injuries normally connected to hitting obstacles but somehow we seemed to escape unscathed.

However another big danger with some 30 other parachutes in close proximity was collision with another parachute. This could cause a total collapse of one or both parachutes with fatal results. Whilst it was possible to steer these parachutes, as we were trained, they were not very manoeuvrable. There was a drill to try and prevent you entering another parachute by extending both your arms and legs out in a weird fashion which could result in you bouncing off the rigging lines.

I was trying to work out where we were as there were no recognisable landmarks that I could see when suddenly I was kicked in the back of the head. I realised straight away that another had entangled with my parachute probably collapsing his chute so he was now slipping down past me.

Not a word was said between us and once the body had cleared the rigging it started to slip past me. It was then I heard my intruder screaming and I was desperately trying to catch the lines as they passed me but I just could not get a hold. However when the fabric of his parachute started to slide past me I then managed to get a grip and yes I could hold him but it was painful on the finger nails.

I knew that it was only going to be a matter of seconds before we hit the ground and was fearfully aware that my rig could collapse or at least with two of us with our equipment would be descending at a faster than normal rate of descent.

I felt my intruder's gear go slack as he landed and then there was flash as my knees hit me hard in the face due to the rapid descent and my unusual position knocking me out. I regained consciousness after some time. As always it seemed as if I was awaking from a nightmare and slowly realised where I was and what had happened. I then remembered that there were two of us and quickly released myself from my harness and jumped up to check my 'passenger'.

My left ankle was extremely painful and I could not put weight on it so I crawled down the rigging lines and then found the other harness empty. I started to think that this was indeed a nightmare but the pain of my left ankle brought me back to reality. Who was he and why had he left me unconscious especially after what I had done for him?

I unpacked my container, grabbed my rifle, put my kit on and looked for the RV which of course was not prominent as we were in the wrong place. Suddenly with relief I heard my Platoon Sergeant shouting for the men to RV on him and the red light some 300 metres away. I crawled to the RV through the wet grass to be greeted by my Sergeant who wanted to know where the f….

had I been. He quickly realised that I was injured and instructed the medic to attend to me. At the same time he told me that I was the last man in and was the only injury. He then asked me if I had any idea where we were to which I gave a negative reply. After a brief discussion we decided that we would stay put until first light when we would then put out reconnaissance patrols to try and discover where we were.

At first light the familiar sound of helicopters were heard nearby so we put up a flare (with our vary pistol), and smoke. Sure enough this was seen by a pilot who landed nearby. The observer instructed the Platoon Sergeant where he was and gave instructions on where to rendezvous with the rest of the company. I was then flown to Tidworth Hospital where my injuries were diagnosed as a broken left ankle and concussion which of course meant that I had to stay in hospital. Strangely I felt relieved over this and accepted the situation relaxing and resting. I was soon discharged on crutches with a plaster on my left lower leg this time. However when I returned to my unit I was put on 'light duties' attending Courts Martial and being the proverbial 'soldier's friend' in a number of civil court cases. I also assisted the Adjutant, which was actually very interesting, along with visiting my platoon to ensure that everything was running smoothly in my absence, which of course it was under the control of my Platoon Sergeant.

 I soon made a full recovery over some six weeks ensuring that I retained my upper body fitness during this time. However a question that I was now being asked was 'who was the soldier that I had saved'? I did not have an answer and it started to become a little embarrassing as it was suggested on one occasion that perhaps I had made this story up to go with my injury thus perhaps making me bit of a hero. I found this upsetting and had not even thought about it in that way so I put the whole episode away in my mind although my Platoon Sergeant was sure that he knew who it was! He maintained that it was probable that the unfortunate felt so embarrassed over his actions of screaming and perhaps leaving me unattended resulted in the silence that was the only option considered to retain his credibility.

The mystery of who I did possibly save remains to this day and maybe after all this time, if you are still about, it would be great if you could contact me! I bear no grudge.

Chapter 18
Surival After Being Entombed - 1967/68

We started to get into a routine consisting of normal military training with the emphasis on fitness and stamina interspersed with the monthly night parachute jumps. It was made all the more interesting when we were dropped into other countries such as Germany, France, Libya, etc. These drops were normally followed by a patrolling exercise lasting for anything up to some ten days. Strangely most of the lads found this interesting and enjoyable as we were being tested for what we joined for and it was challenging. Some of the soldiers equated these foreign drops as 'going for a holiday abroad' and what better way to see the countryside, as long as their leader didn't get lost.

The RAF normally dropped us in the correct place and surprisingly injuries were uncommon. In all my military jumping I only experienced one dramatic drop when the RAF did drop us in a totally wrong position in Germany which resulted in a number of serious injuries (covered in Chapter 20).

However I noticed that my Platoon Sergeant, Sergeant 'V', was not very happy and after an in depth discussion with him discovered that he had just received joining instructions to attend a senior NCOs course at the Parachute Regiment's Battle School based in Brecon, Wales.

This course was renowned to be stamina and physically testing for a good reason as it was important that all senior NCOs in the Parachute Regiment were of the required high standard. Sergeant 'V' was concerned that at his age of forty-five he would not survive the physical side of it. I decided to approach our Company Commander, Major 'H', on the matter as this NCO had a wealth of experience, having fought at the Battle of Arnhem during World War II not to mention other conflict areas such as Suez and Aden.

Whilst Major 'H' was sympathetic he told me that he could not alter the policy on this and then went on to inform me that I, as a young officer, would also have to attend this course as a 'non participating' observer. However I only had to attend the final two weeks of the course that was four weeks in duration. I was informed that it was important for young officers to understand what our senior NCOs were made of and more importantly we had to undergo the Escape and Evasion that covered current known methods of interrogation, held on the final week of the course.

I reported back to Sergeant 'V' with the information who seemed relieved as obviously there was no possible escape here. He seemed to have accepted the fact that he would not complete the course and would therefore not be able to continue in his present position. He then went on to suggest that perhaps we should start looking for a replacement, hopefully from within the platoon, suggesting one particular Corporal. I tried to encourage him to adopt a positive attitude over this as with the platoon he seemed to survive the physical onslaught most of the time.

He was soon off and I joined him at Brecon just as he was leaving. He had given up due to physical problems and was sent back to his unit. I saw him before he left and tried to cheer him up but 'it was written'. I reported to the Adjutant and Training Major of the Battle School on arrival who informed me of the situation and actually it all seemed to make sense, sad as it was.

There was another young officer joining the course with me named Rowan, from the First Parachute Battalion, and we immediately got on well together. We were briefed on the course, consisting of some 30 Sergeants from within the Parachute Regiment Brigade. Emphasis was again placed on the fact that we must attend the Escape and Evasion exercise on the last week. We would be introduced to and briefed on the methods of interrogation that were currently being used at the time by various countries and would be given the chance to evade capture.

This would be done by letting us loose on the Brecon Hills with no food or equipment, and would then be hunted down with use of all types of methods including dogs. It all sounded rather challenging and exciting!

The first week of the course I attended was indeed physically testing, starting at 06.00 hrs in the morning with a run completed with the assault course. Following this platoon tactics were practised in the hills day and night, sometimes finishing in the late hours, to be followed by the early morning physical assault every morning. The morale of the Sergeants within this course was remarkably high as they had adopted the attitude that nothing was going to break those that had got this far and nothing did break them.

The final week arrived and we spent a day being lectured by the Intelligence Forces on the most recent methods of interrogation including what was called then 'The Water Treatment' now titled 'Water Boarding', where you are secured flat on your back with a cloth placed over your face and then water is poured over your face. This prevents you from breathing with the idea being that if you answer questions the treatment would be stopped. This did not physically injure or mark those that were being interrogated so evidence of any physical abuse was at a minimum. However we were warned that there was a risk that you could drown during this form of interrogation and we would have to undergo it without fail.

Another form of interrogation that we would undergo was sleep deprivation whereby you would be watched by your jailer in your cell and when you started to sleep a bucket of cold water would be thrown over you awaking you with a shock. You would then be taken to friendly interrogators where you would be questioned in comfort by them, which would disorientate you thus making you vulnerable to answering questions inadvertently. However, the good news was that we would only endure this treatment for supposedly a continual seventy-two hours, but this did not include the time we had 'evaded' and the capture time that could be anything up to two days.

Rowan and I decided that the best thing to do here would be to escape for as long as possible thus perhaps avoiding the full time of interrogation or missing it all together. We would not trust anybody once on the run.

The final briefing for this exercise took place that Monday evening and we were given 'top secret information' that should not be divulged at any cost! Having been searched to ensure that we were not carrying food, compasses etc., although we carried one water bottle on our belt, we then boarded three trucks that were totally enclosed. There were two guards sitting by the tail gates to ensure that we did not look out. After forty-five minutes the trucks suddenly stopped and we were ordered out and away. We could hear hounds or dogs baying in the distance and were informed that they were after us so speed was of the essence.

Having disembarked the convoy commander informed us that we could hear the baying of the only surviving pack of Blood Hounds that were going to be employed in finding us and with that the trucks departed leaving us to our own devices. I was not quite sure whether to believe the story of the Blood Hounds but one thing for sure was that there were dogs about.

Much to my surprise the majority of Sergeants sat down on the side of the road stating that they wished to be captured now whilst they were fresh so that they could undergo the interrogation and may even be finished by Friday. One actually produced a cigarette but then realised he had a problem as he had no form of lighting it, much to the amusement of the others who were suggesting we should look for a couple of sticks to light it for him.

It was last light on a pleasant summer's evening in the hills of Brecon. Rowan and I decided that we were going to run for it and having shaken hands and wished each other luck we started running our separate ways heading south according to my smuggled miniature compass.

I ran for some miles and it was getting dark that impeded my progress as I could not travel as fast due to the failing light. However one thing for sure was that the barking and baying of the dogs were getting closer. I, therefore, decided to hide in a large thicket of brambles that had a stream running through it. I paddled up hill in the stream and lodged myself in a concealed position by the side of the stream. I could just see out over the valley from which I had travelled.

It was hoped that by using the stream my scent would not be obvious to the dogs and waited in anticipation. Much to my surprise I saw another fleeing figure, possibly Rowan, pass close by and the dogs were now close behind. They passed near to me in full cry with their handlers trying to keep control and did not stop. I was suddenly left in peace although I could hear the baying recede in the distance and then it went quiet.

I decided to stay put as it was quite comfortable where I was laid up by the side of the burbling brook and before long I was asleep. I awoke wet and cold at first light to be greeted by a wonderful view down the valley that I had fled up and the first rays of sunshine along with the dawn chorus. The warmth of the sun soon started to dry me and I fell asleep again, this time in the comfort and warmth of the sun.

I slept until mid-day when my hunger woke me up. I treated myself to lunch of one finger of a Kit Kat chocolate bar (I had smuggled through three bars), and it was delicious. I savoured every moment of that chocolate dissolving in my mouth and then washed it down with some water from my water bottle.

I felt good and was getting impatient to start my route back to base as I could see the weather was worsening. I planned to return to the road where we were dropped off to find a sign post to confirm my position and the route plus direction that I should be travelling. We had been advised that it is sensible when evading the enemy to travel by night and to hide up during daylight hours but I was getting short on time as we had been informed that we would be captured by tomorrow without fail. I had no intention of being captured now.

I started my homeward march in the early evening running down the hills and walking as fast as I could up them, a routine I had learnt in 'P' Company, which enabled you to cover as much ground as quickly as possible without exhausting you too quickly. The weather had got worse and it was now raining and did so all night. I had estimated that we were some 30 miles from base on drop off and that it would take about two days to get back.

I found a signpost that confirmed my position and route home that was comforting so I intended to lie up for one more night before returning. However I decided that it was important that I should find some form of shelter as there was now a high wind blowing along with the rain and I was aware of the exposure risk although by keeping on the move I felt fine. The thought of hiding under a bush in an exposed position did not seem very attractive.

Come first light I had covered a lot of ground and then I came across a farm complete with a barn. This was an ideal place to lie up so I cautiously approached. There was a large sliding door covering the entrance that I quietly opened and saw that the barn was in fact full of small bales of hay and it smelt so inviting.

Entering the barn I climbed up the haystack to find a 'plateau' halfway up. I then pulled out five or six bales, near the edge to make a form of tomb in which I would rest. I also moved some edge bales so that I would have a small slit window, measuring some 9 inches through which I could keep an eye on the entrance and would have some form of ventilation as my construction consisted of overhead bales thus completing the 'entombment'. I did this just in case the hounds were used to search the stack.

The wind was howling, rattling the sliding metal door and the rain lashing the barn. I stripped my soaking clothing off to discover that in fact the sweet smelling hay was quite warm so I had a heated den. What could be better and I celebrated my new home with a chocolate bar and water and slept in the warmth and security of it.

I was suddenly awakened after a short while by the large metal door of the barn being opened and there below me was the farmer with a uniformed policeman. I immediately thought that I had been seen entering the barn but this assumption was quickly dispelled as I heard the policeman explaining to the farmer that military were concerned about this young officer that had gone missing on the hills in this weather. Apparently he had not been wearing any weather proof clothing, did not have any food nor any form of communication. I was the only one missing as the others were all accounted for so a massive search was in progress as they feared that he could be out on the hills suffering from exposure.

Realising that he was talking about me I nearly gave myself up but suddenly remembered the golden rule of not trusting anybody. I thought that this may well be a trick so I kept quiet. The policeman then had a good look around the barn and after a while they both left with the metal door being slid closed again. I felt elated as I knew that I had evaded capture due to being cautious. I noted that it was lunchtime so I had another Kit Kat bar followed by an afternoon rest.

I awoke that evening by what I thought was the haystack vibrating which I thought was a little odd. I started to open my tomb by removing the top bales and much to my horror I found that I just could not move them. I later discovered that part of the stack above my 'plateau' had collapsed burying me with bales.

In panic I started shouting for assistance but soon realised that this was futile and I was just burning up much needed energy. I had to get a grip, relax and think. The answer for escape was of course to make my slit window larger so that I could crawl out of it. To make it larger I could pull handfuls of hay from the two bordering bales and I found that in fact I could quite easily do this but I had an awful lot of hay to move and it was now getting dark and I had no form of light.

Handful by handful I did this, dropping the removed hay down the edge of the stack. I would rest about every thirty minutes although I was now fearful that my window could collapse that would indeed entomb me for good.

After some six hours, at dawn with a cockerel crowing merrily nearby, I eventually crawled out of my cocoon falling onto the hay below. After this I decided that I would ask for assistance as I now felt quite weak. Hunger and dehydration was really taking effect as I had not eaten properly for some two days and my water intake had been sparse.

I eventually decided to approach the farmhouse to explain my situation and ask for help. Much to my surprise as I approached the house I saw the farmer and his wife get into their Land Rover and drive off obviously without seeing me.

I now had to make up my mind whether I should continue with my march back to base or perhaps find some food and water first. I cautiously knocked and opened the unlocked house door and shouted to see if anyone was in. There was a chained collie dog nearby that was barking and straining to get free and apart from that the house was empty.

I entered and made my way to the kitchen. The house was really untidy and I found the kitchen in some disarray. This was good as I felt that if I did help myself to food and drink it would not be noticed. My hunger and weakness overcame my conscience and with the intention of repayment for the food that I was about to take I started my search. I found a tin of baked beans, bread, eggs, bacon and tea bags. I had a great breakfast and really felt better for it. I thought that I really ought to wait for the return of the farmer and his wife so that I could explain things and perhaps offer some form of apology and repayment.

However by mid-afternoon there was no sign of them so with reluctance I started my weary journey back to base, that was some 15 miles away, after another good meal. I stayed on the roads following the sign posts as I wished to return as fast as possible now as it was Thursday. There was indeed a possibility that they were looking for me and perhaps what I recently heard the policeman state was not a trick.

Despite my urgency for speed night soon came about as I spent a lot of time taking cover from vehicles and helicopters that seemed abundant and was actually quite impressive. This delayed me further as it is difficult to push on in the dark without any form of light and I was exhausted.

After a rest in a roadside shed, I kept going and first light soon came. I was now on the home straight recognising the road leading to the Battle School.

Suddenly around a bend I came across a car and caravan parked by the side of the road.

It was a lovely early morning and the door of the caravan opened and out climbed an attractive naked middle aged lady who started to do exercises in front of me totally oblivious of my presence. I felt so embarrassed and I had no idea on what to do as I had frozen still with the onslaught of this sight.

Eventually after some five minutes I thought that I had better announce my presence somehow so I coughed loudly and walked by trying to look in the opposite direction. Much to my surprise this lady without any hesitation approached me and asked if I was the missing young officer as I looked rough and was in uniform? I answered that I had been out for some days and so she asked me into the caravan for breakfast with her husband.

It was such a surreal situation and here I was enjoying another cooked breakfast with coffee and good company (fully apparelled now). I did feel a little tired as I had been going all night and informed them that I really had to get back as apparently they were searching for me and this had now been confirmed. So after thanking them for their hospitality and refusing a lift in their car I walked the final 2 miles to camp.

I knew a way into the camp through a hole in the perimeter fence so that I did not have to go through the main gate. I thought that by reporting direct to the orderly room where they would be doing all the admin I would make quite an entry.

I noticed a yellow Air Sea Rescue Wessex helicopter on the parade ground along with two Army Scout helicopters. There were also a number of Army Land Rovers parked nearby which seemed a little unusual as there was no other exercise in progress as far as I was aware.

I strolled into the orderly room where I saw the pilots, drivers and observers being briefed by the Training Major with a large map of the training area that was hanging on the wall.

Suddenly he saw me, stopping his briefing stating 'Where the fuck have you been'? There was an immediate response of cheering and clapping from the assembled group, some of whom approached me patting me on the back and shaking my hand. It was then that I realised that the policeman was stating the truth and a full scale search for me had been in progress since yesterday.

With confirmation from the Training Major they then stated that they would be on their way and the room quickly emptied leaving me with the Training Major and Adjutant. I was asked when I last had any food and stated that I had just had a cooked breakfast with a nude lady and her husband which perhaps was not the best of responses.

A thorough debriefing then followed with the Adjutant mentioning the fact that it had been suggested that perhaps I had taken a lift to London, where my girlfriend of the time lived. I was shocked at this suggestion and it eventually transpired that the time and date when the exercise would end (endex), did not actually appear in the initial exercise instructions.

I was exonerated although it was made quite clear that I would have to participate the next Escape and Evasion exercise to undergo interrogation, which I did some weeks later although this time it was suggested that I should not attempt an escape.

The course was closed that lunchtime with many of the Sergeants asking me how London was! However I noticed that Rowan was not about until lunch in the Officers' Mess when he made an appearance looking a bit odd. It was good to see him again and I approached him to ask him how he had got on. I noticed that the Adjutant accompanied me stating that Rowan was not too good. I shook hands with Rowan and was shocked to hear that he now had a profound stutter, hardly being able to speak.

Rowan explained with some effort that this had happened following inter-rogation and the Adjutant quickly interceded by stating that Rowan was getting the best treatment for his disorder that was obviously inherent, and that it was expected that he would soon make a full recovery.

I could not really converse with my friend who eventually broke down in tears and left for transport that was taking him home. This experience left me shocked and I never saw or heard of Rowan again despite efforts to contact him. This was my first experience of the Parachute Regiment Battle School.

Chapter 19
Life Threatening Skydiving Incidents - 1967/68

It was good to get back to my platoon and battalion and I soon realised that my exploits in The Brecon Beacons had spread and I was questioned by my fellow officers at tea in the mess on the first day back. I was amazed that I had a captive audience whilst explaining my adventures and it was quite clear that I had now been 'initiated' into the battalion. So much so, one friend, Captain 'H' Jones called for a celebration in a well known pub, The Bunch Of Grapes, located in Hammersmith, London.

We would have an early supper and then drive to Hammersmith, 'H' leading the way in his Lotus Elan, with the last in to buy first round. These trips were great fun and on one of these excursions I met two gorgeous girls who turned out to be models, in underwear!

My new Platoon Sergeant, who had been on the Battle Course in Brecon with me and whom I liked, was selected to take over from my existing Sergeant. It was sad to see my old mentor move on but he had been placed into an administration post which he was looking forward to. He had played an important role with me, taking me on as a young Platoon Commander, acting very much as a father figure, gaining me that essential experience. It was time to move forward and the oldest soldier in the platoon now was one of twenty-seven years. We were fit, mean lean fighting machines!

I was now getting some weekends and evenings off. This offered the opportunity to explore the possibility of expanding my skydiving experience. I had learnt that the National Skydiving Championships were to be held at the Army Parachute Association (APA), base located in Netheravon in Wiltshire. This was only a short drive from Aldershot, and not only that you could also book basic overnight accommodation, with catering, at the centre. It was great for the early morning starts when we would be jumping at first light. The wind was more often than not slackest at this time.

I had just progressed on my 35th jump to a thirty second delay before deploying the parachute. That meant that you would jump from the centre's aircraft, the De Haviland Rapide, from 7000 ft. With this type of time delay you could carry out skydiving manoeuvres such as flat turns, back loops, forward loops, tracking, (where you would move across the sky at an angle of anything up to about 70 degrees covering a lot of ground) and of course relative to when you would link up with others in free fall.

For competition purposes a flat turn would have to be executed fast and accurately. Any overshoot would be penalised. With loops the somersault must be smooth and exact. There was a timed sequence, known as 'style' that was monitored from the ground through high powered binoculars: it was a 360 degree turn to the left, then turn to the right followed by a back loop, then the turn sequence again followed by a forward loop. You had to deploy your parachute no lower than 2200 ft and then land in a sand pit aiming for a foam circular disc. This was known as 'accuracy'. Your distance from the disc would be measured. The competitor would spot their own exit from the aircraft. In other words they would direct the pilot over the target and jump when at the right spot having given the pilot instructions to 'cut' the engines.

I had a lot to learn and soon found an experienced coach who monitored me on the ground giving me advice which was invaluable. I eventually learnt to 'spot' in the aircraft although there was a lot of walking involved at times following wide landings. However I always landed somewhere on the 500 acre airfield which was something.

The APA at Netheravon became my second home, and every spare moment I had being spent there. I again met Colin, another young Para officer, who I had trained with at Mons. He, like me, was training for the competition and we were the best of friends. Having completed his university course he had a lot of letters after his name and somehow also had the time to qualify for a Private Pilot's Licence and was keen to take me up flying one day.

On my 79th jump I suffered my first parachute malfunction. It was what is classified as a blown periphery, whereby some of the rigging lines on opening looped themselves over the canopy of the parachute, thus causing the chute to spin around at speed with a rapid descent. The drill should be to deploy your reserve parachute, in this case worn on the front of the harness. However unbelievably I tried to knock the fouling lines off the canopy.

Whilst doing this I realised that not only was I losing height rapidly and was soon spinning at speed with every possibility of the parachute collapsing. I instinctively pulled my chest mounted reserve parachute and threw it into the direction of the spin. It opened immediately with a jerk just before I hit the ground. I landed gently on my backside as the reserve was now holding me up from the chest rather than the shoulders.

I just sat there wondering why I had been so foolish and feeling really grateful that I had survived. My thoughts were soon interrupted by the centre's Land Rover that had driven out with the chief and assistant instructors, who were obviously expecting the worst. No comment was made by either instructor; they just helped me up, having checked the fact that I was uninjured, and in silence I was driven back to the buildings. The matter was closed with a debrief and the chief instructor wrote 'canopy handling' in my log book. He then got me booked on the next jump which would be later that evening. I had learnt my lesson and survived, promising that in future I would never think or muck about but just stick to the drills.

Thankfully I had hired the parachute from the APA and it was examined by the chief rigger of the Association, Jo, following the incident. He was a small tough wiry looking man who had served many years in the SAS and Parachute Regiment being a veteran of Arnhem and other battles. He casually informed me that the rig was a 'write off', showing me the shredded fabric. This was quickly followed by a question whether I would like to consider purchasing my own rig, pointing to a packed parachute lying on a nearby table.

It was a modern parachute of the type known as a 'Para Commander', which had a forward speed of up to 18 knots along with the fact you could stall it out so that you would loose height rapidly by pulling hard down on the control toggles at the same time, not to be recommended near the ground. This was ideal for accuracy work and Jo informed me that it only had some five jumps on it. The previous owner was a SAS man who had just been posted to a country where he would not be using it and was desperate for cash. I was told that with my experience it would be ideal for accuracy and it could be mine for £70 cash.

Colin and I carefully inspected the rig and it did not have a mark on it. Colin stated that he would buy it if I did not do so, I agreed to the purchase, although I had to drive to Gillingham to borrow the cash off Father as it was the weekend. I had to hand the money over before 17.00 hrs, which was the time of my next lift that evening.

I was successful in my mission with mother and father seeming keen to support me in my new purchase. Even more rewarding on that evening jump with my new parachute I landed only a metre away from the central disc.

Later after the final lift just before we made our way to the bar, Colin and I were approached by the Chief Instructor asking if we would consider being trained up to become ground instructors at the centre. This would entail completing a course that would certify us to train students on the ground and to perform and sign off the various checks required during the student's packing of their parachutes.

After some thought and discussion we accepted the invitation and started our training that lasted a week. The responsibility did not seem an issue at the time and in fact we both really enjoyed our new position, feeling that we were repaying what we had taken and so much enjoyed in the past, by giving something back to other fellow jumpers, as of course we were not paid for what we were doing.

Despite the experience and training there were still traps waiting for the careless and the unwary. On my 104th jump from 5000 ft I found that my chest mounted reserve parachute had not been secured properly and it had come loose, blocking my vision and hitting me in the face with some force. I opened my parachute high and that was a weird experience being suspended at over 4000 ft in absolute silence and with everything looking so small below. I concentrated on landing as close to the APA centre as possible as I would have some minutes under the canopy due to my height, to go adrift. I landed in the pit and have written in my log book that my reserve belly band broke which I explained to the Chief Instructor.

Shortly after this whilst practising my style routine from 7000ft, I completed what I had to do. I checked my altimeter and it read 3500, which gave me time to carry out another back and forward somersault. This went well so I stabilised getting ready to open my parachute and noticed that I still had 3500 ft on my altimeter. Amazingly and without further thought I went for another somersault and halfway through this sequence suddenly realised that everything around me was green and the horizon was where it should not be.

I stabilised again for opening and with horror saw the ground speeding up to me as I was far lower than I should be. I instinctively pulled my rip cord and whilst waiting for my chute to open I noticed a dark haired woman below me wearing a white pullover, looking up at me. I was transfixed by this sight with the ground and her rushing up towards me. There was no fear just amazement of the experience and then there was the familiar jerk of the parachute opening just before I hit the ground.

It only took seconds for me to land under my deployed parachute and it was a hard but successful landing. I sat there in shock until the woman, who was the wife of a close friend, came running up to me asking if I was OK. I calmly replied that I was fine and she then broke down into tears giving me a large hug, thanking God for sparing me. It was not long before the familiar sight of the centre's Land Rover complete with the Chief and Assistant Instructors appeared.

I was asked what had happened and produced the jammed altimeter that was still showing 3500ft. I mentioned the fact that I had hired this instrument from the APA. I was given a lift back to the centre and had to make a statement and all the altimeters had to be checked. I believe a spider was found in mine and I still have nightmares over this incident.

I was now amassing the jumps and the experience. The National Freefall Championships were approaching and I started meeting the experienced skydivers some of whom had thousands of jumps to their name and many were in Special Forces. I realised that the competition was going to be stiff but the whole thing was a tremendous experience. I was actually placed 13th in accuracy so I felt well rewarded and I had opened a passion that I would follow for some years.

Chapter 20
My Platoon - Disastrous Night Parachute Jump - 1967/1968

I was at this time, commanding a platoon of some 28 men ranging in age from eighteen to twenty-eight years. We were all reasonably experienced soldiers although to date had not seen any action and not unnaturally we were all yearning for that in some form. I preached the fact that we were here to keep the peace and not fight for it.

Every month we seemed to participate in a night parachute drop to be followed by a patrolling and/or platoon exercise sometimes competing against another platoon that at times was testing. On one occasion the battalion was part of a large North Atlantic Treaty Organisation (NATO), exercise.

We were split into differing sections and patrols and briefed accordingly. It was a seven day exercise located in the Black Forest in Germany with the German army acting as the enemy. I commanded a patrol of some 16 soldiers and was ordered to lay up on the edge of a large wood overlooking a trunk road. Further instructions were to be given as the exercise progressed although we had to observe a radio silence. This meant that we could not transmit on our radios until we received a message breaking this silence. The Russians were actually good at intercepting messages and causing havoc which at times could be dangerous when there was any live firing.

We were issued with all our kit etc., including twenty-four-hour ration packs. This filled us with a bit of concern as it was probable that we would have to survive some five days without food, although we were promised replenishment whenever possible. The parachute drop took place at night with strict instructions not to break a radio silence that had been imposed by the commanding officer unless there was an emergency.

The drop went well and we were soon in position as instructed. As dawn broke on a lovely morning a wonderful view confronted us and there we lay concealed under some thick undergrowth in a defensive position. Nothing happened the first day and it seemed strange to be able to relax in relative warmth, sleep and eat our twenty-four-hour ration pack.

The following day there was some activity on the road with some light German Army vehicles passing by that were soon followed by a 'snake' of tanks, artillery and heavy lorries that had queued up on the route that we were observing. I was amazed at the size of this German Army that we were watching rolling past as I thought following the last war much of it had been disbanded, but this was not the case as there was indeed a threat now from Russia. Some of the soldiers reckoned that they were going around in a circle using this wood as cover and that it was not just one long column of vehicles that no doubt was presented to impress the Russians.

I waited eagerly for instructions for action but nothing came through. I was concerned that our radio was not functioning but was assured by my radio operator that it was. We had also exhausted our food supplies, as this was now the third day, not to mention water, although we had discovered a fresh clear spring nearby.

Then much to our unease some of the vehicles turned up from the road we were observing and used our wood as a harbour area so there was much noise and disturbance all around us. Even more upsetting our patch of undergrowth under which we were hiding was being used by the German soldiers as a latrine area.

It was clear to me that without any form of instruction in this situation I had to move. One of my soldiers was of German descent and spoke fluent German so I ordered him to come with me so that we would find the feed area, which we could smell. I instructed him to inform the officer in command that we were a special force patrol that needed feeding and that there were 16 of us. Much to my surprise this explanation was accepted and was organised. Within an hour we were all enjoying a delicious sausage stew with tea under strict orders from me that no one was to speak unless they spoke fluent German.

I then decided that following our feast we had to make a break for it so again with my bi- lingual scout ahead of me we escaped at last light without being questioned or challenged. None of us could believe that we had pulled that tactic off as we had passed many tanks, lorries and soldiers all of whom were the 'enemy'. I calmly announced that if you act as if you are meant to be there you would not be questioned.

We now faced the task of working out where to go and what to do. I thought that if we followed the trunk route that we were meant to be observing we may be able to blow up a bridge or carry an ambush out so I nervously broke the radio silence announcing my presence. Much to my surprise my message was received and I was informed to wait.

It was arranged that a British exercise umpire would be joining us shortly and that once he had done this we were to cause maximum disruption to the enemy. We guided the umpire's vehicle to our position, greeting our umpire who jovially explained that we had been forgotten about. We then proceeded to a bridge not far away that we intended to blow up. However in the morning again hunger was causing a problem but there just ahead of us was a German tank that had lost a track. The crew were striving to replace it so we captured them, tied them up and devoured any goodies we could find within the tank, much to the consternation of our umpire who was trying to stop us. We were then further rewarded by the ration truck arriving with breakfast, which we ambushed and emptied. At this stage the umpire stepped in strictly instructing us to release our prisoners and their vehicles so once again we hit the road.

Having 'blown the bridge up' we then proceeded back to our battalion base under instructions from our umpire to be involved in a company attack against an enemy position that was below us. The only problem being our route took us through some orchards of cherries and apples and not unnaturally with the soldiers being so hungry more attention was being paid to picking apples and cherries rather than attacking the enemy.

Following this attack the end of the exercise was announced and having said farewell to our umpire who confirmed that we had caused maximum disruption, even if it was for the wrong motive (that being food), we went our separate ways. My patrol was transported back to a large harbour area complete with tents in which we could sleep, feeding areas and showers. We were also issued with clean, fresh clothing and it was bliss.

However, when suddenly after two days in this heaven we were briefed that another night jump was to take place onto a DZ not far away within a matter of hours. We were not sure why this was happening as there were no patrolling or military objectives following this jump. It just seemed empty.

The battalion was soon airborne and jumping into the night yet once again. Having carried out my checks under my canopy I tried to establish my position on the ground. It did not make sense as it appeared that we were over a dark wooded area with the DZ some distance away.

There was a joke that in a situation like this you had to keep your legs crossed when landing in trees to try and protect your 'family parts'. You also had to try and protect your face. There was no doubt that I was about to land into a forest at night along with some of my soldiers. I closed my eyes, crossed my legs, waited and prayed.

After a brief period I carefully opened my eyes to find that I was swinging under my parachute caught up in some branches. I had not felt or heard anything but was now well and truly hung up in a tree. I was about to release my container and self as I had the firm impression that I was hanging just above the ground, when I heard my neighbour do the same thing.

There was a crashing sound as he plummeted to ground some 60 feet below landing with a disturbing thump below. This was then followed by a shocked consistent scream of pain and it was obvious that this unfortunate was badly injured and required assistance fast.

I had to get down with all speed so I released my container and weapon that crashed its way earthwards and was left wondering what to do next. I pulled my reserve as per the drill with the intention of climbing down it to the ground. However this just caught up in the branches in front of me.

I then had the brainwave of getting a swing going so that I could hook a leg around a branch or something that would bear my weight and then I could release myself and climb down the nearest tree. I started to swing and felt my parachute starting to slip through the top canopy of branches above me. I somehow managed to get a leg around a branch and released myself.

Being free now I could climb down the tree, which I did in haste as I was eager to get to the injured man below. I jumped from the tree as soon as I thought that it was safe but I was still some height above ground, landing hard and awkwardly in the dark on my right ankle.

Strangely there was no pain just numbness although I found it painful to put weight on this ankle and it was now imperative that I should reach the casualty. I started to crawl towards the screaming but then it went very quiet, apart from somebody else shouting some distance away.

I realised that I was on a steep slope and that the DZ and clear ground was up the hill so I decided that I should crawl or hobble up hill towards the DZ, checking my compass bearing as I did so. I eventually broke through the wood and found the company RV that was now using a red light. Having been greeted in the normal fashion with the Company Commander demanding to know where I had been and where was my rifle and kit? I explained that there were some casualties in the wood who needed immediate attention.

He quickly realised that I was also injured and having summoned medical assistance for me, declared that a search would take place at first light and he would radio for assistance. We found all the casualties and they were recovered with assistance from the Royal Engineers and the medics. My container and rifle were also found so all seemed well, with casualty evacuations by helicopter to the nearest military hospital, at Prum in South East Germany. This was a large American hospital attached to the American air base in this location. I was once again issued with crutches as I had problems with my right ankle that was very painful.

We were transported back to the harbour area and were informed that we would be flying home shortly. I was treated by the battalion doctor, who reckoned that I had sprained my ankle and then asked if I would like to accompany him to Prum hospital to visit two of my soldiers, who had been badly injured. I jumped at the chance and we grabbed a Land Rover for the 90 mile journey. The injured lads were thrilled to see us as it all seemed a bit daunting for them in this huge American hospital but they made a full recovery, although one who had landed on a plough was eventually medically discharged due to his injuries.

Having carried out the visit we stopped off at a local hostelry that appeared to be full of British Special Air Service (SAS). We had a good meal with our new comrades and then suddenly we were attacked by a number of Nazi youth who burst into the club wielding chains and knives.

The SAS jumped into action, easily disarming the youth, and then set about throwing them out of the windows and we were three floors up. The doctor quickly and very correctly ushered and assisted me out of the building as he was concerned that the American Military Police would soon be on the scene. That would be very unhealthy for us officers, who really should not be present here and after all I was on crutches!

We made a quick escape and returned to the harbour area where I enjoyed a good sleep with brunch the next day followed by a flight back to the UK. Gossip had it that there had been an ambush on British servicemen in a club near Prum where a number of youths had been seriously injured and one soldier had been arrested for causing serious bodily harm to a police dog whilst carrying out its duty. It was alleged that this soldier had bitten this dog's nose off that resulted in the animal being destroyed. An unpleasant story and nobody knew that we had witnessed this attack.

Chapter 21
Sky Diving Fatality - 1968

It was good to get back to Aldershot despite being on crutches and I was soon was back to full fitness. The routine returned to normal which again offered me the chance to spend more time at the Army Parachute Centre at Netheravon.

I was enjoying the parachuting as I had now progressed onto 'relative work' where two or more jump at the same time from the aircraft and then link up in free fall. I was soon jumping with a group of three others, Johnny, Kevin and Pete, who wanted another to join them. They claimed that they were in the Royal Corps of Transport (RCT), and appeared to be led by an experienced skydiver named Pete, who had hundreds of jumps to his name.

This group seemed to wield a fair amount of power and many jumps took place free of charge from differing military aircraft, including the Scout helicopter and Beaver over various parts of the country. My position due to my inexperience was to be 'the dummy' being the first to jump and then just maintaining a stable position waiting for the others to move around the sky and latch onto me.

I was also invited to join them in various parachuting displays that at times were exciting. On one occasion, over Tangmere, the cloud was low, around 1000 feet, but despite this Pete decided to go for it and we all somehow survived a hairy 'hop and pop'. It was normally recognised as safe practice to deploy your parachute at around 2200 feet. Pete was duly castigated later that evening in the pub over the matter.

On one 'relative' jump from 7000 feet over Netheravon with the group I was performing my 'dummy act'. Johnny was the first planned to connect and with concern I noticed that he was approaching me from the front at an excessive speed. It all happened so fast and the next thing I knew was that he collided with me hitting me hard in the face with his helmet. There was flash on impact and that was all I remembered until I regained consciousness under my parachute feeling very dazed and wondering where I was which was some 1500 feet above ground level.

I noticed that my white jump suit was covered in blood that seemed to be coming from my face. My right eye was swollen and my nose and mouth were painful and bleeding. I noticed that Pete and Johnny were circling under their parachutes nearby and Pete actually shouting out at me asking if I was OK. I started to regain my senses and realised that I had to control my parachute for the impending landing which was no problem. Once on the ground I remembered what had happened and started a self examination.

I was shortly joined by the gang with Johnny full of apologies. Pete quietly handed me back my rip cord and explained what had happened. After the collision it was obvious that I was unconscious and I rolled over onto my back, doing the 'dead fly' act. Johnny was dazed after the impact and remained in a stable descent nearby. Pete moved into a position whereby he could pull my ripcord, which he did around 3000 feet, thus opening my parachute that thankfully opened without problem as I was actually in an unusual opening position being on my back.

Johnny opened at the correct height although he also suffered cuts and bruising to his face and Kevin maintained that he was standing by in case he was wanted!

We walked back to the hangar in silence and nobody in the centre was aware of what had happened up there until later. I decided that I would not go to hospital for a check up but I was grounded by the chief instructor and Pete for the rest of the day, although the others continued with their practice. I was indebted to Pete for saving my life and we had a good session in the pub that evening.

I used the rest of the day to have a modified seat sown into my parachute harness by the rigger, Jo. Whilst doing this he asked me whether I was in the SAS to which I proudly replied that I was actually in Para.

He then informed me the reason for the question was that the three others in my group were actually SAS and that he just wondered why I had been accepted by them. I was flattered by this information and it all began to make sense although the question remained why they were claiming that they were in the RCT.

Jo then went on to quietly tell me the sad news that my friend Colin, who I had trained with at Mons, often jumped with and completed the ground instructors course, had just been killed. Apparently whilst attempting to take off in a Cessna 172 aircraft from a remote field in thick fog he flew into a hill. The chief instructor was about to break the news to me as his family had asked whether his ashes could be spread from the Rapide aircraft above Netheravon. I of course would be the obvious person to carry this task out. I had been forewarned but was left shocked. At the end of the day I buried my woes with my newly recognised SAS comrades later that evening in The Dog and Duck.

The next week back at Aldershot with the battalion every body, including my soldiers, wished to know how I had sustained my facial injuries. I informed them that I had walked into a lamp post whilst looking at something. This satisfied most although one or two such as my friend 'H' Jones did not believe me and I had to relate the true story over tea in the Officers' Mess.

The weekend was soon upon us again and I made the early morning trip across Salisbury Plain on a beautiful day in my green Ford Thames van with my parachuting kit behind me. I used to listen to the BBC Light programme with John Dunne presenting the morning show on my transistor radio tied down on the passenger's seat. On this occasion there was a course of young Guardsmen completing their introductory jumps and I had volunteered to be a ground instructor, checking their packing and so on. I was hopeful that if there was any time I might just get the chance of a jump or two.

It was a good high spirited group, well supervised and the weather was perfect. On one of my morning breaks I was making my way to the canteen from the packing hall, passing those that were waiting for the next lift outside. I noticed the Rapide overhead dropping the first to jump that day. I watched them exit the aircraft on a five second delay from 3800 feet. Then with horror I noticed one of them tumbling towards the ground with no parachute deploying.

I started to run towards where I thought the point of impact would be and noticed that I was accompanied by an attractive nurse, named Kay, beside me. I suddenly realised that we were running into a danger area as the body descending above us was as good as a missile that could kill if it hit us. I stopped running grabbing Kay and we watched as the parachutist hit the ground at terminal velocity just ahead of us with a tremendous boom, similar to that of a artillery gun going off. He then bounced some 40 feet in the air to once again contact the ground with force.

We were soon attending the body and I was amazed at the two craters that had been created in the chalky soil by the impacts. The body of this young man looked strange with his limbs at weird angles and the straps of his harness had been buried in his flesh. He had landed on his back and the black track suit top that he was wearing was shredded. His eyes were open and there was blood trickling from all facial orifices. It was a dreadful sight and I was not sure what to do as it was quite obvious that this unfortunate was dead. I gently closed his eyes.

Kay felt his neck pulse and exclaimed that he still had one and that we should carry out CPR on him. I quietly stated that was up to her and she then opened his mouth to clear his air way. It was a repulsive sight seeing blood and broken teeth ooze out and Kay was then sick, following which she threw herself into my arms sobbing. I was filled with revulsion and was desperately trying to control myself as I thought that I was about to throw up as well.

The situation was saved by the arrival of the chief instructor in the Land Rover. He asked if we had witnessed the accident and whether we had touched anything as this area was now 'a scene of a crime'. We explained what we had done and seen. He started taking photographs and asked me what I had observed as I was a ground instructor.

This made me feel better and I started looking at the corpse for clues. I noticed that the finger nails had been ripped off caused by attempts to open the reserve and then saw that the elastics used for opening the chest mounted reserve parachute when deployed, were closed over. This action was often used to prevent inadvertent opening of the parachute on the ground. I pointed this out and then realised that the same had happened to his main parachute so it was quite obvious that this student had not been checked before boarding or jumping from the aircraft. Photographs were taken and we were asked to leave the scene as others joined the chief instructor in the initial investigation to this fatality.

Kay and I walked back to the hangar where the course was packing up preparing to return to their base as it had been decided to suspend any further activity until further notice. I invited Kay home to meet mother and father and maybe to stay the night but she declined stating that she was meeting a friend that evening.

We heard nothing more on this fatality although I was introduced to the parents of the deceased some weeks later when once again I was doing my ground instructor duties. His mother quietly asked me if I had seen her son hit the ground to which I replied that I had. She then asked if I had heard him screaming before and whether his death had been instantaneous. I was also asked by her if it was 'messy'.

I was taken aback by these questions and honestly replied that there had been no screaming and that his death without doubt would have been immediate and that he looked peaceful. She seemed to be happy to hear this and thanked me for trying to help him. The father then shook my hand warmly explaining that he was ex-parachutist and begged me to try and understand why these questions were being asked.

It left me rather shaken and later that evening, just to complete a sad day, I was asked if I would spread the ashes of my old friend, Colin, from the Rapide over Netheravon Airfield. Colin had been killed in that flying accident as described earlier in this chapter. This was a bit of a disaster as he insisted on blowing back into the cabin covering everything including me in ash. However his parents were very grateful and could see the amusing side of it.

That was a hard day and I went home to my parents determined not feel down. It was good to have the support from mother and father despite the fact that I was late for supper for which I was in trouble but it 'brought me home'!

Chapter 22
Gliding Incident - 1967/1968

Netheravon Airfield started to become my 'play centre' where I would be found at any time whenever I had leave. I soon discovered that the Army Gliding Association operated on the same airfield well away from the skydiving centre.

My first flight as a student pilot with a flying instructor was in a tandem two-seated glider known as a Slingsby T21. It was an enthralling experience and I was sold on gliding. Furthermore, it would fall neatly into place with my skydiving as at times when the wind or cloud base were out of limits for jumping I could possibly enjoy flying a glider on the same airfield.

There are a number of methods of launching gliders. The two main systems being used at Netheravon at the time were an aero-tow or winch. An aero-tow is when another small aircraft with a single engine would tow you up to a reasonable height. This would give the glider a good chance of finding an updraft of air known as thermal upon which you could fly upwards thus giving the pilot time in the air and to cover ground. The longest I remained airborne in a glider unassisted was thirty-five minutes which was quite a thrill. The winch launch was cheap and easy as a large former German winch was used at Netheravon. The only problem with this was that the height of launch was restricted to some 800 feet.

I started to put a lot of time into learning to glide at the expense of my skydiving making me strangely guilty when I watched the jumping taking place not far away. However it was not long before I was cleared for my first solo flight in a small single-seated glider called a Grunau. The story had it that it was actually 'captured' from the Germans during the last war when it was found hidden in a rather large haystack.

I enjoyed many solo flights in this little old 'booty of war' although the average flight time was only around ten minutes per trip and it had the reputation as the 'gliding brick'. I needed to progress to a higher performance type of glider so I started flying another aircraft under instruction known as the K13 where the instructor would sit behind you in a fully enclosed cockpit and not beside you in an open cockpit as in the T21.

This seemed to be flying at its best and with instruction I was soon soaring the skies for a good length of time. On one memorable occasion somehow we got a bit close to a large cloud known as a cumulonimbus, (a large thunder cloud). It was an exhilarating rough ride and I was whooping with joy as I watched the altimeter wind itself up from 2000 to 8000 feet in a matter of minutes. My instructor, Peter, was not quite so excited at what was happening and at 8000 feet quietly asked me to deploy the air brakes as time had come to descend and he was concerned that we were gaining height rather too fast.

I did as asked and much to our surprise we still continued to rapidly gain height and Peter, an experienced glider pilot, took over control. He tried descending at maximum speed with the speed brakes out and still we were going up now being tossed around like a cork with the altimeter showing us approaching 10,000 feet.

It was obvious that we had been sucked into this thunder cloud and there was every possibility that the aircraft could disintegrate and I suddenly felt terrified. However it was comforting to remember that we were actually wearing parachutes and it would seem strange to get an unofficial sixty second delay jump from a doomed glider from this height.

Peter calmly asked when I had last done spin checks and then warned me that he was about to put the aircraft into a spin to try and get out of this up draft reminding me that I had a parachute if needs be.

With that we entered a spin and at around 7000 feet Peter gently pulled her out. It worked and all once again seemed calm and quiet apart from the odd bit of turbulence. The aeroplane seemed intact and all controls functioned as they should and we could now enjoy a gentle descent back to the airfield, although wary of any sudden updrafts that we may encounter. I put in a good landing and we got out with Peter exclaiming that whilst he had heard of this happening he had never experienced it before and that we were fortunate to have escaped.

I continued gliding for another five years without incident and eventually turned to powered flying gaining my Private Pilot's licence in 1973.

Chapter 23
Lybian Airstrip Argosy Crash - 1968

Following the stressful time I had recently experienced whilst gliding at Netheravon, I was pleased to get back to my Army duties and the platoon. We were now performing well as a team, winning various competitions such as inter platoon patrolling exercises, shooting matches etc. However my Company Commander did not seem too pleased with me as I was accused of spending too much time away fraternising with the SAS and jumping out of aeroplanes. He made it clear that my position was with my platoon as their commander not behaving like a 'gladiator'.

It just happened that the company was leaving for El Adem airfield in Libya for patrolling and defence exercises over a period of some five days. After the normal preparations we boarded the aircraft, an Armstrong Whitworth AW.660 Argosy. We were to carry out a day parachute jump onto El Adem which was a treat as normally all our jumps were done at night.

It all went as planned without any hitches and we soon discovered that following a phase of patrolling out in the desert we were to be transported to an improvised desert air strip that the RAF were using. It was in a remote part of the desert and had the nick name of 'Strip Spillane'. Our task was to defend the strip until we were evacuated, so trenches were dug around the runway and we looked forward to eventually flying out.

Our boredom was punctuated by watching the RAF landing and taking off. A take off was invariably followed up by the pilots 'buzzing the camp'. This was exciting to watch as it was something to watch these large aircraft skim over the desert at full speed with only feet to spare above the ground appearing to fly directly over us. We were pleased to be in our trenches and no doubt the 'crabs' (slang for the RAF), were highly amused to watch us 'Pongos' (slang for soldiers), taking cover in our trenches.

On our final day I had just visited the 'Hilton' which was a large tent boasting a water tower that fed showers and was used for reception etc. I bumped into a skydiving friend of mine, John, who was loading a field gun, Land Rover and five of his crew onto an Argosy. He was due out shortly and we discussed the possibility of meeting at Netheravon Skydiving Centre this coming weekend. He could join the 'relative gang' and with that he was called to board the aircraft. We waved each other farewell and I made my way back to the platoon position by the end of the runway.

I returned to my command trench greeted by my Platoon Sergeant who had made me a mug of tea and together we watched John's Argosy take off whistling close over us. The pilot then turned for what was considered the 'flypast' and my Sergeant and I thought that on this occasion the flight path did not look right as it appeared that his wing tip was about to hit the 'Hilton' water tower'.

It did hit the water tower, cartwheeling into the runway and blew up in huge ball of flame. Whilst we were in our trenches we watched in horror and a wheel most probably from the gun or Land Rover sped towards us bouncing well over our heads. I was fearful that debris would come our way but it didn't.

Without further thought I gathered six 'volunteers' and proceeded as fast as we could to the crash site with the hope of finding survivors. On the way my thoughts were of John to whom I had just bidden farewell. Would he have survived?

Five crew and six passengers including John lost their lives in that fatal accident. We found no bodies just ears, hands and feet. The stench of aviation fuel mixed with burning flesh and rubber was quite overpowering so I quickly withdrew as it was now obvious that there were no survivors. On returning to our position I noticed a gaggle of four soldiers staring at something in the sand and shouted at them to get a move on which they did.

Once back in the position I was quickly informed by one of the 'gaggle' that they had found a forearm and hand that was grasping an erect penis. The soldiers were quick to question whether the penis belonged to the owner of the hand. It was really quite grotesque but somehow this type of humour kept us sane when required.

We were flown home very shortly after this in another Argosy that with relief did a normal takeoff. We were left scarred by what we had seen. One particular soldier did not recover and I believe was medically discharged at a later date.

Chapter 24
The Grenade Range - 1968

Having been accused of behaving similar to a gladiator by my Company Commander, I obediently 'toed the line' and spent more time with the platoon. The next big event was with the battalion travelling to Lydd Camp on the Romney Marshes in Kent for live firing exercises. Live firing is when you perform various tactics with live munitions including grenades and it is thought that it is the closest you will get to real action, so as such could be considered as hazardous if not controlled correctly.

A new Lieutenant, George, joined the company as a Platoon Commander. He was fresh from Sandhurst and we quickly became friends despite the fact that we would be competing against each other with the varying platoon competitions.

To start the training we were to carry out grenade training followed by Fighting In Built Up Areas, (FIBUA), that involved clearing houses that were specifically designed for the task and then range work. We would complete the week with live firing on the ranges day and night. It all sounded interesting and we were looking forward to it.

Transport to Lydd was by train, which seemed a little odd as we were mixing with the public in our 'fighting gear', less our weapons that were being transported by truck. However we felt that we were on show, proudly wearing our maroon berets and wings, the insignia and uniform for paratroopers.

Whilst waiting on one station I was standing separately from my platoon trying to behave and look like an officer. One of my soldiers then approached me discreetly pointing out the fact that he and his comrades had been watching an attractive woman sitting nearby who apparently had been studying me intently and they reckoned that she had the 'hots' on me. I, of course immediately looked in the direction of my so called admirer and she realised that all were watching her and she started to blush and quickly exited the scene followed by wolf whistles from the assembled soldiery. I felt sorry for her but resisted the temptation to catch up and attempt to console her.

Lydd Camp was of the basic Nissen hut construction which would accommodate up to 12 of you sharing ablutions (toilets and showers). There was one cook house and mess hall where we ate our food. The officers, senior NCOs and soldiers were segregated, by simple screens, which to me being a young 'lefty' seemed weird but I was instructed that this separation of ranks was essential for discipline as at times some soldiers would try and get familiar.

On arrival I was informed by my Company Commander that I would be the range control officer for the grenade range. The battalion was being refreshed on live grenade handling as the following day we were to have two days of FIBUA training using live munitions including grenades.

I soon discovered that I was to be assisted by three experienced senior NCOs who were going to be my directing staff (DS). They would be responsible for the handling and control of the troops coming through the range and I would simply be in command.

We assembled at 08.00 hrs on the grenade range and the weather was good. Crates of grenades along with their fuses were stacked in a special bay. My only experience of throwing live grenades was in my basic recruit training and at Mons Officer Cadet School, so everything with this task was a little daunting. I explained this to my DS who immediately put me at ease stating that we would do a live rehearsal before arrival of the 'punters' and that my position would be up in an armoured lookout hut. This overlooked the range with a narrow slit at about face height through which I would give my commands. It was also important to watch for the fall of the grenades when they were thrown, in case one did not explode. If this happened another drill would come into effect and I, as the range control officer would have to place an explosive charge next to the dud grenade to dispose of it. A task that not many relished as it was known for these 'duds' to suddenly explode.

So the rehearsal started by each of us taking two of these 36 Mills grenades to a concrete bay where we were then issued with a detonation fuse that had to be placed into the grenade. I was informed by my DS that this type of grenade was used during the First World War (1915), and was still being used by the British Army. However it was an effective weapon that packed quite a punch with a killing area of up to 100 metres especially if you got hit in the head by the base plug. There then followed a lurid description by one of the DS who had witnessed how the head of an unfortunate had been split in half, revealing trembling brain matter, after suffering this injury. I was then instructed not to linger after I had seen where the grenade had fallen, and to get my head down.

Once we had primed our grenades we rehearsed the sequence and commands throwing two grenades each. All went well and I now felt confident over what had to be done and achieved. I was then given instruction on how to dispose of any grenades that did not go off using plastic explosive. It all seemed reasonably straightforward.

The 'punters' started to arrive on time at 09.00hrs and I disappeared up into my lookout. All went well and we had pushed through the majority of the battalion by 18.00hrs. However two base plugs did actually hit my hut with a resounding clank and one actually shattered the red danger flag pole beside me.

I also had to dispose of one dud grenade as practised. The grenade was correctly thrown and nothing happened. I had noted exactly where it had fallen and the drill was then to wait for some fifteen minutes to ensure that it would not suddenly explode. I was dispatched by my DS complete with my bomb disposal kit. One of my DS offered to come with me as it was my first time, but this I refused. I walked steadily up to the offending bomb and as I approached, it rolled down the side of a small crater.

I froze as I was expecting the worse after this agitation and there was nowhere to take cover on the range apart from a few shallow depressions in the shingle.

Strangely I was more concerned over being watched by my audience, the DS, and to be seen to be diving about for no reason would not do my credibility much good. Fortunately nothing happened and I approached this grenade that was now well lodged at the bottom of this crater. However in my enthusiasm to lay my charge I found myself sliding down the edge of this depression, not only burying the grenade in loose shingle but I actually landed on top of it. The good Lord was looking after me, as he had done so many times before, and nothing happened.

I was now left with the task of carefully uncovering this Mills bomb which I did successfully and I laid my explosive beside it. Having primed the charge I set the fuse off that gave me some three minutes before it went off and walked casually back to the shelter of the throwing bay. Once there I heard the double explosion and was congratulated by my observing DS who stated that I had completed the task successfully.

The following day it was back to my platoon and house clearing. We were briefed accordingly and the clearance began under the supervision of two DS The first thing that happened after we had started to clear a house was that I saw one of my Corporals throw a live grenade into a room through a window. However the next thing I noticed was that he started to climb through the window before the grenade had exploded.

Fortunately I was within reach and without hesitation I grabbed him by his shoulder harness and pulled him back onto the ground. His adrenaline was obviously running high and despite me trying to hold him on the ground he attempted to get up again to go through the window. Fortunately one of the DS, a big man, assisted me by diving on top of him and between us we held this man firm until after the grenade had detonated.

We then let him go and off he went though the window, smoke and dust shouting commands to his section as if nothing had happened. The DS informed me that strangely this can happen frequently although most times prevention avoids the consequent fatality. It was a good day with no further incidents and we soon learnt that FIBUA is a hazardous, tiring and drawn out task, as many films have depicted.

Chapter 25
Army Range Fatality - 1968

Live firing on the ranges was next on the list and whilst we were zeroing our weapons for this task I was briefed by the company commander that I had to design and plan a live night firing exercise for tomorrow night. I stressed the fact that I did not have any range qualifications that would cover me for this, but I was ordered to plan an exercise and that emphasis must be placed on realism.

I mentioned this to my Platoon Sergeant, who suggested that perhaps we could simulate an ambush on the firing point but it did not seem all that realistic. I spoke to the new Platoon Commander, George, but he did not wish to get involved and informed me that he also had a night firing task that he was organising.

I decided on a night ambush that would consist of some 25 riflemen with their Self Loading Rifles (SLRs), and one General Purpose Machine Gun, (GPMG) that was manned by two gunners. The plan would be to load and make ready the weapons on one firing point and then advance forward to the firing point that we were going to use, some 100 metres from the targets. The targets were to be moving and illuminated by trip flares along with spot lights attached to vehicle batteries.

It was simple but I had no knowledge of range procedures. It seemed realistic enough and what I understood as range disciplines were still being followed. I nervously discussed my plan with the Company Commander who confirmed that it sounded good to him as long as it was realistic. I asked, if perhaps, he could be present on the night and he assured me that he would be and told me to pull myself together as I was an experienced and good shot knowing what should and should not be done on rifle ranges.

This did fill me with confidence and, with three senior Directing Staff NCOs, set about organising and rehearsing the exercise the afternoon before. All went as planned and the soldiers arrived.

I gave them their orders and we carried out brief rehearsals. All were clear what their tasks were. As night fell rifles were made ready by the soldiers to one side of the GPMG. I went over to the GPMG and ordered the gunners to make ready. This would mean that they would lie behind the gun and that the belted live rounds would be placed in the weapon that would now be cocked with the safety catch applied. Having carried out this action the platoon would then proceed into the ambush site, or in this case, the firing point. I thought that I noticed my company commander nearby and as nothing was said all seemed good.

However when the gunner cocked the GPMG it started to fire. Much to my horror I saw the gunner get up from lying behind the GPMG and run away

Author in free fall at 4000 ft over Salisbury Plain.

Author and Simon with Mother, 1952.

Charioteer *lost at sea 1979.*

The home-built 'Goldwing' being flown by the author. (Photo by Tracey Elliot-Reep)

Alona with a Dartmoor pony.

Elizabeth milking the cow with help from Alona.

The photo of the house included in the time capsule year 2000.

The fourth daughter's wedding.

The girls. (Photo by Tracey Elliot-Reep)

The Author at work.

'Tranquillity'.

We grow old together – A 'Stagging Oak' on the farm.

Sailing out to sea.

along with his number 2. The immediate action in an accidental discharge of this nature is for the gunner or number 2 to break the belt of bullets, thus stopping the firing. With no gunners nearby the machine gun spewed high velocity rounds in all directions similar to a loose high pressure water hose and probably nothing would stop this until the belt ran out.

I ran towards the spitting monster and saw it slowly revolving towards me. I felt some form of commotion around my lower right leg where bullets were smashing into the ground around me complete with the familiar high pitched cracking of the high velocity rounds passing by. I jumped onto this GPMG kicking and stamping on it and then it stopped.

I then heard a horrible screaming coming from the direction of the riflemen and I heard my Company Commander shouting at me asking 'what had I done?' I ignored this and quickly made my way over to the platoon where I met the Platoon Sergeant who informed me that we had one man down but that seemed to be it and then calmly asked for instructions.

I ordered that he should line the men up on the firing point and unload their weapons and he was then to clear each rifle by torch. This was done and I attended the man down at the same time shouting for the range medic who did not seem to be present. It was one of my Corporals that had been hit. I knew him and his family well and we were the best of comrades.

I carried out a medical assessment and noticed that a bullet had hit his left leg in the femur shattering it and it appeared that his leg had just about been ripped off. He was initially conscious and I cradled him in my arms calling for the medic whilst at the same time trying to tie a form of tourniquet around the upper part of his leg with my shell dressing.

In between his screams he asked if I could give his two young boys some mint rock that were in his chest pocket, that he had purchased that afternoon at the sea front and to give his wife some personal messages. The medic arrived with his bag and with shaking hands administered a morphine injection. The casualty then went silent but still had a pulse and was breathing.

The range warden informed me that he had summoned an ambulance and that it should be here within minutes. My Company Commander reappeared on the scene blaming me for this accident and again asking 'what had I done?' and much to my surprise my Platoon Sergeant politely asked if the Company Commander could assist perhaps by taking over control as I was preoccupied with the man down.

The ambulance then arrived complete with a trauma doctor on board and the casualty was speedily placed on a stretcher and put in the vehicle along with another soldier who apparently had been hit in his right calf muscle. I asked the doctor if I could come to the hospital in the ambulance and he invited me in. I handed over my command to my Platoon Sergeant and we then were driven at speed with blue flashing lights to Lydd Hospital.

I stood by the doctor as he desperately tried to save my Corporal but pronounced him dead in the ambulance after a short while. We then turned our attention to the other casualty in the ambulance and sure enough there were two neat holes through the calf muscle of this soldier who looked shocked and shaken but apart from that the doctor reckoned he would be fine.

My head was spinning at this stage and we arrived at the hospital where the body was taken to the morgue and the injured soldier to a treatment area. I was amazed to see a police constable standing by the entrance to the morgue and he explained to me that this was now actually a scene of a crime in connection with the Army range accident and that was why he was there.

The doctor who had come in the ambulance informed me that he was to write a report and that he would give me a lift back to the camp. I gratefully accepted and then suddenly remembered that my late Corporal had live munitions on him. I approached another doctor who was passing and he spoke to the policeman who agreed to enter the morgue with me so that I could clear the corpse of explosives.

We entered the morgue together and it was an unpleasant sight with the stench of blood and death being quite overcoming. So much so the young police officer started to spew and the accompanying doctor cared for him producing a bucket. I quickly searched the body finding the munitions and the mint rock. I gently closed the wide open eyes and bid him farewell.

Following this I was met by the ambulance doctor who insisted on taking me back to his home to give me time to rest before taking me back to camp, informing me that he had got it all organised. On arrival at the doctor's home it was pointed out that I was covered in blood and that perhaps I might like to clean up. I was offered a shower and dressing gown whilst his wife cooked me some scrambled egg and toast and I was given a large glass of whisky; it was 02.00 hrs and I was in a complete daze and totally shattered. I had noticed whilst removing my trousers and boots that my right trouser leg had two holes through the fabric and the rubber heel of my boot also had a hole through it. On closer examination of my leg I noticed a red pencil line that crossed my calf at the back. The doctor examined it and informed me that this could only be a mark left by a high velocity round that had skimmed my leg with another going through the heel of my boot.

The doctor then notified me that it had been organised that he would drop me off at the camp gates at 07.00 hrs tomorrow morning where the Adjutant, who I knew well, would meet me. Oddly enough I slept well wondering at how fortunate I had been and also asking the question why?

Chapter 26
The Board of Inquiry and Self Harming - 1968

I was awoken with a cup of tea and the doctor told me that it would take fifteen minutes to get to Lydd Camp from here so perhaps we ought to get moving. I thanked his wife for her kindness and hospitality and she gave me a hug, wishing me luck. We departed arriving at Lydd Camp at 07.00 to be met by the Adjutant as planned. I was, and am still, so grateful to this doctor for everything that he and his wife had done for me at this critical time. He had gently explained to me that this would be a life changing experience and that I was to remain positive throughout. We shook hands and he wished me all the best.

With that I was met by the Adjutant who in his turn shook hands with me and then gave me a pat on the back stating that this could have happened to anyone and that he was there to help. This filled me with relief as I was not sure whether I would be facing immediate disciplining, as I knew that my Company Commander was blaming me for this horrendous event. However it would appear that this would not be the case and I was receiving sympathy not discipline.

The Adjutant then took me into breakfast in the officers' section of the cook house and again everybody, without exception, was friendly and full of sympathy. I started to feel better and over breakfast the Adjutant explained that a board of inquiry would be convened next week. It was stressed that this was not any form of legal proceedings and that the intention of the board would be to report on what actually happened on that fateful night. The president selected was the Military Transport Officer (MTO), who was a Captain with many years of military service behind him and above all I knew him well. I felt this was good as I knew that this man would do a good job and be fair.

The MTO, Adjutant, second in command of the battalion and myself after breakfast were to be taken in the battalion Scout helicopter back to Aldershot where things would be set up for the board of inquiry next week.

After breakfast, having packed my equipment, we boarded the helicopter and were flown to Aldershot landing on the square as was normal. We completed some forms in the Adjutant's office and I was then ordered to go home for the weekend which rather surprised me. The Adjutant asked me to telephone my parents to warn them and to be back here in his office by 08.00 hrs on Monday morning. He also instructed me to try relax and forget what had happened as 'what will be will be'.

With that I went back to my room in the Officers' Mess, unpacked my kit, cleaned myself up, changed into a shirt and jeans, bundling my bloodied uniform into a kit bag and then drove to Gillingham, in Dorset, where my parents lived, having briefly explained the situation to them by telephone.

As I approached home I suddenly began to get concerned over exactly what I should tell them, especially my mother. I arrived to be met by father, who took my kit bag and showed me into the house. Mother as always gave me a big hug and that was it. I was instructed to get changed for supper and father gave me a glass of beer. Suddenly I was back to normality back in my home, it all seemed surreal.

Not a thing was said about the accident over that supper and I had an early bed. I started to sleep well to awake in a sweat, hearing that screaming, feeling that warm bloody mass of a shattered leg and looking into those wide open dead eyes. Was I really to blame as after all I gave that command to load that GPMG. This was to haunt me for years and that question 'why' materialized in my mind time and time again and still does.

Later that week end I spoke to my father over the situation. I felt that as an experienced and accomplished soldier himself he would be in a position to offer assistance. He listened to what I had to say. He advised me that at this time I should not talk to anybody in the battalion over this until after the board of inquiry. To him there appeared to be some conflicting evidence, with reference to my Company Commander, who seemed to be blaming me. Father stated that from what I had told him I was not to blame and that it was likely that the board would come to this conclusion. I found this steady advice at such a time of turmoil in my mind comforting.

I left home on the Sunday evening after supper and drove back in my green Ford Thames van to Aldershot, arriving at the Officers' Mess later that evening where I managed to get into my room without seeing anybody which was a relief. I unpacked my clean clothes and got my service dress ready for tomorrow morning when the board of inquiry would be starting.

I did not sleep that night, thus avoiding the nightmares but leaving me totally shattered for the day. I knew that I had to give evidence and was not looking forward to it. After breakfast when everybody wished me luck I reported to the Adjutant's office. He comforted me and took me down to the gymnasium where an amphitheatre had been constructed for the board of inquiry. There were three officers sitting on the board at a long table with the president, who I knew, in the centre. When I entered the room I was cordially greeted by those on the board who shook my hand. There were some 30 witnesses most of whom were my soldiers who were intent on giving evidence. There was also my Company Commander sitting on the other side of the room to me. There were two military policemen standing guard by the door.

It seemed strange as, whilst this was a formal hearing, we were again in-structed that we had to give evidence under oath. However this was not in any way a legal proceeding and in fact there were no lawyers present, apart from an observer sitting on the board. The purpose of this investigation was to establish exactly what had happened and that a report would be written and submitted to the Brigade Commander who would decide on any actions if any that should be taken.

It was hard but I managed to withdraw into myself as if I was observing matters from another place. When I spoke I did so clearly and without emotion and being in this dream certainly assisted me in this. I noticed that when the company commander spoke some of the soldiers became agitated to such a degree that they were warned that they would be expelled from the room. It lasted three days and I got the firm impression that the Company Commander was indeed blaming me for this accident as I should have known better as range officer. He claimed that he was not present at the time of accidental discharge so could not in any way be held responsible.

However, whilst walking up to the Officers' Mess from the gymnasium for lunch on the third day I was suddenly approached by the president of the board who walked beside me. He informed me that, in strictest confidence, he wished to tell me that to quote an American expression I, a young Second Lieutenant who was half way though a three-year short service commission, was to be the 'fall guy' in this whole ugly mess. I responded by confirming with him that I was, therefore, found to be responsible for this incident and he agreed stating that he had no control over this. He then went onto say that I must know that I was not really to blame and that perhaps after this I could put it all behind me and start life again with a clear conscience. With that he patted me on the back and we went into lunch.

I was not only totally dazed living in another world, but was now confused as I had been assured that only the truth could be given in this report. It was all too much and I began to feel a bit of a hero being the 'sacrificial lamb' no doubt saving others from early discharge from the Army. I really could not care any more and if I was to be dishonourably discharged so be it.

Nothing happened after the inquiry and the report was not divulged. I was not dismissed and was actually congratulated by my commanding officer on my performance at the time of the accident and during the board of inquiry. I was instructed to return to normal duties as Platoon Commander under my Company Commander, who obviously found this difficult. With all the confidence I could muster I went back to my soldiers who were full of praise, some stating that they would follow me anywhere (which only soldiers could do), but I got the message and remembered that they had supported me during this hearing.

I began to feel better over the whole situation although I had been warned that the findings of the report would manifest itself at some stage. When this was to be I and others were not sure and I was informed that it was up to the Brigade Commander. In the meantime I had to endure a confidential report from my Company Commander who opened with the fact that I was 'an enigma' who lacked common sense and was immature. He thought that this was amusing and it was now obvious to me, which way this horrible mess was going despite reassurances.

There was one other task that I had to complete and this I was dreading. I had to visit the widow of my late Corporal and give her the mint rock for his two young boys, aged three and four years. I also had to inform her of what he had said to me before his death. I knew where she lived as I had been invited to tea there, by him, to meet the family not long ago.

I decided to visit in uniform and unannounced. I knocked on her door and to my surprise she greeted me warmly inviting me in stating that she had spoken to one or two who were present at the accident and was looking forward to speaking to me. She informed me that the boys were away with their grandmother for the day. She then went on to thank me for everything I had attempted to do to try and save her husband. I was not sure of how to respond to this and managed to blurt out that I had been blamed for the death of her husband.

She looked shocked and asked why this was. I told her the truth and after tea she firmly exclaimed that in no way was she holding me responsible and rather oddly then asked whether the weapon involved was serviceable. Why a Corporal's wife should know the condition of our weapons was beyond me although she did qualify this question. She explained that her late husband had shown some concern over the serviceable state of one of the machine guns. I did remember something about this and that he had reported the matter that I thought had been sorted.

This matter had not been mentioned during the board of inquiry and I felt that it was not my position to challenge the serviceability of our weapons or equipment as I thought that I was already in enough trouble.

Before leaving I presented her with the mint rock and we parted weeping. It was very difficult as this Corporal would be sorely missed by his family and indeed by his platoon.

I returned to the Officers' Mess that evening and decided that enough was enough. I was going to commit suicide by slashing my wrist in the bath. I ran a hot bath, selected a new razor blade, locked myself into the bathroom and got into the bath. I carried out three deep slashes that I thought would suffice and watched my blood pour into the bathwater.

I relaxed, feeling that I had taken the correct decision and that now it was all over. I said some prayers and wondered how long it was going to take. After 15 minutes I was amazed to see how much blood I had lost but still felt as if nothing had happened. The water was now thick with blood with the stench being prominent.

I was about to carry out more slashes to my wrist when I heard somebody outside the bathroom door asking what was going on. It was the battalion doctor who had smelt the blood and without further hesitation he kicked the door down.

He asked me what I was trying to do and then went on to explain that I had not slashed my artery but had cut some veins. He went onto tell me that the bleeding would eventually clot and that my only achievement would be an awful smelly mess in the bathroom and a sore left wrist.

The doctor cleaned me up, bandaged me and then put me to bed, having given me a strong sleeping pill instructing me to stay in my room until tomorrow morning when he would visit me again. I slept well that night in a drug induced coma without nightmares.

The next morning the doctor redressed my wounds and stated that I was to take some sick leave suggesting that I should go home to my parents. I did this and a brief recovery period started as I felt that I had reached the lowest point and was now to look forward positively as advised by that Samaritan doctor at Lydd.

Chapter 27
Malta and SCUBA Diving Accident - 1969

Once again I was keen to get back to my battalion, now in Malta, so I reported back to Aldershot where I was medically assessed as 'returned to my normal cheery self'. This enabled me to fly out to Malta to join my platoon. However before this happened I had to appear in front of the Brigade Commander who had decided on the findings of the inquiry. As a young officer, aged nineteen, I was blamed for the death of my Corporal although he went onto say that no further action would be taken and that I should resume normal duties. Despite being warned about this 'finding' I found it all devastating and desperately tried to put it all behind me.

I boarded the aircraft, which was an RAF Britannia, in a total daze and was met at Luqa by two soldiers from Support Company who had arrived to collect me in an open Land Rover in desert camouflage and full of sand fresh from Libya. It was great and whilst driving through a town known as Sliema on the way to our barracks, which were known as Saint Andrew's, the driver suddenly stopped for what appeared to be no reason.

I did not know what was happening and noticed that both the driver and the other soldier sitting in the back of the vehicle, were gazing skywards. I was getting concerned as I thought that this could be some form of crazy joke but then managed to trace the direction of their gaze assisted by a furtive point of the finger of the driver to a balcony. On the balcony was a Maltese girl wearing a short skirt bending over to scrub the floor. She seemed to be enjoying the audience by adopting different poses.

I ordered the driver to proceed without any further delay, as we were now beginning to hold the traffic up, which he did and then a discussion took place about whether the young lady in question was actually wearing any underwear. It was good to get back to basics with the soldiers again and it brought me back to reality which was great

I was dropped off at the Officers' Mess and was shown to my room by one of the mess stewards. This mess and barracks were built from the 1890s designed to accommodate at least 1000 infantrymen, their officers and spouses and not much modernising had taken place since. I had a spacious second floor corner room with a fan, balcony, fireplace and wonderful views. My bed was large and was covered in a mosquito net so I was quite comfortable.

I met up with my comrades over tea and was warmly greeted with tea turning into an impromptu party welcoming me. However I noticed that my Company Commander was not present but was informed that he seldom came into the mess as he was married and lived in a married quarter with his wife, as did other married officers and soldiers.

With the celebrations over I got stuck into the routine of military life on Malta. As warned the main problem being that of boredom with constant weapon training etc. along with range work and fitness training. I decided to break the monotony by starting a SCUBA (Self Contained Breathing Apparatus), diving club within the battalion. This was greeted with enthusiasm, but then I was left with the task of organising procurement of equipment and instructors.

Much to my surprise I discovered that one of my soldiers in the platoon had been a North Sea oil rig diver and claimed that he held a diving instructor's certificate. I was made, and asked him where he thought the best place would be to get all the equipment that we would require. It was suggested that perhaps I could approach the Royal Navy as they would surely be able to assist.

After many enquiries I discovered the correct contacts and was warmly greeted by the Navy who were only too happy to provide everything we needed, including air for the bottles, and instructors. Training started in the local swimming pool and membership was strong. I felt pleased at the progress of my 'club' and all were enjoying it with great support from the Royal Navy for which I was very grateful.

We soon progressed to diving in the sea and learnt that it was essential to follow all safety precautions that we had been given. Above all it was essential that nobody dived on their own and that all diving had to be supervised and carried out with a 'buddy', who you would never let out of sight whilst underwater.

After a number of dives I arranged an excursion onto a wreck of a British Second World War destroyer, HMS *Maori* that had been sunk on her mooring, by a German bomb in 1942. It lay in some 45 to 90 feet of water and had been broken into two parts. The bow section contained the front gun turret where a large octopus, named Oscar, could be found. It was customary to feed Oscar fish placed on the end of your spear gun and fascinating to watch his tentacles wrap around the food and then disappear into the turret. Artefacts such as plates with the ships emblem still visible, cigarette lighters and cases, lanterns etc could still be found around the site.

I had chosen the right day for this excursion as visibility underwater was good which in this area was unusual. There were ten of us diving in pairs using the naval equipment that had been carefully checked and we were supervised by two Royal Naval instructors.

It was wonderful to swim about the wreck and my thoughts were with those that had perished in this sinking. I was looking inside the wreck when suddenly at about 16 meters of depth I got a mouthful of water instead of air. At the same time there were bubbles coming out of my breathing regulator. The drill would be to swim over to your diving 'buddy' making a sign and he would offer his breathing regulator from which you could share the air whilst making a controlled ascent to the surface. We had practised this essential drill a number of times and were fully conversant with it.

However in this instance I had a problem in that I could not see my partner anywhere so without further hesitation I swam for the surface as I was quickly running out of air and at the same time had to exhale. I should have ascended at the same rate as my bubbles but I didn't as I was now panicking to get a breath of air as soon as possible. I had breathed in some of the water that I already ingested and was beginning an uncontrollable spluttering fit.

I broke the surface of the water at speed but it was wonderful to breathe air. I was promptly sick and was choking at the same time but I had survived and was still alive although I was feeling quite dizzy and odd. My mind suddenly started to function again and I called for assistance from the instructors not far away as I remembered that my partner was now down there on his own.

The instructors were soon with me getting me on board the rubber dinghy and one dived to collect my 'buddy' who still had not surfaced despite my problem. They both surfaced shortly after, with my companion unaware that I had disappeared. I was fine although the instructors questioned me closely on what depth I had been, for how long and what speed I had come up to the surface as they were considering taking me to a decompression chamber nearby.

I assured them that I was OK, which was a stupid thing to have done, as about a week later I suffered a terrible bout of bronchial coughing that developed into pleural pneumonia, whilst on board a Royal Naval frigate acting as an Army interrogation officer.

I underwent a casualty evacuation by helicopter to Bighi Hospital, in Malta, where after ten days I recovered. However I was advised by a consultant that my x-rays clearly showed a shadow on one of my lungs indicating that I had suffered a lung over expansion injury. I was advised that this would mean that I should not dive again and that I was fortunate not to have suffered any other injuries such as decompression sickness or a blood embolism.

It was confirmed later by the Royal Navy, whose equipment I had borrowed, that it was thought that the reason for this incident was that the swivel 'o' ring for the mouth regulator had failed.

Another lesson had been confirmed in as much as that to ignore or flaunt safety rules and procedures in any way is highly dangerous practice. I was of course fully aware of this through my previous experience of life. Following this incident I was interviewed by my commanding officer who asked me what I was trying to prove, to which I could not provide an answer. It was left that I should learn from all this and remember that I was not immortal and that if I wished to live to 'a ripe old age', I was to take care. More importantly I was reminded that I also commanded soldiers for whom I was responsible.

Shortly after this I was given the nick name within the Officers' Mess as 'One Lung'.

Chapter 28

Me in Trouble and a Para Ascending Incident - 1969

We were warned that boredom would be the enemy whilst posted in Malta, although this seemed hard to believe. However not much was happening on the war front worldwide, apart from Vietnam, so as I was constantly reminding my soldiers we were doing a good job keeping the peace!

With my latest restriction on SCUBA diving following my accident I started to look about for other activities that would help to alleviate the constant routine. I became interested in sailing and was invited for a sail on a lovely old Hillyard 12 ton sloop by the owner, a wealthy businessman whom I had met at a British Embassy party.

I joined the family on her mooring, for a sedate sail out of Valetta Harbour and following this was invited on board at any time if I wished to do some maintenance such as sanding down the woodwork etc. and was shown where the keys were hidden. I made maximum use of this offer being able to relax on this yacht whilst on her mooring.

I started to meet many sailing enthusiasts and one day was asked if I would like to take part on the following day in a dinghy race being held by the local sailing club. I accepted and recruited my crew who was my Company Sergeant Major (CSM), who was also a skydiver, so we knew each other well.

It was a windy day for the race with many capsizes, including us, and we managed to right ourselves and completed the race without problem although we were not placed. It was actually great fun and both the CSM and I enjoyed it stating that we would do this again.

On the same day, our commanding officer (CO), who had taken up wind surfing had also capsized and was unable to recover. He was seen to be blown out to sea so the alarm was raised resulting in a rescue where a Royal Naval Wessex helicopter managed to rescue our CO complete with his windsurfer.

This incident was kept reasonably quiet although it came out over tea in the Officers' Mess the following day.

Shortly after the sailing adventures I was summoned into the office of my Company Commander (who apparently had blamed me for the range accident). I was informed that it had been reported to him that I had capsized a dinghy in a race and that this was thoroughly irresponsible and that it could also debase the reputation of the Parachute Regiment.

He then went on to state that he was, therefore, charging me for irresponsible behaviour unbecoming of an officer and asked me whether I would accept the punishment that he was about to impose on me. (This was normal and correct procedure if you were charged by a superior officer.)

I responded with a firm 'no sir' and looked at him in defiance. He then told me that this could most probably result in a Court Martial and advised me to 'accept the award'. I steadfastly refused to do this and insisted on seeing the CO over this matter, as in my opinion this charge was unjust and discriminatory, knowing full well that the CO had to be rescued from the sea on that same day.

The response from my Company Commander was that of frustration with him claiming that I was always challenging him. I felt rather sorry for him and after lunch I was marched in front of the CO by the Adjutant, who could not understand what was happening. The CO read through my charge sheet and then blew his nose very loudly asking whether I was aware of the problem that he had on the day in question. I noticed that the Adjutant was attempting to suppress a smile as I claimed that I had heard all about it at tea in the Officers' Mess not long ago.

With that the CO dismissed the charge stating that my Company Commander had obviously misunderstood the situation and that he would speak to him. I was then asked if I had any other projects in my mind.

I explained that it just happened that I was researching the possibility of parascending, where a person is towed behind a four-wheel-drive-vehicle, or as in many cases a boat while attached to a specially designed canopy that looks similar to a parachute. A parachute harness connects the pilot to the parasail which is coupled to the towing vehicle by a detachable rope so once the intended height is reached (that could be anything up to 400 feet depending on length of tow rope), the parascender could parachute to ground carrying out a normal parachute landing. It was, however, primarily intended as a 'fun ride'.

I went on to inform him that, by coincidence, during a sail in the well known Hillyard sloop the skipper had also discussed the possibility of carrying out some research on the island in a project he was interested in, being parascending. He had found a new type of parachute rig that could be of some commercial interest. I was intrigued by this and promised to explore some possibilities to make this possible such as finding trained parachutists, vehicles and land where this could take place. The CO seemed interested and asked me to keep him informed, so I had killed two birds with one stone on this occasion.

I went back to the 'skipper' of the Hillyard sloop and informed him that my CO was interested in this venture and perhaps the next move would be to procure the parachute. This arrived a few days later complete to go including a tow rope and helmets. All I needed now were volunteers, who were trained free fall parachutists, a Land Rover and permission to use a remote rifle range situated at Ghan Tuffieha that I had chosen as the ideal site for the job. They had just started to build a large hotel next to this lovely site, which was a shame.

I soon recruited some suitable volunteers and gained permission to use a Land Rover at Ghan Tuffieha. My CSM was my number two in this operation and it was exciting inspecting the new equipment before the first flight. I was given the honour of carrying that out and of course it went without a hitch with me doing a stand up landing inches from the makeshift landing target that we had placed on the ground.

All the volunteers then completed a flight successfully and it was great fun but as my CSM remarked it was not like the real thing and asked me if I could sort something out on that score, in other words organise some proper skydiving.

We continued with this parascending programme and on one particular day the wind was blowing hard down the range towards the sea. We were now experienced in this activity and I could see no harm in launching even if it was gusting around 25 to 30 knots! I volunteered for the first flight.

I estimated that the Land Rover would not need to be driven forward in this wind and I was right. As soon as the canopy was presented to the wind I shot upwards and remained at a steady 300 to 400 feet, violently swinging from side to side. I did not wish to release myself as I thought that the wind really was out of limits for a safe parachute landing. In other words I was now in an unsafe situation stuck up there with every possibility of being smashed into the ground on one of these wild gyrations.

I then saw the Land Rover slowly reversing and thought that the CSM was trying to lower me by driving the vehicle backwards with the wind but then realised that in fact it was being dragged backwards with all four wheels locked and skidding on the grass. I saw the lads running about looking for rocks to place under the tyres to act as chocks as the Land Rover and I and were on the move, gradually approaching the cliffs now.

Without warning there was what seemed a tremendous gust of wind that resulted in a loud 'twang' from my parachute and I nearly completed a backward somersault in my harness. I also dipped towards the ground again but then quickly gained height. One of the rigging lines had parted from the fabric of the rig. This happened two more times and I was now fearful that my end had finally arrived with the parachute about to collapse.

Suddenly there was a lull and everything became calm. Without hesitation I released myself carrying out a successful landing to be caught and assisted by those on the ground who quickly packed the parachute up before the next gust of wind. I had survived fifteen minutes of hell up there but as the CSM stated 'all's well that ends well'.

This terminated the parascending project and I returned the broken equipment to our sponsor with a report of what had happened. He was grateful for the information that was to be used in future applications and marketing enabling the use of limitations. I now started to concentrate on the skydiving possibility on the island.

Chapter 29
Russian Roulette and Crazy Party Games - 1969

Following a boring embassy party one evening we were driven back to the Officers' Mess just in time to catch the bar that was about to close. Alcohol in Malta was cheap and most of us took advantage of this which probably was not good for our health, but it was enjoyable and relieved the boredom.

On this occasion there were four of us young officers and Brian who was a Captain. The party in the mess continued, having tipped the barman for his efforts and Brian introduced us to a party trick that normally gained attention when at tedious upper class type of parties, one of which we had just attended.

It was quite simply eating your glass, having drunk the contents first. (You were normally restricted to one glass full throughout the evening on these occasions.) He assured us that the glass to be found at these smart occasions were like their owners brittle, fragile and easily consumable. A demonstration, with instruction, was then given and we were surprised to note that Brian actually swallowed the glass having ground it up well with his teeth.

He then ordered four glasses from the barman for human consumption and we all tucked in and quite remarkably there was no blood or cuts and we stopped at the glass stems although Brian had eaten his. The amazed barman was cleared to put the consumed glasses on our mess bills so it was decided to try another activity and this was to become a 'fire eater' and blowing fire similar to a dragon.

A tin of lighter fuel was ordered and Brian once again gave us instructions on what to do. A mouthful of fuel was taken and then with force you exhaled the air mixed with the lighter fuel from your mouth and lit the exhalation with a match or lighter, ensuring that after the exhalation you firmly closed your mouth. Failure to do this could result in a 'blow back' with possible fatal results. It was not long before there were four of us dancing around the bar spitting fire at each other.

There was, however, on this occasion one casualty with our gunner, who had a smart moustache. He did suffer a blow back and his moustache was burnt off. We put the fire out with a couple of soda siphons but he looked a little odd without his 'tache'.

Then from somewhere a Smith & Wesson revolver appeared on the table in front of us. The words Russian roulette were mentioned by Brian and it all went very quiet.

Whilst we quietly gulped our drinks, mainly to try to get the taste of lighter fuel out of our mouths, Brian went on to explained what Russian roulette was about.

He stated that it is a lethal game of chance in which a player places a single round into the cylinder of the revolver, spins it and places the muzzle against their head and pulls the trigger.

He went onto explain that the name of the game was supposed to have originated from Russia and roulette referred to the spinning of the revolver's cylinder, which was similar to the spinning roulette wheel found in casinos etc.

Because only one chamber in most cases is loaded the player has a one in x chance of hitting the loaded chamber. As most revolvers hold six rounds there is, therefore, the chance of blowing your brains out as one in six. However, Brian quickly explained that with an old and worn firearm that had been properly maintained and cleaned it was highly probable that due to gravity, the weight of the single round would normally end up at the bottom of the cylinder once spun. It was essential to hold the weapon horizontally whilst spinning the chamber.

This would very much alter the odds in the favour of the player especially if the cylinder was spun outside the pistol. (Money or further free drinks could be won here.)

He produced a box of bullets and placed one into the cylinder and gave a demonstration and sure enough the loaded chamber on a number of occasions did rest at the bottom of the cycle. So without further hesitation he span the cylinder, locked it back into the revolver pointed it at his head and pulled the trigger. There was a click as the firing pin hammer struck an empty chamber.

We all breathed a sigh of relief and I asked to have a go. Brian unloaded the weapon and handed it to me, along with the bullet. I placed the shell into the chamber gave it a good spin and hesitated asking if I could have a quick look to make sure that it was at the bottom of the cylinder. This attracted much amusement from my comrades so without further hesitation without looking I quickly locked the cylinder into the correct position, pointed it at my head with care and pulled the trigger. I cannot relate on how I was feeling at this stage but when I heard that resounding click the feeling of relief was overwhelming. I did this two more times and placed two bullets next to each other into the chamber on the third attempt. Brian reckoned that I had pushed my luck enough and that I still lived to tell the tale which was as it should end!

Two others played the game and I am happy to say that there were no casualties. In fact our gaming was suddenly stopped by the entry of a particularly stuffy and strict single Major, who lived in the mess, who was wondering what we were up to. He could not understand why we were all so quiet and fortunately Brian had disposed of any evidence that may have given our previous antics away. However, one bullet had been left on the table and this I retrieved as quickly as I could and then departed for bed wishing everybody goodnight.

Once in bed I recalled what I had done and it all seemed unbelievable. Had I really pulled that trigger three times with the final one having two rounds in the chamber? Maybe I could survive anything that would come my way.

I have never played Russian roulette again.

Chapter 30
Malta & Cyprus - Skydiving - 1969

Military routine continued as before although the men were getting restless at times. I encouraged them to make the most of what they had here, an island that many tourists spend money to come and stay on. One or two remarks were made about the food and accommodation that this 'holiday camp' seemed to produce and it was a problem to keep everybody occupied and happy, which was understandable.

The other Platoon Commander, George, and I were notified by our CO that our Company Commander was leaving to be replaced by another Parachute Regiment officer who had just completed a successful tour with 22 Special Air Service (SAS).

We soon discovered that this man was a quiet and strong type who listened to everything one said before making decisions. He was also meticulous in researching different characters within his company and it was all very refreshing. The first interview I had with him he asked if I would consider competing in a skydiving competition to be held in Cyprus in a couple of weeks' time. It was the Near and Middle East Forces free fall championship competition and it appeared that 3 Para was unable to produce any suitable competitors experienced enough to participate, which seemed odd.

I had actually brought my skydiving equipment over to Malta, just in case, so I 'jumped' at the chance and enthusiastically volunteered myself. This was approved by the CO and I was shortly flying over to Cyprus to be met by an old skydiving friend, Nick, who was a Captain in the Royal Corps of Transport. I was accommodated in the Officers' Mess next to a local airstrip which was going to be used for the competition.

There were some 30 competitors at the initial briefing the evening before the opening day of the five-day event. It was to start with a mass jump of all those competing. This had been designed and advertised as a 'crowd puller' and went off well with many spectators.

I carried out a good jump landing in the centre of the arena achieving a stand up landing and released my parachute from my shoulder risers. This was a 'flashy' manoeuvre not normally recommended due to safety as timing for this was critical. The crowd showed their appreciation of my entry and then, having removed my helmet, I noticed an attractive blond haired girl running towards me shouting my name.

She flung herself into my arms much to the amusement of all. I suddenly realised that she was an old childhood sweetheart, Patricia, whose father was commanding an infantry battalion out here. It really could not have got much better but I had now to concentrate on the competition ahead of me as I explained to Patricia. She enthusiastically stated that she would assist me in packing my chute between the six jumps during the week.

We were jumping mainly from Cessnas. The weather was good and all jumps were made as planned. It was an accuracy competition which meant that most jumps were made from between 3200 and 4000 feet with individual jumpers spotting for themselves. In other words they had to decide when to jump from the aircraft.

On the final jump I had been allocated a Piper Colt aircraft to jump from which was being flown by an experienced Cypriot pilot. It was a small aeroplane that was a tail dragger and I could just fit into it wearing my parachutes although it was a struggle to strap in. The doors had been removed so I could hang out, which gave the pilot more room and it was the first time I had jumped from this type of aircraft.

Following takeoff after clawing our way to about 1000 feet I noticed that the engine started to die. I looked at the pilot who was pointing earthwards. We had no form of vocal communication as I was wearing a helmet and he earphones.

There was no doubt we were now descending rapidly and that we were making a forced landing. An arid level open area with what seemed many rocks lying about had been selected and we made a perfect slow controlled landing somehow avoiding large rocks and stones.

We both got out and having removed my helmet I congratulated and shook hands with the pilot who stated that he had put out a radio call, so assistance will be with us shortly. He then opened the engine cowling to investigate the problem.

I did not have to wait long before I was recovered by a Land Rover which also arrived with a mechanic. It was later discovered that the engine failure was caused by dirt in the carburettor.

I carried out my final jump from a Cessna 172 and did well in this competition winning the championship and being placed first in all events. I returned to Malta with an armful of trophies. Maybe it was the support and encouragement of my new found admirer, Patricia, who was without doubt as was confirmed by Nick, an absolute stunner both in looks and character. I was invited to dinner by Patricia's parents on my final evening in Cyprus and following that I never saw her again.

It seemed strange to get back to the battalion in Malta and I was congratulated by my new Company Commander and CO who posted my victory on battalion orders which was embarrassing.

My final winter with the battalion was approaching and I discovered water skiing. Somehow we managed to get hold of a speed boat that was powerful and big enough for the job. Those that participated were soon on one ski and we spent many a happy hour skiing around St Paul's Bay. On one occasion we were put on standby to entertain HRH Prince Charles as he had expressed an interest in water skiing on one of his trips to Malta. However he did not have the time so we were stood down but we got some new skis out of this.

My final feat was to organise some skydiving from a Royal Naval Wessex helicopter. The Royal Navy had been wonderful in supporting us in our mundane duty and the pilots thought nothing of producing their helicopters early in the morning ready for jumping. Those soldiers that became interested in free falling steadily grew in number.

After Christmas the time had come to leave the battalion and I carried out my last jump, dispatching five jumpers from 7000 ft early one morning. I was attached to the helicopter and wearing just a small dispatch parachute as I had no intention of jumping. My CSM was the final jumper and somehow I became unattached from the aircraft and was pulled out by him.

We descended together and carried out some relative work and when the CSM deployed his parachute I pulled my little emergency despatch chute. It opened with no problem and I landed on the airfield. However the pilots of the helicopter were concerned and they came running over to discover that I was safe. I apologised for the alarm that had been caused and the incident was light-heartedly concluded proving that these emergency chutes do have their function!

Chapter 31

Mountain Leadership - Fall off a Climb - 1970

I left the 3rd Battalion the Parachute Regiment in Malta early in 1970. However during my farewell interview with my CO I was informed that it had emerged that the weapon involved in the Lydd Range accident in 1968 had been found to be unserviceable with worn parts. It was thought that these defects most probably caused the accidental discharge that killed a Corporal and injured a soldier. He went on to inform me that he was telling me this as he had felt upset over this matter and that now I could do what I wished with this information. I was shocked at this and on return to the UK had a lengthy discussion with father over the matter. It was decided for the benefit of all concerned it would be best to let 'sleeping dogs lie' and not take any action.

A twelve week resettlement course to qualify for a Mountain Leadership Certificate had been organised for me at the Army Outward Bound School based at Towyn in North Wales and I was looking forward to this. I had to undergo instructor training in mountain walking, climbing and rock climbing. I was partly experienced in these activities through my Army experience but had to undergo recognised instructor training to qualify for my certificate that is now recognised as an award. Following this I planned to get a job as an instructor in an outward bound school somewhere in the U.K.

I joined the outward bound centre at Towyn and started to enjoy the routine of a typical outward bound centre where a swim in the sea at first light would be enjoyed followed by a hearty breakfast. Some classroom work would then have to be endured learning various disciplines including the tying of rope knots etc. This was interspersed by an occasional race over the assault course that for some unknown reason always resulted in an injury or two.

When the classroom work had been completed successfully the students ventured out onto the hills to complete recognised walks and some basic climbing. I was an instructor under supervision and all started well.

After some four weeks I was then sent on a Rescue Search and Survival course being organised and held at the Mountain Rescue Centre based in Snowdonia. I was to join two SAS soldiers who were experienced mountain leaders. I learnt a lot on this course and to conclude the course we marched to the top of Snowdon to spend the night in a snow hole and then to complete a rescue the next day.

We arrived at the summit of Snowdon in bad weather. However it was not snowing as was normal at this time of year, but raining hard being driven by gale force winds, which of course was good exposure making weather. It was cold but we soon found shelter in amongst some rocks. Over mugs of tea that we had brewed we decided as there was no snow that we would return on a night march and have supper in the centre, which we did and a good evening was had. With hangovers we carried out the rescue exercise with stretchers successfully.

Having completed this course I could now join the local mountain rescue group and it was only a month before I was involved in a rescue on Aran Fawddwy, south of Snowdon mountain, where a 'boy' with exposure had to be extracted by stretcher at night. We were successful in our mission that was carried out in deplorable weather. It was very satisfying and I was involved in three other successful rescues during my time at Towyn.

I was doing more rock climbing now, leading the students, and when the opportunity presented itself, leading two fellow instructors on a more difficult climb. On this climb I was leading a 'very severe' route with two other instructors. The weather was not good with freezing rain and at a critical stage whilst traversing a buttress with an exposure of some 300 feet I lost my hand hold on ice and fell.

I remember free falling through the air, the rope gradually taking the strain. Would my runners remain secure and would my belayer (one of those that I was leading), hold me? I started to bounce sedately about on the end of the rope. My companion and runners had held me successfully and whilst I had gashed my hand and bruised my right arm I was in a fit state to rappel down the slope to a point where I could safely alight and perhaps find an easier route either up or down. It was always better to go up rather than try to descend.

I reached the top without problem and the three of us completed the climb without further incident. My life was literally in the hands of my fellow friend cum instructor, who had held me securely on the belay preventing a fall that would have most probably killed me.

I continued leading students on simple climbs emphasising safety and how important it is to always ensure that the correct equipment (that should always be checked) is being used and that strict climbing discipline is at all times adhered to, relating my story of the fall.

After some three months the time had come to leave Towyn, and the Army, complete with a Mountain Leadership certificate. Strangely, I never used this qualification in any future employment prospects as it was not required. My log book now lies redundant in my old brief case.

Chapter 32
Civilian Life, Attempted Suicide and Two Flying Mishaps

Having left the Army I descended upon my parents who seemed pleased to provide accommodation whilst I was searching for employment. This was one of the better moments in my life as not only was I living in the comfort of my old home enjoying mother's cooking but I received my gratuity from the Army for completing my three year short service commission. I also owned a new MG Midget car so I was fully mobile to attend those employment interviews. Not unnaturally I found my way to Netheravon for parachuting and gliding on numerous occasions as well.

However I was falling in love with a sweet girl who I had known for many years. There was talk about a wedding and children so things were getting exciting. However one evening I noticed a friend's car outside her flat, in London, whilst on an unannounced visit. On entering the premises I found my friend in bed with my fiancée. I was shocked and drove home shattered in the early morning.

I entered home in the early hours and went to bed. Strangely I slept well and father woke me as usual at 07.30 hrs. I thought that I had just suffered a nightmare but it soon became apparent that I had not after speaking to father about the matter. 'Oh dear, that's not very good is it? However its best you found this out now rather than after the wedding. I must go to work, we will talk about it this evening. OK?' Off he went in his new Triumph Herald car. I did not speak to mother about the matter.

I suddenly felt very depressed having been totally deceived by the love of my life of the time. My trust had been abused and taken advantage of. It was all too much. I was going to end it all by shooting myself in the mouth with my 12 bore shotgun, which I used frequently. I prepared for the action and found that I could just reach the trigger with the end of the barrels in my mouth. This did need practice

I drove to a beautiful spot on The Deverills, near Mere in Wiltshire and spent the afternoon contemplating my fate. In the end I decided to carry out the suicide. I place a cartridge in the right hand barrel. I pushed the barrel well into my mouth, said a prayer, and pulled the trigger. There was a resounding click. The cartridge had failed to discharge and this had never happened before.

I felt sickened and to have another go I would have to break the gun open to reset the firing pin. This I did and at the same time had a good look at the failed cartridge that was in the barrel. It had a shallow indentation on its percussion cap so maybe on this occasion for some unknown reason the cartridge just had not gone off. I did not have another cartridge so I would have to use the same round. This, for some unknown reason, did not seem an attractive action.

Whilst thinking about this I realised that I had been joined by a yellow Labrador, wagging its tail and also to be joined by the owner, an attractive girl, named Jane, who lived nearby mother and father. She recognised me and asked what I was shooting? 'Rabbit' I replied. 'I have not heard any shots and I have been up here for the last hour, you are obviously not seeing much'

'Oh yes I have seen plenty,' I replied.

'How many cartridges have you got and shall we go back to the car park?' She questioned. I did not answer the question about the cartridges. 'Rod, are you alright?' She questioned a number of times, 'you do not look your normal self'. Little did she know and I never told her.

We made our way back along a track with my head spinning what was happening? We reached the cars and Jane suddenly asked if I would like a drink at a local pub, The Dolphin.

The drink turned into dinner and a relationship that lasted four years. I should now be dead but was enjoying the company of a person that I would never forget. Suddenly my world had been turned about.

The next day I took my gun into the local gunsmith who informed me that I had a broken firing pin. All I could think of at the time was that **'It is written'.**

In retrospect I would urge anybody considering taking their own life to consider the future and the suffering that a suicide death causes. There is always a method of dealing with the distress and anxiety that is being endured and after some further thought the sun may shine again during the next day as it did with me.

Shortly after this I started sailing again, being invited to join the crew of a Contessa 32 yacht based in Lymington. The vessel was owned by the brother in law, known as 'G' and his wife Pauline, of my parents' next door neighbour. They operated a successful business from Bristol and it was enjoyable and rewarding crewing for them. They were keen to broaden their racing career and felt that with my support as crew this would be possible.

It was possible to enjoy this activity at the same time as being employed although with parachuting and gliding I was under a fair amount of pressure. The main problem I found was not so much finding the time but trying to decide which pursuit I should choose at any one time. It was a hard life!

We entered The Admiral's Cup series of sailing races between the period of 1970 to 1973. Many yacht races were completed successfully including two Round the Island (the Isle Of Wight), and two Fastnet Races. It was a wonderful experience sailing with this couple. I learnt a great deal about sailing and we were placed on a number of occasions, which was satisfying. Despite sailing in some difficult and challenging conditions I do not remember any incidents during this time. This said a lot for our skipper's ability not to mention that of the crew and the yacht!

I then found a job with an insurance broker known as 'Wilsons' based in Salisbury. I was to receive initial training and then my task would be to visit mainly military establishments to sell insurance, particularly life insurance.

I did not feel comfortable doing this as many times I met up with old friends who were still serving. Consequently my sales results were not as vibrant as they should have been, particularly in this area. Despite this, after a year I was given another area to operate in and that was in Surrey. I concentrated on selling insurance to non military individuals and started getting the results with the assistance of an experienced broker, who was my manager.

I rented a flat at the top of a large remote house, near Elstead on Hankley Common in Surrey. It was bliss living in the middle of nowhere accessible by a long drive. I knew Hankley Common well from my Army days, having taken part in military exercises and jumped many times from the balloon that was based there.

My parents seemed sad to bid me farewell but this was my chance to leave home which was the only correct thing to do now. I still was not happy with selling insurance although it provided me with a good steady salary that was not commission based. I therefore decided to sign up with a recruitment agency and start looking for another form of employment.

It was not long before I was contacted by the agency who informed me that they had found just the job! It was to become a medical representative with a well-known medical company, Cyanamid of Great Britain, then based at Bush House in London. I would have to undergo a six week training programme and then would be selling antibiotics, vitamins, vaccines, absorbable surgical sutures to doctors and hospitals etc. I would receive a good salary plus expenses having completed the training programme. A company car would also be provided.

It sounded too good to be true so I applied for the position and was interviewed twice. I was always wary of the interview procedure and carried out extensive research into the company. I discovered that this company was actually listed in various editions of the *Guiness Book of World Records* as the victim of the largest industrial theft in history.

It was reported that Cyanamid maintained a legal patent protected monopoly on the antibiotic tetracycline for many years. However it was alleged that a visitor to the factory, where the tetracycline was fermented, managed to furtively scoop up a sample of the mix and smuggle it out. This enabled a generic version of this antibiotic to be propagated thus breaking the lucrative monopoly that Cyanamid had enjoyed on this drug. It was thought that this action had cost the Company hundreds of millions of dollars in sales as other companies now entered the antibiotic market. To this day it seems amazing to me that a 'casual' action of one individual could cause such damage to a company of this size.

I asked whether this was correct at the interview. I think it rather took my interviewers aback and it was confirmed that this had happened. I was also offered the job, which was an achievement as there were many applicants some of whom were experienced medical sales representatives.

I gave notice to Wilsons as required and left on a friendly basis. This had been my first 'real' employment and they had looked after me well despite my poor performance.

I started my six-week training with Cyanamid in the De Vere Hotel in London where I was booked into a spacious suite overlooking a park. The hotel was comfortable and I was the only one undergoing this course that mainly concentrated initially on biology to start and concluded with methods of selling. I had different tutors who visited me in my suite and other characters such as my area manager, Derek, also visited. It was rather like being in hospital!

On one occasion I was joined by another candidate, Tony, who had just left the Police Force. He was destined to 'rep' in another area, but had to undergo what was left of the course with me. Tony was not a happy man alleging that the corruption in the police was rife and that he intended to 'blow the whistle'. Apparently he had kept a diary with names and events in it and wanted me to harbour it for him. I felt uncomfortable over all this and the following day he failed to appear for the course. I never saw him again as apparently he had changed his mind over employment with Cyanamid.

With the course complete I was let loose in my area visiting doctors selling mainly antibiotics, initially under the supervision of Derek who would debrief me after each visit. Eventually I was on my own and quickly discovered that it was easy and simple selling to Asian doctors especially if you were liberal with your samples. I was so successful at one stage I won an award and was warmly congratulated by head office and of course Derek.

However, after a while monotony started to set in, following the same routine day in and day out. As a form of distraction I started to learn Russian doing my work in the waiting rooms of my doctor customers, as I was normally seen after all patients had been attended to.

One day whilst driving past Blackbushe Airport for my first appointment nearby at 09.00 hours I noticed an advertisement up on a board by the entrance to the airfield. *'Book a flying lesson for £6 &10 shillings for one hour and get a free half hour flight'*. My mind started working overtime and learning to fly in my spare time would be a wonderful distraction and give me something constructive and useful to do over and above my job. Furthermore, it may open the door for an alternative employment such as becoming a pilot. (The British currency was decimalised shortly after in February 1971.)

I completed my day's work and on the return journey home dropped into the flying club at Blackbushe Airport. I was received by an attractive receptionist called Eve who I quickly discovered was married to an Army officer instructing at the Sandhurst Military Academy based nearby in Camberley.

I made enquiries about the advertisement and Eve suggested that if I was interested in taking up flying lessons start booking now as the offer of the free half hour flight was only on for the next few days and the price of lessons were about to rise. She went on to point out the aircraft that I would be flying. It was a Piper Cub that was parked nearby the club house. I booked 10 lessons there and then and, much to my surprise, was offered my free half hour by a flying instructor named David, as it was such a lovely evening and he had a free hour to spare.

With the paperwork quickly out of the way I walked out to the aircraft with him. This was an old small 'tail dragging' twin seated plane that had to be started by hand swinging the prop and was used to train American Second World War pilots. The instrumentation was basic and it was all very exciting. David strapped me into the front seat and then he showed me which switches to turn on and explained the start up sequence for a hand swing start up. He was to swing the prop.

It all went as planned and the engine started without problem. David clambered into the back seat and started to show me the controls in more detail. We were soon taxiing to the active runway where we lined up and took off. It was wonderful to get airborne again and this time flying the 'ship' not jumping from it. We flew for some forty five minutes on that beautiful evening and following that magic I was sold on learning to fly.

My first lesson was to be on the following day for an hour and, as before, it was a great evening, weather wise. Once again David was my instructor and on this flight I was handed the controls so that I could fly the aircraft straight and level progressing onto banking turns. He then demonstrated a 'practice' engine failure. When this happens a suitable site to land the aircraft has to be quickly identified and then a number of checks are to be made as it may be possible to restart the engine.

In this case David pointed out a small field that he had chosen as our landing area. As it was a practice he would instruct me to apply the throttle to recover and we would then climb up to suitable height. Nothing could be simpler and I watched and listened to my instructor performing all the necessary actions. We skimmed over a nearby wood and the field that we were aiming for seemed in the correct position and was now getting close. At this stage I was told to apply the throttle which I did with some enthusiasm but nothing happened. The engine continued to tick over with the prop spinning slowly around in front of us.

'Recover now' shouted my instructor. 'I am trying to do that' I replied, now desperately pumping the throttle lever backwards and forward. This is situated by the left shoulder of the front pilot in these aircraft. 'No don't do that' responded my instructor, 'you are flooding the carburettor and that is why we have lost our power. 'Right I have control as it seems that we are now forced into a forced landing'.

David landed our stricken aircraft without any problem and we managed to stop just before a large hedge. He instructed me to turn the motor off as it was still just ticking over. I did as was told and he then stated, 'I have got to have a fag and just admire that wonderful view'.

We got out and sat by the aeroplane in the grass looking out over the Hampshire countryside as we were on the side of a small hill with David drawing heavily on his cigarette. It was so quiet and the birds were singing away. It could have been dreamland had it not been for the fact that we were sitting in someone's remote field with the likelihood of getting our aeroplane out being slim, following this unintended crash landing.

The question was then asked by David whether or not he had informed me about pumping the throttle as it could cause carburettor flooding problems. 'No I don't seem to remember you mentioning it', I replied and he then apologised. 'No sorry Rod I don't think I did; all this is my fault, you just cannot get the instructors anymore'! I felt sorry for him and truthfully stated that I was enjoying every moment of this experience.

With that he quickly responded whilst putting his cigarette out, 'Well that's good because I have some bad news for you, I am afraid that only one of us will be able to take off in this aircraft, assuming that we can get it going again, as I am concerned about the length of the take off run and the grass. It is going to be tight and as you cannot fly that means that you will have to walk home and I will take my life in my hands and fly back, sorry'.

'How do I get back?' I asked rather taken aback. 'I think there is a road down there somewhere and the airfield is about 25 miles in that direction. I am sure that a man of your ability and experience will be back in no time. Oh by the way can you just open that gate at the bottom of the hill in case I have to fly through it'.

I was not sure whether David was joking but he made it clear that he was not and reminded me to close the gate after he had left. With that he started fiddling with the engine and I opened the gate as requested. When I returned I was given instructions on how to swing the prop with emphasis being placed on the fact that if I lost my balance at any time I must not fall forward into the prop as it would not do it any good at all. I had to fall backwards.

I swung the prop without problem and the engine started fine. David ran her up to full revs and then lined up for takeoff. I watched in trepidation and was pleasantly surprised to see that he was airborne after about one hundred yards which was half the distance that was available. He passed high overhead and set course for Blackbushe leaving me in the peace and quiet of that summer's evening. I closed the gate and found the road that he had mentioned to me.

I felt conspicuous walking on this isolated country road in my smart shirt, suit trousers and shiny black shoes (my selling gear), intending to hitch a lift from a passing vehicle, if any vehicle did pass of course. However, it was not long before a new Mercedes car drove past and I stuck my thumb up, which is the pedestrian sign to hitch a lift. Much to my surprise the driver stopped. 'Where are you going'? An attractive middle-aged dark haired lady asked. 'Blackbushe Airport' I answered and with that she instructed me to get in.

We started our journey and she asked me my name and if I was alright. 'My name is Rod and everything is fine, I am just an ejaculated pilot,' I responded, using the incorrect word in all innocence. I noticed that she seemed amused over the matter and went on to ask me, 'at what height did you ejaculate'?

'Ground level,' I stated and then went on to explain the situation: 'my instructor told me to get out of the aeroplane after a forced landing. He fixed the engine problem and thought that the weight with two of us in the aircraft would be too much for such a short takeoff run so here I am.'

By now my driver appeared to be in fits of giggles, which was alarming, and then she put me right over my misuse of the English language. 'Rod I think that you meant that you were ejected from your plane not that other word you used.' I did not understand what she was going on about until eventually it soon it dawned on me how I had inadvertently used the wrong word.

We were soon at Blackbushe Airport and I noticed that David had landed safely and parked up our little yellow bird in her normal spot by the club house. He was signing the aircraft off and was just about to get in a car to collect me. I thanked my Samaritan, Jane, and she departed giving me a hug and kiss as well as wishing me luck in my new flying career. Somebody then mentioned the fact that she was the wife of a well known racing driver who lived in this area.

David and I then had supper in the pub and my future flying routine was explained to me. It would start with circuits, where the student learns the basics in aircraft handling, including landing and taking off, followed by cross country flights where landings would take place at different airfields mixed with practising recoveries from engine failures, spins, stalls and 'unusual attitudes'. I had passed my medical but would also have to take written examinations in air law and navigation. If I had successfully completed all this I could then take a General Flying Test (GFT), which if I passed would be awarded with my Private Pilot's Licence.

At the time it did not seem too daunting but challenging and I spent nearly all of my spare time at Blackbushe Airport flying whenever I could and this was very much governed by the weather. I did a lot of my book work and revision whilst waiting to see my doctor customers. I was happy doing this and my job was going well, meeting targets set.

One weekend on the Saturday there was a cross wind on the active runway and I was keen to fly circuits carrying out cross wind landings which I enjoyed doing previously. There is a technique with these types of landings as the pilot has to descend whilst facing into the wind although the landing strip could be at an angle. To get it right the yaw has to be 'kicked off' at the last minute thus straightening the aircraft in line with the runway.

The chief instructor relented as long as I could prove to him that I could do a successful landing with him initially. This I did with no problem so I was cleared to fly solo in these conditions. However I was warned that these aircraft are known to 'weather cock into the wind if out of limits' and this was commonly called 'ground looping' that could be disastrous if unlucky. It all seemed quite exciting.

I took off and carried out my first landing with no problem kicking off the cross wind yaw at the right time and then took off again to carry out a second landing. I noticed that the wind had seemed to have increased and when coming in to land I had to increase the yaw into wind. I managed to land without problem but then it happened. I suddenly started to spin around on the tarmac runway with terrific screeching of the tyres and the 'g' force being held firmly in place by my harness. It was not a pleasant experience. To make things worse I noticed that one of my wings started to dip on one of the spins. If it contacted the ground it would flip me over.

Somehow it did not and I was left on the threshold of the active runway facing the direction I had originally landed after two and a half spins. I could clearly smell the aroma of burning rubber that emitted from my undercarriage tyres. I noticed an aircraft with twin engines, which was landing behind me, retract its undercarriage and fly low overhead waggling its wings as it did so, it was quite a sight.

I regained my composure and taxied back to the parking area where I closed down and signed off. 'Everything OK Rod?' asked my instructor, 'No problem and I know what a ground loop is now,' came my response and I assured him that everything was fine pointing out that she still had two wings. My instructor was not amused and together we inspected the aircraft. Somehow no damage had been sustained apart to my confidence and ego.

I successfully passed my GFT in that little old Piper Cub, registration G-AYPP, after four months and just over thirty-five hours flying time. This was a great thrill and I felt that I had achieved a lot in a short time even if I had suffered two mishaps. So now I could fly, parachute, glide, climb and sail to mention some of my hobbies. There just was not enough time.

Chapter 33
Loss of Keel and Sinking of a Yacht - 1973

I decided one weekend in August to take a break from everything and went sailing on a friend's old yacht for a change.

Peter, a work colleague and friend, one day announced that he had just purchased a wooden one-off design 24ft yacht that he was keeping at Gosport. He had purchased her some six months before and on top of the purchase survey had done a lot of work on her including the basic electrical installations.

As he knew that my girl friend of the time, Jane, and I had done a reasonable amount of sailing, he asked us to join him on a weekend in August 1973 for a sailing trip from Gosport to the Isle Of Wight. We gladly accepted the invitation.

The yacht was indeed of the old type design with a raised bow section and boasted the fact that she was a 'Little Ship' that had been used to assist in the evacuation of Dunkirk, which as Peter claimed was one of the main reasons why he had purchased her. Peter was an experienced yachtsman and as the purchase survey had suggested, despite her age, she seemed in good working order and the small engine functioned well.

Having been fitted with our lifejackets and been briefed by the skipper on emergency drills we slipped on the Friday afternoon and sailed across to the Isle of Wight where we dropped anchor in Yarmouth for the night. The weather forecast for the weekend was good with plenty of sunshine and it was a lovely evening.

The following day we raised our anchor, stowed the half inflated rubber dinghy on the cabin roof and sailed out of Yarmouth on a light southerly breeze heading west. It was enjoyable with a slight sea and breeze and the old girl was going well. We had lunch, which Jane had prepared below, underway, and Peter was on the helm sitting to windward with Jane. I was sitting on the leeward side of the cockpit (nearest the water), reading a magazine. It was all very relaxing and we were not wearing our lifejackets in such benign warm conditions. They were stashed below. I had just volunteered to go below to clear up the lunch things and started to move accordingly.

We were on a port reach (going forward with the boat leaning over to the right), when suddenly there was a 'clonk' from below and the yacht continued to keel over. I realized that something was wrong when the sea started slopping over me and my magazine. I saw with horror, the cabin fill within seconds with a huge swirl of water that flowed through the open main cabin hatch. The yacht quickly settled on her side and started to sink with the air pressure in the cabin blowing the cabin windows out with loud bangs.

We scrambled onto what was left of the hull that was not submerged. Jane calmly and quietly announced that she could not swim and really did not want to get wet. It's strange how comments like this in dour situations can change things and both Peter and I both laughed and it helped getting our minds around survival. I then remembered that I always carried a sharp knife on me when sailing. I produced it and with help from Peter we cut the half inflated rubber dinghy away from the sinking vessel. Jane stepped into it, complaining that she was actually getting wet now and the yacht then sank beneath Peter and I who were left clinging to the partly inflated dinghy.

It was a strange sensation to feel that reasonably firm platform you are standing on quickly sinking and to be suddenly left in the water, without a life-jacket, hanging onto a semi inflated and submerged rubber dinghy. We started to wave our arms about and shout for assistance as there were many other vessels on the water enjoying the weather. Much to our relief a large motor launch suddenly changed course and headed towards us.

The skipper of this launch was obviously experienced and placed his vessel in a position whereby we could easily clamber aboard on the stern bathing platform being assisted by two capable middle-aged ladies. Once we were on board we were shown into the main cabin where we were made comfortable, despite our sodden state, blankets were produced along with cups of tea. It all seemed surreal.

Much to our surprise Peter and the skipper of the launch, Ken, suddenly realized that they knew each other well. Discussions started between them as to how and why this had happened and I heard Peter state that in his opinion the keel bolts had failed, which was why we heard the 'clonk', hence dropping her keel resulting in the capsize.

He had not run aground with her during the time he had owned the boat and the survey had not produced anything untoward so to him this was a mystery, especially as he had done quite a bit of work on the boat out of and in the water.

During this conversation it transpired that Peter had installed some electrical equipment using the keel bolts as an earth, which he considered normal practice. Ken immediately stated that there could have been every possibility that, by doing this, electrolysis of the bolts could have taken place thus making them brittle, hence the failure if the age of the bolts were also considered.

Whilst all this was going on Ken had decided to remain in the area of the sinking as he was aware that the inshore lifeboat had been called by another vessel and it was only a matter of minutes before we saw the inflatable lifeboat approaching us at speed. The lifeboat came up to us and asked if there were any casualties.

They were informed that all three crew of the stricken craft had been rescued successfully and were safely aboard in a good state. The lifeboat then started to search the sea around the area as a surprising amount of clothing and floatable articles started to appear on the surface, including lacy knickers and a treasured woollen climbing shirt of mine. These were all carefully retrieved by the lifeboat crew who handed them over to us.

Eventually the lifeboat returned to station and having got the semi-submerged rubber dinghy on board Ken took us back to Gosport where we rejoined the real world.

A great deal was discussed about the incident with many and indeed it was thought that it was highly probable that she had dropped her keel due to electrolysis within the aged bolts that had turned brittle due to this action. The main lesson learnt here, of course, was that if any initial electrical work is carried out on a vessel it should be done professionally and with care.

The yacht sank within minutes and if I had been in the cabin at the time the water flooded into the cabin it was questionable whether I would have survived due to the sheer force of water ingress that I had witnessed, fortunately from the outside. I was only seconds away from entering the cabin.

Lifejackets should be worn at all times, as we witnessed in this situation, as it was impossible to retrieve them from below. We were fortunate to have had some form of flotation available and this may well have saved our lives.

A simple action such as carrying a sharp knife on one when sailing also saved the day as we managed to cut free our flotation device with ease and speed. Divers and military pilots always carry a knife on them for emergency use.

There is no doubt that keeping calm, as demonstrated by the skipper and Jane was also a life saver. So often in these types of situations individuals can 'close down' or become hysterical thus being a liability to all including themselves.

To conclude we were fortunate to have been where we were at that time. It would have been different if we had been crossing the Channel or the Atlantic at night. We probably would have become another statistic involving a missing vessel with a crew that had disappeared.

Chapter 34
Flying with a Suicide Pilot - 1973

Having survived the sinking of Peter's yacht it seemed strange to meet Derek on my first call the next day and to launch into my work selling antibiotics to doctors as before. All was going well with my job as a medical representative although I was now beginning to find that the work was becoming repetitive despite my distraction of flying.

Whenever the weather was suitable at the correct time (normally evenings or weekends) I would be found at the Flying Club at Blackbushe. Now that I had my PPL my next ambition was to learn aerobatics and to assist me in this I decided to convert onto another aircraft, a Beagle Pup 100. This was a low-wing two-seated aircraft that, after the Piper Cub, was simple to fly and it even had an electric starter, so by just turning the ignition key one could start the engine.

With the conversion complete I started to learn the basics of aerobatics under instruction. This activity was governed by weather and expense but I soon learnt how to loop, roll and carry out stall turns not to mention spinning and stalling.

It was enjoyable, and then I met another individual who was a member of the club who was more experienced than I was and who shared the same passion for throwing aeroplanes around the sky. His name was Martin and he was a former Royal Marine who had somehow become a stockbroker and appeared to be doing well.

Martin was a happy content man who was married with two young daughters and had a good sense of humour. We became great friends and it was not long before we decided that we could share our flights in the Pup as we had both been cleared to carry out certain manoeuvres solo and together we could enjoy the aerobatics. We would take it in turns to fly with the strict understanding that neither of us would interfere even if things were going wrong.

We did this for a number of months without problem and one afternoon I noticed that Martin was not quite his normal cheerful self. I thought nothing further of this and it was my turn to take off and to climb to the correct height where we had decided to carry out some aerobatic manoeuvres. Whilst climbing out I noticed that Martin appeared to be crying.

'Martin what's the problem?' I asked.

'I have been involved in a serious financial fraud and the police are now onto me. They will probably be waiting for me when we land and I just will not be able to cope with prison not to mention the disgrace I have brought upon my family and self.'

I was flabbergasted at what he had just told me and asked if this was correct or just his perception of the situation. He assured me that it was correct and things were not looking good. I started to feel unsafe with what could now be a suicidal pilot sitting next to me.

He started his aerobatic routine and it was obvious that he was not flying safely, to such a degree that I insisted on taking over stating; 'you may wish to kill yourself but I want to live, please let me take over and we will land now.'

Much to my relief he handed over to me and he broke down into convulsive sobbing next to me on the return trip to the airfield. I landed the aircraft and we refuelled as was normal practice. He seemed to make a recovery and apologised for his behaviour and returned to his normal cheery self.

We signed the plane off and then Martin suddenly announced that as it was such a lovely evening he was going up for another hour on a cross country to fly over his house nearby. As there was another aircraft spare I did the same with the intention of flying over my uncle's house in Old Alresford.

Martin took off first and after some delay I got airborne and flew for some thirty minutes over Alresford. On return I noticed a twin engine Civil Aviation Authority (CAA), aircraft parked nearby. I signed my aircraft off and noticed two men in suits watching me. Eve, the club receptionist, also seemed tense and was not behaving her normal flirty self.

Having completed the paperwork I said good evening to Eve and went to my car (the Cyanamid company car) for the journey home. It would not start and I was then approached by the two men who had been watching me. They informed me that they were police officers and that they had immobilised my car by removing the rotary head and asked me to accompany them back into the Flying Club building.

This I did and was shown into the office of the chief instructor where there were two CAA officials, who had obviously arrived in the aeroplane parked outside. I was introduced and by now I was fearful of the fact that perhaps Martin and I had done something dreadful whilst practicing our aerobatics earlier that afternoon.

I was questioned in depth on how well I knew Martin and what state of mind he had been in earlier that afternoon. I informed them about how we had practised aerobatic manoeuvres together and that everything had gone to plan, although he did at times appear depressed. However he had gone on to hire another plane for a short cross country flight as indeed I had done.

I was again cross examined on exactly what we had done earlier that day, on Martin's behaviour and whether he had shown any form of 'anti-establishment' tendencies. As far as I was aware this was not the case and I told them so.

By now I was getting inquisitive and in my turn started to ask why I had been apprehended and questioned in this manner. One of the CAA officials then informed me that the aircraft that Martin had signed out earlier this afternoon had very recently flown under Tower Bridge in London, totally illegally. After that he had carried out some 'unsafe' flying antics at minimum height over the River Thames in front of the House Of Commons. This aircraft was last seen flying north at low level. Royal Air Force fighters had been scrambled as it had been considered that this could be a terrorist attack.

I was astounded and just did not know what to say. The telephone then rang and was answered by the chief instructor who handed over to a CAA officer. He immediately reported that the aircraft in question had been reported as flying into the ground up in the Lake District, killing the pilot who was the only occupant.

There was a brief silence and I was then released, having made a written statement and returned home late that night with my head spinning. I was later informed that Martin's parents lived in the Lake District and that he had flown into a hill near his parental home. It was very sad.

The following day I was met by Derek, my area manager, on one of my calls in Slough, who asked me to telephone the training manager in Bush House as soon as possible. At the same time he asked why I had asked for time off yesterday afternoon. I informed him that it was a long story and that I would tell him after I had telephoned the training manager.

The training manager had been contacted by the police yesterday afternoon. They were carrying out an urgent character screening on me and wished to know all about me. Not unnaturally this caused alarm and the first question asked was why my company car had been parked at Blackbushe Airport that afternoon. I should have been working. It was, however, fortunate that I had signed off early with Derek, that day, a point I confirmed with him following this telephone call.

It was all cleared up and my explanation for my absence from work was accepted although Derek had not informed Bush House when perhaps he should have done. I spent that lunchtime relating my story to him and he listened in amazement stating the fact that it is not every day that one of his 'reps' had been dicing with death in a small aircraft with a suicide pilot!

Chapter 35

Army Air Corps and Some Flying Escapes - 1973-1974

On one of my calls to a doctor's surgery whilst waiting for my slot I noticed a large advertisement in a well known newspaper: 'The Army is looking for pilots, no previous experience required'. I just could not believe it and following my visit I purchased the newspaper for the information I required to make further enquiries on this advert.

That afternoon I telephoned the number given and was sent an application form which I completed and within a week was then invited to my first interview at the Army Air Corps Centre, based at Middle Wallop in Hampshire.

As before I carried out extensive research into interview techniques and this held me in good stead. It was agreed that I should attend the four day aircrew selection that was then operated by the Royal Air Force at Biggin Hill. This was designed to test my aptitude and medical suitability for pilot training and if I passed I would then attend another interview with the Army Air Corps Directorate.

This sounded good to me and I started to investigate what to expect on the aircrew selection to discover that the first day after the stringent aircrew medical, candidates had to complete an intelligence test (you can now take an online IQ test and receive a certificate with your score).

This filled me with fear as after my school days I had a complex that I was not very intelligent. I soon found a book to train me up, explaining what to expect on these tests and how to perform well in them. I learnt that only a round peg would fit into a round hole and so on but I took this information with all seriousness.

There were some twenty candidates, including two females, who attended this course with me and we were warned that not all of us would succeed and some would leave early if they were not successful in what they were being tested for.

The accommodation was comfortable and we settled into the course taking the IQ test after the medical on the first day as warned. Four were invited to leave after that first day and I felt that I had actually done well so the main hurdle was over.

The remaining tests were mainly connected to physical co-ordination and suitability to flying, where again a few more struggled and were asked to leave. The two girls appeared to be enjoying themselves and it was good to have them around as they seemed to alleviate the tense atmosphere about us with their sense of humour. They were proudly announcing that they had been chosen through the RAF ranks to become fighter pilots and were performing accordingly.

I was amongst twelve who completed the selection and had to wait for the results on which I would be notified shortly when I would be contacted by the Army Air Corps inviting me to attend an interview. This happened the following week and apparently my results were satisfactory and I was offered a position as a student officer pilot, resuming my service at the rank at which I had left the Army previously, which was a Lieutenant. I had to sign a contract that directed that my employment with the Army could be terminated at any time if I failed any part of the Army Pilots Flying Course. In turn I could leave at any time up to my passing out parade when I would receive my wings. After this I would be contracted for five years to remain in the Army.

I accepted these terms and handed my notice into Cyanamid accordingly. Derek my area manager appeared upset to lose me and pointed out the fact that I had been working effectively with him for over three years. He was concerned over the fact that I had been upset in some way over my employment with Cyanamid, which of course was not the case. I stressed the fact that I was just moving on and that I had always been happy working for this company which I considered was under good management.

It seemed odd to be working as a medical representative on the Friday and then to become an Army student pilot on the Monday but that is what happened.

As instructed I reported to Middle Wallop to discover that there were thirty two of us starting on the flying course. We were warned that only about 40% would pass out and be awarded our flying wings and this was one of the toughest courses in the Army. The course consisted of some young serving officers, of whom I was the oldest, and a collection of senior NCOs. Spirits were high on that first day as we started to gel together whilst collecting our flying uniform and equipment.

I was accommodated in a spacious room on the second floor of the Officers' Mess and had a 'batman', Mr Smith. He would bring me tea in the morning as well as polish my boots, press my shirts etc. as he had done for previous officers over countless years. It all seemed luxurious and I soon integrated into the old Army system that I had been used to four years before. I was also looking forward to the challenge that lay ahead.

On the second day we started settling into the routine of the course that would initially consist of half a day in the class room studying air law, navigation, meteorology, engineering and so on. All this would be concluded by examinations and to pass we had to attain at least 60% in our markings. The other half of the day would consist of flying and every trip was scored by a color marking system.

Green was acceptable, brown borderline and red non acceptable. One red trip could put the student 'on review' whereby they would be given a certain amount of time to correct things and then be tested. Three brown trips would result in the same fate. Failing the test would terminate flying training and the student would be RTUd.

The students also had the option to pull out of training whenever they so wished during the course as in some cases the pressure was found to be just too much.

On the second day of the course we enjoyed our first 'air experience' flight with our instructors in the fixed wing aircraft known as the Chipmunk (now a vintage aircraft), that was used to complete the initial elementary flying training of some twenty five hours. Following this progression would be made onto the helicopter known as the Bell 47 G4, and then onto Advanced Rotary Wing and operational training phase flying the Sioux helicopter.

My first flight experience in the Chipmunk went well and I desperately attempted to conceal from my instructor, a former Spitfire pilot, the fact that I had flown before. After we had landed he asked: 'So how many hours flying time have you got and do you hold a PPL?' I was shocked that after such a simple flight it had been detected that I had previous flying experience so I answered truthfully. 'I have seventy-five hours private flying time logged on light fixed wing and yes I do hold a PPL'. 'Well that's good because from now on I expect some accurate flying. When I say fly at 2000 feet at 80 knots I expect you to do exactly that and not be out by any fraction, do you understand?' This left me feeling concerned as I had been dreading the fact that previous experience could be used to make student pilots work even harder than those without.

So flying training commenced with me trying so hard to be as accurate as I could possibly be. I was somehow getting through with green trips and then my first navigation exercise with an instructor came up. It was all going to plan and I was rigidly flying at the height and speed that had been instructed.

I had found all my navigation points and was returning to the airfield in good visibility at 2000 feet. I heard my instructor who was sitting behind me snoring so obviously he had confidence in me and was enjoying an afternoon snooze. I thought that I had seen something to our front at the same height at some distance away and paid no further attention to it.

I was checking ground references (Bullers Cross on the A303), on the map and enjoying the view when I looked to the front. With horror there very close, directly in front of us and heading in the opposite direction at the same height was a twin engine DC3 airplane. It seemed that there was no escape of a collision but I rammed the control stick forward as quickly as I could, that left us suspended by our seat harness. I closed my eyes waiting for the impact and heard the thunder of the two engines passing very close overhead.

I had somehow averted a disaster and there were grunts and groans coming from the back as my instructor had been rudely awoken. 'What the hell is going on?' he asked. 'I think I have just avoided a head on collision,' I responded, 'can you hear him?'. 'OK I have control and was it that DC 3 up there?'

'Yes it sure was; I really did think that we were going to collide, perhaps you ought to send an Air Miss Report?' I asked.

With that, much to my surprise whilst circling around my instructor did file an Air Miss Report and apparently it was an aircraft from Boscombe Down which was carrying out air radar research at the time.

We completed this exercise without further incident and I was congratulated for my action which made me feel good.

I did the fixed wing phase of the flying training with three hours to spare. When asked what exercises I would like to complete to use the flying time up, I asked for aerobatic training, which was gladly given by my former fighter pilot instructor.

Having completed our fixed wing flying training we now started flying helicopters. To start emphasis was placed in being able to control and safely land the aircraft if the engine failed. Every trip included an 'engine off' landing when on some occasions the instructor would actually shut the engine down and the student would then make a genuine forced landing on the airfield.

After a number of trips carrying this procedure out the first solo flight performed would be a genuine engine off landing whereby the student pilot would cut the engine out and make an 'engine off landing' in front of their instructor on the aerodrome. As dramatic as it sounds as students we all managed this training without incident and it filled us with confidence.

Hovering was the next challenge along with landing on sloping ground not to mention engine failures whilst hovering, tail rotor failures etc. This was followed by solo cross country flights and landing in clearings that could be found in wooded areas.

On my second solo cross country flight whilst flying over a disused airfield at 2000 feet my engine suddenly stopped. I immediately adopted the drill that had been rehearsed time and time again deciding where to land, which actually was no particular problem as I had plenty of space. However I could get the final part of the landing wrong that could result in an unhappy result of crashing to the ground.

I had time to think whilst descending with nothing but the sound of the rotor blades revolving above me so I transmitted a 'Mayday' call on the radio. Sweat was pouring off me to such a degree that I found it difficult to see as I could not clear my brow with my hands or arms which were engaged in controlling the aircraft.

It was possible to try restarting the engine by pressing a button on the throttle control levers, which I did. Much to my surprise and relief the engine suddenly burst into life again. I 'rejoined the needles' which meant that I could join the engine up with the rotor blades once again and virtually fly as normal resulting in a 'running landing' on the spot that I had decided to land on.

Once on the ground safely I cancelled my 'Mayday' call and was not sure what to do next. The answer soon came as my instructor, who had been flying with another student nearby, having heard my Mayday call, knew my position and immediately flew there. He landed next to me, closed down and got out of his helicopter.

My engine was still running so he got in and tried running her up and hovering.

'What's the problem Rod?' he asked over the headphones. 'The engine stopped but I managed to get it going again on the way down and I have not closed her down yet,' I answered. 'How very interesting, there does not seem to be much wrong with it now so fly it back to Middle Wallop, which is not far from here, OK I will see you there.'

I was a little taken aback as I felt that he did not believe me, but I had no choice. He got out, gave me a smile and thumbs up and returned to his helicopter. I nervously started to increase the revs for takeoff, transmitting on the radio the fact that I was now about to take off again and return to Middle Wallop. I then heard the chief instructor telling me to stay where I was and to close the aircraft down informing me that he would be there in a matter of minutes.

My instructor took off obviously unaware of that last transmission and I was left on my own closing down as I had been told. I waited for some five minutes and the chief instructor arrived. He informed me that this aircraft was to be recovered by road and that a team would be there shortly when I could then get a lift back. I was to remain on site with the aircraft until the recovery had been completed.

I eventually returned to the Officers' Mess that evening for a late supper feeling awful about what would happen to my instructor. However it was fascinating to watch the recovery and my engine was closely examined that night. Dirt was found in the carburetor thus causing the engine failure and it was fortunate that I did not attempt to fly back that afternoon as another failure could have happened at any time, perhaps this time with disastrous results.

Following this I successfully completed my training without any further incident until a few days before my passing out parade.

Chapter 36

Survival Training with the SAS - 1974

Part of the Advanced Rotary Wing syllabus included survival training with the SAS in Hereford. We were to spend a number of days in the field learning how to forage from the countryside, thus simulating being shot down over enemy lines. It all seemed a bit far-fetched but it was a welcome break from the pressure of the flying school.

We were to operate on a large estate within Herefordshire and our instructors were some well-known SAS characters. Edible indigenous plants were described and shown to us. We trapped rabbit and were shown how to slaughter a live sheep sampling the warm raw liver afterwards. Camps were set up and we enjoyed a barbecue of rabbit and mutton. That evening an orienteering race was organized to ensure that we would learn to move at night; The area was to be patrolled by an enemy that had to be avoided.

This seemed simple enough to start but we soon discovered that 'the enemy' was the SAS patrolling the area in open-topped stripped-down Land Rovers and lamps ostensibly shooting rabbit with twelve bore pump action shotguns. In fact it was apparent that they would blast away at anything that moved using a high shot cartridge so it was essential to avoid them.

On one occasion they latched onto me and chased me at a distance in their open topped vehicle blasting away. I lured them onto a steep slope and unbelievably they followed me. Sure enough the Land Rover overturned rolling and crashing to the bottom of the hill accompanied by the three occupants who were cursing loudly. We soon got the impression that we were in a different world here and that you do not mess about with the SAS. They will act first and then answer the questions later.

River and lake crossings were also practiced where we had to swim across a fast flowing river and then a wide lake complete with any equipment we were carrying. There were two safety boats in the lake being used as a safety back up in case any of us got into difficulties. We were swimming across in full uniform with boots on and half way across I suddenly got cramp in my legs.

I tried to relax on my back but sank due to the weight of my clothing and boots. I raised my hand and shouted for assistance as I sank to the bottom. I managed to push myself back to the surface from the bottom and again raised my arm shouting but there was no reaction from the safety boat. In fact the crew of one boat actually started to wave back to me.

Fortunately two of my brother officers, Andy and Pete were swimming close by and they saved me from drowning, getting me onshore and caring for me. Andy roundly criticized the safety boat crews who claimed that they thought that I was 'larking about' and they were just waving back. We began to feel fearful as it was becoming apparent that causing a Land Rover to roll the night before had been taken exception to and that our instructors could well make life difficult for us. The following evening we were shown how to put a fishing line across a river and the use of eel traps where a sack of straw would be filled with rotten meat, weighted and then placed in a quiet pool. Not many thought that this was going to be productive so they did not bother as the weather was beginning to close in and the shelter of the camp was calling.

Two of us persevered as instructed as well as placing our rabbit snares. We were beginning to get hungry by now so this was an incentive, even if there was only one more day to go. Early the next morning we inspected our lines and they were weighed down with some good trout, our eel sacks were full and we had caught three rabbit. The weather had improved so we enjoyed a good breakfast.

On the final day we were being trained on how to avoid and, failing that, how to deal with dogs, namely condemned German Shepherd police dogs that had tasted human blood. We were concerned over this final day with what had happened in the past few days. It seemed as if there was almost a feud between our SAS instructors and us the students.

Obviously it would make sense to avoid dogs, but we had to know how they behaved and what systems could be used to tackle them if attacked. It was described to us that if a dog attacks a human it would normally lunge for the throat and either it could be kicked over your head in a Judo type kick or both front legs of the dog could be grabbed and pulled apart. This we were told would kill the dog.

A volunteer was asked to act as the dummy and I was pushed to the front, something I normally did but someone got there first with me. Well I felt reasonably confident and would be wearing a fibre glass arm upon which the chasing German Shepherd dog would latch onto as practised a number of times before. The very fact that we had been informed that these were condemned dogs did not enter our minds.

I was instructed on how to wear 'the arm' and told to run in a straight line away from the assembled course. This I did and heard the dog approaching me and grabbing my false arm. The moment this happened I stood still as I had been instructed, but with alarm noticed that this dog was not going to let go, as it should and in fact it was now laying into 'the arm' with some force.

I felt it falling apart and it disintegrated into bits and I knew that I was in trouble so I turned to face this growling monster with bared teeth. It was obvious that it was going to attack, which it did and I somehow managed to kick it over my head as we had been instructed to do. The handler and another officer armed with a rifle were now running towards me but again I had to face another attack and this time I only had time to defend my throat with my arm which was grabbed by my frenzied aggressor.

I heard the handler who was by now approaching me telling me to remain still and not to move in any way, which I did. There was a shot and the poor animal dropped dead at my feet and then I felt the pain in my right arm that had been badly mauled.

First aid was administered and it was thought that in fact it was an arterial wound as I was losing much blood. A tourniquet was applied and one of the SAS stripped down Land Rovers, with a leading character driving, came rushing up. I was helped into the front seat with another holding my arm up in the air and the three of us departed at speed heading for Hereford Hospital.

The rescue crew were reassuring, both stating that they do not like officers but in this case they could like me! I felt conspicuous speeding though Hereford obviously in a SAS vehicle being tended by those that despised officers.

We arrived at the hospital and I was taken straight into the operating theatre to have my arm tended. It was an arterial wound that was stitched and after some while I was discharged. Much to my surprise the two 'officer haters' had waited for me to come out and were pleased to see that I had survived suggesting that we could get some fish and chips on the way back. I pointed out that I did not have any money on me and they insisted that this treat would be on them, although I really did not feel like eating anything.

My fish and chips were shared between the two of them although I was given plenty of water to drink. I was getting concerned about getting back in time to catch the transport back to Middle Wallop but this of course was waiting. I was greeted by my comrades all of whom were sympathetic and, indeed, as were the instructors who seemed almost apologetic as obviously that arm should not have fallen apart.

My arm was in plaster for some two weeks and conveniently it was a two week leave period. On return I had a medical which I passed and this meant that I did not miss any flying training and after that I was flying again completing the final phase of the flying course.

Following our two weeks leave I had the plaster on my arm removed and I underwent a medical which I passed. I was back on track for the flying training that was now being completed. We received letters from our designated squadrons describing our future roles and it was interesting for most of us.

However I was not happy as I had been informed by my future squadron commander that my role would be principally one of administration in Germany. He promised me that he would do everything possible to ensure that I would complete the eight hours flying per year required to keep me current and for me to receive flying pay.

I spoke to my friends Andy and Pete over the matter and they suggested that perhaps I could write back explaining that I had joined the Army Air Corps to fly and not to become an administrator. Andy and Pete light heartedly pointed out that I would be flying 'The Mahogany Bomber' and in fact from thereon I was referred to as 'The Mahogany Bomber Pilot', much to the amusement of the others.

This aggravated me and without hesitation I wrote a letter to my prospective squadron commander informing him that I was not happy with this posting and requested that he should review the situation. I shortly received a response informing me that I will do what I was ordered to do.

I began to feel that I had been misled and that the Army Air Corps were in fact searching for administrators not pilots. The flying course was just bait to recruit individuals into the Corps.

The flying training that we were undergoing now at the end of the course was almost a formality with emphasis being placed on flying in the field from strategic positions. This was interesting but I was beginning to lose my enthusiasm for it all and to think that all this was a waste of time.

However, there were lighter moments and one afternoon we were undergoing firefighting instructions. We were taken out to a remote area on the airfield from where different portable fire extinguishers were demonstrated and set off. The powder extinguisher was introduced to us and handed around.

I just could not resist setting it off upwind over the course causing absolute mayhem with everyone running in different directions getting covered in the fine white powder. It was great fun.

What I had not noticed was that a very important person (VIP), in the form of a General, who was being accompanied by two senior Army Air Corps officers, had joined us on a quick tour. After my little exploit I rejoined the course that was now covered in the residue. Andy was pointing at something and I then noticed this 'white' man and his escorts, who I did not recognize, standing there away from the melee. He cleared his badges of rank with his gloves and asked me my name. I noticed that he was a General so I told him and to my surprise he replied that he thought that this showed excellent spirit within the course and congratulated me.

However one of his escorts, the chief instructor, who was also covered white, was not quite so entranced and instructed me to report to his office at 17.00 hours that afternoon. The VIP party then departed a little whiter than when they arrived.

My comrades applauded me on my performance and it was pointed out that obviously I was about to attend an interview without coffee or tea or indeed a carpet. They all hoped that I would be there tomorrow morning. With that the firefighting instructor closed the session down and we returned to the classroom to clean up.

The interview was without coffee and I was accused of irresponsible behavior, but as the General had pointed out this could be taken as high spirits and would be accepted as such in this instance although an 'eye' would now be kept on me.

I took this opportunity to speak to the chief instructor about my discontentment over my future posting being an administrative one; amazingly he seemed to understand my situation and stated that he had heard that I was to be 'a Mahogany Bomber Pilot'. He went on to tell me that there was nothing he could do and strongly suggested that at this stage I should accept the situation.

Chapter 37
Love and Resignation

So I was still there the next day and we finished for Christmas leave. I had been invited to stay some days with my god father, Mike, a well known character who lived on Dartmoor. He was a great friend of my father and together they seemed to have driven the Nazis out of Italy during the last war. I never did quite get the story out of either of them, but both were decorated for their efforts. Mike was keen that I should spend some time with him helping on his small farm at Huckworthy near Yelverton with his five horses. Apart from short periods of training in the Army this was my first time on Dartmoor.

The day would start at 6 am when he would bring me a cup of tea and then we would get the horses that we were exercising ready. I was given a large bay horse known as 'Coppa' to ride and together we would set off over the moor as soon as it got light. Sometimes the weather was not too good but that did not make any difference, with the only thing that could stop us being ice.

I had done some riding when I was younger but in no way was I experienced and Mike looked after me well. We would get back for a late breakfast and then muck the horses out. During the day sometimes we would go to Tavistock to get provisions and drop in to see friends.

One evening had been reserved for the local Hunt Ball and we were to meet at a friend's house near Widecombe-In-The-Moor. Val and Allan had invited eight other people to drinks and dinner first and then we were going to travel to the hunt ball together. I was concerned that I would be on my own but Mike assured me that he had partnered me up with an attractive woman so it all sounded good.

We met, suitably dressed for the occasion, as arranged at Val and Allan's house that was a spacious property in the middle of nowhere. There was an interesting collection of people there and then my 'partner' entered the room. Her name was Elizabeth; she was a very attractive, slim, dark-haired woman and I immediately felt my heart beating overtime when I saw her. She was introduced to me and our eyes met.

It was an enjoyable evening I held Elizabeth close to me for the last dance and then it all suddenly ended. For some unknown reason I had not secured her contact details and we went our separate ways. It was my last night staying at Mike's and the following day I was driving home to my parents, at Gillingham, Dorset for Christmas.

The next day I tried to think of how I was going to ask Mike for Elizabeth's telephone number and her address. I was not sure how he would take it but my problem was quickly solved. After breakfast Mike said: 'By the way Elizabeth has just telephoned, she has left her torch in my car and was wondering if you could drop it off on your way back today.' Then with a quiet giggle he stated: 'I have put it on the table for you.'

After packing I thanked him for a great stay and he asked me to let him know how I got on with dropping the torch off. With that I departed and eventually found my way to Elizabeth's farm the other side of the moor. It all looked very smart and before lunch, that she had prepared, I was shown around.

The first thing I noticed was that there were yellow labels stuck on the machinery stating that it was the property of HM Customs & Excise (VAT). When I asked what all this was about Elizabeth replied: 'It's a long story, but to cut it short I owe a lot of money to these people along with others and we cannot even sell any cattle as we have a TB and brucellosis standstill order on us'.

'What has happened to your husband?' I asked in all innocence.

'He is the problem, he left us last summer on the August bank holiday and is now in Australia. As you can see I think that I need help.'

I felt shocked at what she had just told me and we entered the large warm farm kitchen complete with its Aga. Elizabeth then told me that I would be shortly meeting her four daughters that had just returned together from riding their ponies. Sure enough shortly after this I met Nikki, with the other three, Claire, Tracey and Jo who politely greeted me and quietly sat at the kitchen table.

I knew that I was being covertly examined by them all and I was on my best behaviour. It was a magical lunch and when completed the four girls went about clearing the table and did the washing up. Following this they then informed us that the ponies needed mucking out and feeding and off they went.

'What do you think?' asked Elizabeth.

'They are great,' I responded, 'you are totally on your own?'

'Judy, who has been helping me has been a tremendous support. In fact I do not think I would have got this far without her, she just loves her cows and is good at looking after them. I am concerned over how we are going to cope this spring as it is going to be a struggle. Somehow we have to carry out the farm work as I am not going to be able to afford contractors. The accountant has been doing a good job but there is no money as the existing business account has been frozen.'

I found this statement interesting and started thinking that maybe I could come down on weekends and help on the farm. I then remembered that I was about to be posted to Germany to carry out this administrative job. It was certainly food for thought.

I started to get ready to leave and then Elizabeth suggested that perhaps I might like to come down and stay next weekend. I could scrape out the cattle with the tractor and if the weather was good there were hedge trimmings that needed burning. I could stay in the spare room and without hesitation I accepted this invitation. Elizabeth appeared pleased and gave me a hug stating that she was looking forward to seeing me again next weekend.

I departed for home at Gillingham in Dorset and was warmly greeted by mother and father who were looking forward to seeing me. It was good to sleep in my bed again and to enjoy mother's cooking. I met a few of my boyhood friends most of whom were now running their own businesses and it was a happy Christmas.

I discussed my future with mother and father who seemed to understand my predicament especially with the latest development of meeting Elizabeth. It was quite clear to them both that I was in love as mother put it. It began to become apparent that I had reached a 'y' junction in my life. I could either continue in the Army in an occupation that I possibly would not enjoy or resign and join Elizabeth who desperately needed help, accepting the challenge of the unknown.

Father as always stressed that this was an accurate deduction of the situation and that it would have to be my decision. However, he did suggest that perhaps I should carry out more research and thought on the 'farming front' that would undoubtedly prove to be challenging. I should not make any hasty decisions.

The weekend arrived and I was so looking forward to driving down to Devon and seeing Elizabeth or Liz as I now called her. I said farewell to my parents on the Friday afternoon and drove with great excitement down to the farm arriving at 5 pm. Liz and the four girls welcomed me with tea and cake and I heard all about the various adventures of the previous week. It seemed as if I was already part of the establishment which was almost frightening.

I learnt to drive the tractor and how to scrape the cattle out with help from Judy. Judy had been working on the farm for some three years helping to look after the horses and cattle. She was a single girl with long brown hair who originally came from London and this was her first job away from home. It was obvious that she enjoyed her employment here and was undoubtedly a tremendous support to Elizabeth.

I was then presented by Liz with a chain saw, which I had not used before. I decided to take advantage of this situation to meet the neighbouring farmer, Peter, and asked him how to start and operate this saw. He showed me, warning that the chain saw was the most dangerous machine on the farm. I heeded this advice.

That weekend I learnt how to drive the tractor, an old David Brown 780 (now vintage machinery), operate the chain saw and much more about the situation in connection with the business. It was obvious that whilst Liz's husband had not communicated with her it would not be long before he would either want to take the estate and business over or be paid for his share. In the meantime somehow the bills had to be paid and the existing business of pony trekking had to go forward, thus bringing some money in.

I had some savings that would be sufficient to pay off HM Customs & Excise and to kick-start the riding business this coming summer. However, if I was thinking this way I would have to consider resigning from the Army that would free me up and then I would be able to assist with this business. I was quite entitled to resign now before I passed out with my flying wings. Furthermore if I wished to continue flying at a later date this Army flying experience would stand me in good stead.

The choice of which direction I should go was becoming obvious, especially as I was fully aware of my feelings for Elizabeth, who I now adored. She had proved to me that she was strong, confident and capable. She was also a superb mother nurturing her four lovely daughters. If I was looking for a partner I could not find anyone better.

I returned to Middle Wallop and continued flying. I had another two weeks to decide whether to resign or not. My conscience was now troubling me as I felt that time for a decision had come. Furthermore I noticed that my flying performance was being affected and that I was making stupid mistakes. In other words I was now not flying safely.

I made the decision to leave the Army at the beginning of 1975. I asked for an interview with the chief instructor, who was surprised, stating that a lot of money had been spent on me. I pointed out that in my opinion, as I had already discussed with him, I would not be flying so the whole exercise was a waste of time. He then asked that whilst I was free to resign now whether I would consider staying in the Army. I said that I would consider this.

I informed my comrades what I had done and they all seemed to understand. Andy, who was about to get married to his fiancée, Val, gave me a lecture on how I should be careful in marrying an older woman and that I should always think about the future. He was and is a good friend.

I decided not to stay in the Army and was given one month's paid leave. It was sad to bid the comrades happy landings. That weekend I informed Liz of my decision and she was pleased asking whether I would be moving into the farm. I was hoping that I would get this invitation, as without it life could have now been a little difficult. We celebrated with the girls who were cooking the evening meal and I knew that without a shadow of a doubt I had made the correct decision.

I moved into the farm and started work. We paid off the VAT bill and visited the bank manager who agreed to loan us some money. We got the business going again and the TB and brucellosis standstill orders were lifted so that we could now sell some cattle thus raising more capital.

I worked on the accounts to keep Customs & Excise happy by paying their bills on time and the money from the riding business started to roll in. At the same time the farm had to be cared for as grass was an essential crop and there was also a tenanted farm to look after. It was a challenge and I was fast learning the ropes.

Chapter 38
Farm Accidents, Birth and Marriage - 1975

I soon started to learn that farm work was indeed dangerous and every care along with training should be considered at all times. There was no room for complacency or attempts to cut corners that maybe could save money on occasions.

One lovely spring morning I was working with the tractor. I was driving downhill on a track that runs though a wood on the farm and I had to stop on a downhill slope, to clear the track of a fallen branch. I got off the tractor, having applied the handbrake, and moved in front of it to move the obstacle when I heard a click. The next thing I knew was that my left leg was being run over by the front wheel of the tractor that was rolling forward. I could not move much and the tractor continued to roll over my knee and then thigh somehow catching my left arm at the same time. I managed to wriggle the rest of my body out of the way and the vehicle rumbled on down the track being stopped by a tree.

The pain, especially in the inside of my knee, was outrageous. My right leg and arm were bleeding and were numb and my right elbow was particularly uncomfortable. I could not stand on my leg so I managed to crawl to the stationary tractor, which was still running and somehow managed to struggle on board. I got it into gear and by using the hand throttle lever (found on most tractors), drove it down to the house where I shouted for assistance.

Liz and Tracey who were in the house heard me and came rushing out. They assisted me out of the machine as I was now suffering extreme pain and laid me flat on the ground. Tracey, aged fourteen at the time, was wonderful as apparently she had just completed a first aid course and knew what to do. Liz ran back into the house to phone for an ambulance and get the first aid kit. Between the two of them first aid was given and I was impressed. It was not long before the ambulance arrived.

The medics' main concern was whether my pelvis and soft organs had been crushed but it was obvious from the tyre marks on my thigh that the tractor had missed my torso so I was spared serious life threatening injuries.

'Laughing gas' along with pain killers was administered and I was driven to Torbay Hospital in an ambulance where x-rays were taken. Miraculously I suffered no broken bones and was discharged having been bandaged up.

Liz collected me and I did feel rather sorry for myself with a bandage on my leg as well as my right arm that had also been crushed. I soon learnt that after an accident like this there was little one could do on a farm apart from the dreaded desk work. However, the information got out into the parish and I started to receive visits from the neighboring farmers who came to offer their sympathies and offers of help. Above all this had presented a chance for them to meet me. It was interesting and I felt that I may have made my mark in the area even if it was for the wrong reason and we had the tractor properly serviced after that.

I soon made a recovery and time had come to fell a large dead tree in the garden that I considered a threat to the house, as if it did fall in a certain direction it could smash into the roof. I got a quote for the work from a qualified forester and was concerned at the price even if I was going to assist with the clearance.

There was nothing for it, I decided to drop this tree myself with the 'farm chain saw' that was an old Husqvarna 162. I had been shown how to do this type of work by a friend, who was experienced at using chain saws. I was fully aware that I had to drop this tree specifically in one direction away from the house and I had plenty of space to do this. I spoke to our neighbouring farmer Peter who pleaded with me to take care and to remember that chain saws were dangerous. He went on to state that he would 'have it done professionally, to hell with the cost.'

The challenge was there so I carefully planned what I was going to do and started one warm calm summer's morning. To start it all went well and I was impressed at what I had achieved. I then started the final cut and suddenly realized that if things did go wrong there could be a possibility of the tree falling into the road so I needed two lookouts to stop the traffic at the critical moment, that was about now.

I shouted into the house for Elizabeth and one other. Elizabeth emerged and immediately asked, 'What are you doing, I thought you were going to get a contractor to do this.'

Well I've changed my mind and look it's ready to come down no problem, it's going to land there,' and I pointed to the open stretch of garden which was intended to receive the fallen tree.

'I do hope you know what you are doing, this is a dangerous game if you get it wrong', and with that she called for Nikki who was in the house.

I instructed them what should happen and that when they were in the road stopping traffic I would fell the tree.

They took up their positions and I put the final cut into the tree. Much to my horror I noticed that the trunk of the tree was starting to spin on the stump and it became apparent that in no way was it going to fall where intended. I extricated the saw and for some unknown reason stood there watching. Suddenly there was a tremendous crack at the base of the trunk that extended a shard of wood out beside me, just missing my side, and the tree started falling towards the road and ironically onto one of Peter's wooden gates.

There was a tremendous crash as it landed on the road and Peter's wooden gate, shattering it into many pieces. I then realized what I had done. I had to clear the road as soon as possible so summoned the help of the girls. By lunchtime the road had been cleared and I was left with the task of informing

Peter about his gate.

I visited him after lunch. 'Hello Peter; you know that gate of yours into Jamie's Field, well I've just dropped in to inform you that I have broken it and of course I will replace it as soon as possible.'

'Have you now and how did you do that?'

'Well I have sawed that tree down and it didn't quite go to plan, it was rotten in the middle and it spun around, sorry.'

Peter looked at me with a wry smile asking 'Don't you listen to anything I say? I told you that this was dangerous and you were lucky that you got away with it.'

Shortly after this a forestry contractor was killed nearby under similar circumstances whereby a tree split on felling, catching and virtually splitting him into two pieces. I had learnt my lesson and after this I attended a chain saw course and would never ever fell a tree again without professional assistance.

The hay fields had to be harrowed, fertilized and rolled. When the weather and grass came right it would be time to cut, and the contractor would be called in to do the work leaving me on the David Brown tractor to do the turning. My first attempt went well and we saved some 3000 small bales with help from the neighbouring farmers Peter and Raymond along with a lad, Jamie, who lived next door. It was all carried into the barn where it was stacked sometimes late into the night.

This was enjoyable and rewarding. Elizabeth, who also helped with the carrying, arranged the food and drink to be available when we needed it. However it seemed that it was the drink, especially the cider, which really kept us all going into the early hours. At least there was plenty of hay to see us through our first winter.

The riding business was going well under our supervision although we had an experienced manager to assist. Elizabeth was winning prizes for her well-known Dartmoor ponies and selling them at a good price. The cattle were also selling well so all in all the business was beginning to thrive.

As expected it was not long before Elizabeth's husband suddenly reappeared showing an interest in taking the business over again, buying Elizabeth out, or selling his share to her. Elizabeth was intent in remaining on the farm with her daughters so somehow a half share of the farm and business had to be raised.

When this was to happen seemed to be a grey area and Liz's husband remained in the area. We were warned by our lawyer that he was intent in taking over the farm and business again so any problems with raising the half share money would result in Elizabeth being forced out. We were also advised that there could be a possibility that evidence was being gathered to show to the Courts that we were incapable of operating the business efficiently and, therefore, try and force his way in.

This produced a tremendous strain, but with Liz's positive attitude nothing was impossible and everything was in fact going well. It was agreed that a divorce between Liz and her husband should take place and the formalities were quickly concluded.

This now meant that I could marry the sweetheart of my life, Elizabeth, which I did in July 1975, in between making the hay and running the business. It was a memorable occasion with a quiet Registry Office wedding with my parents present. Following the marriage we drove home to a great lunch, which the girls had prepared in the garden as it was such a lovely day. Father had booked us all into a smart hotel for tea and dinner which was great fun although poor little Joe suddenly developed a fever and we had to return home a little earlier than planned but we all had enjoyed everything and spirits were high despite Joe's upset which she was so desperately trying to hide.

So I now was married to the woman of my dreams and the future was looking promising. Liz reminded me that there was 'just one thing missing and that was a child of mine and perhaps we ought to think about that!' It certainly sounded an attractive option and in July 1976 our daughter Alona was born.

Chapter 39
Business Problems - 1976-1979

Following the elation of the birth of my daughter, Alona, it was time to really concentrate on the business and start raising the capital required to purchase the farm and business.

As father had stated, this venture was going to be challenging and how true this was, especially as it was probable that this money would have to be raised within a deadline. It was decided to sell all the cattle as a herd complete, along with some 20 acres of land. We would also seek additional loans from the bank and mortgage company.

The next problem that was encountered was to agree with Liz's ex-husband on exactly how much capital he was expecting. This had to be done through the Court as many factors had to be considered, not least the children.

At the beginning of 1979 an agreement through a Court Order was reached over the disposal of the estate. It was lower than the other side was hoping for, but what I considered an unrealistic deadline of some four weeks was set to raise the money (hundreds of thousands). I looked upon this as a 'gamble' more than a challenge, but felt confident that we could accomplish this as we had planned accordingly. However the question remained whether we could do this in such a tight time scale.

As a safeguard I had approached my father, as I had anticipated this happening, asking if he would loan us any funds that we may require to cover us if there was any delay in say selling the land. This land was at the time in joint names of Elizabeth and her ex-husband. It would be only too simple to delay in signing the land Deed Of Release, thus causing problems in raising the capital in time resulting in a late payment and failure to comply with the Court Order.

It was not long before we managed to sell the cattle at the asking price and at the same time found a buyer for the land. There were one or two minor problems with the land sale but nothing insurmountable apart from the anticipated attempted delay.

Father was only too happy to assist and raised the money accordingly. I had pleasure in delivering the cheque to Liz's ex-husband's solicitor by hand well in time. He congratulated us, as it was thought that in no way could we meet the deadline, so therefore the farm and business would have to be sold and the proceeds evenly shared. However this now would not happen and we would remain on the farm.

So we had done it and once the land sale eventually went through I repaid my father who refused to accept any interest or cost payments for the sum. He was thrilled that we had pulled this off with his help.

It was not long though before we started to face problems that had not been envisaged. The owner of a small neighbouring farm, which was leased by the business in the name of Elizabeth's ex-husband, had previously assured us that she would be happy for us to continue with the lease instead of the present tenant (Liz's ex-husband). The advantage of farming this leasehold was considered by The Court. However once we had complied with the Court Order this land owner changed her mind and withdrew the lease, which was a little disturbing.

This was devastating as the main part of the riding business then relied on weekly bookings with accommodation and this farm was used not only to house a good proportion of our resident customers but also our manager and her husband.

We had actually foreseen a possible problem here and had discussed our plans to overcome the situation if it ever did arise. We would quite simply change the modus operandi of the business from weekly booking with accommodation to that of taking two hourly rides out with 'casual' bookings being made by holiday makers in the area sometimes on the same day.

The operation would take place here on our farm, which in fact it already did in a low key way. We would charge more per hour and this would also offer us flexibility as if we did not wish to operate certain days we would not take bookings. I had noticed that there was a growing trend in this 'niche market'.

Problem solved and I started marketing the new business in the area and this was received and supported with enthusiasm by a number of businesses. However another problem emerged in as much as that we discovered that the neighbouring landlord, who had withdrawn our lease, had installed our previous manager and husband to continue with the riding and accommodation at her farm under a different trading name.

This was encouragement to now aggressively sell our new product. I did this with support of the local businesses, who promoted us and our casual riding to their holiday makers. It was a success further encouraged by Claire, our number two daughter, taking on the management of the riding. She had just completed a cordon bleu cookery course so this obviously prepared her well!

Claire was a tremendous support to us both during this difficult period and also took on looking after Alona at times when Elizabeth and I wished to make an escape. She was known as 'mummy number two'.

This also gave me time to once again start following my favorite pursuit of sailing. I had met two friends of Elizabeth, both named John and both medical doctors. They had just purchased a 34-foot racing yacht (an OOD34), named *Charioteer*. They were keen for me to join them crewing and assisting them in various sailing races, one of which being considered was the Fastnet. I accepted with enthusiasm and we started to win cross Channel and local events. It was exciting, but little did we know what was about to happen on the Fastnet 1979, which is recorded in the opening three chapters.

Chapter 40
Agricultural Helicopter Flying - 1979-1980

After the Fastnet sailing disaster and the problem we had with the business, I started to get restless and wished for some form of back up if things did not go as planned. Elizabeth suggested that perhaps I could use my flying experience and become a part time commercial helicopter pilot as well as looking after the farm.

All our cattle had been sold so during the coming winter the buildings looked a bit empty. Of course there was plenty to do on the farm such as hedge laying and fencing but this was not urgent.

It just happened at this time that I met an old Army friend, Jake, and his wife Biddy, at a party. Jake was a former experienced Army pilot and lived for his flying. Having left the Army Jake had recently started an aerial agricultural crop spraying business, leasing a helicopter and buying an old fire engine as ground support. He was based in the Cotswolds near Hook Norton, famous for its beer.

He informed me that his new business was a great success and that he was about to expand so if I wished to assist him part time I would be more than welcome. He briefly suggested that I could work on a casual basis assisting his grounds man, Derek, and then maybe consider converting my flying time into a commercial flying licence followed by completing an aerial agricultural helicopter handling course. Jake himself had done this in America recently, as in this country the Civil Aviation Authority (CAA), would recognize American, (FAA), flying qualifications.

The following week I was in the Cotswolds helping Jake as an assistant. I was helping on the ground as planned. Ground operations were mainly run by Derek, who quietly and confidently carried out his tasks. He was a full time employee having been made redundant as a farm worker on a local holding so he knew the area and farmers well. His main task was to drive the fire engine to the various fields and to keep the helicopter refuelled and replenished with whatever it was spreading. However he was not keen on marking out the fields as it did involve extensive walking and he felt that he was too old for that.

I volunteered for that job and got to know the Cotswolds and various large fields, along with their owners, well. It was interesting watching Jake fly with such precision. He would be flying close to the ground with maximum weight, most of the time, so any slight error could prove catastrophic.

After three weeks of doing this Jake suggested that I should now go for a FAA commercial flying licence conversion course. Above all, as he was so grateful for the work that I had done for him to date, (unpaid), he offered to pay for the flying with no strings attached. This was just too good to be true so I accepted.

He knew of the contacts out there, booking me in to the respective courses. During the second week in October I started the commercial conversion course at Meacham Airfield near Fort Worth, Texas. This was to be followed by an agricultural flying course at Gettysburg, Pennsylvania.

I was accommodated in a nearby motel, but I had no form of transport initially. I relied on the flying school's transport and sometimes the buses. On one occasion I got onto a bus and having paid the black driver, started to look for a seat. I then noticed that this vehicle was full of black people and that a large woman just in front of me slid over to occupy two seats so that I could not sit next to her.

I politely asked if she could move over so that I could take the seat. With that in the typical Southern American drawl she asked 'Where are you from boy?' I then started to realize that I had got onto a 'black only' bus and there were some hostile looks directed my way. With the best English accent that I could manage I stated that I was from England. With relief she shouted out to the others that I was from England and asked me to sit next to her, patting the vacant seat. She was very friendly asking me about England and what I was doing over here. There was obvious relief shown by the passengers behind me and when I got off the bus I was bidden farewell by all.

During the course I was befriended by a large man known as Big Ed. He was a former US Army Apache helicopter pilot who, like me, was converting his flying experience into a commercial licence. I explained to him my experience on the 'black bus'. He was horrified at what I had done stating that I was lucky not to have been lynched.

As I was on my own in the evenings, on a number of occasions, he insisted on inviting me back to his home for supper. I would join him, his wife Rita and a little girl he had recently adopted from Vietnam called Jasmine. This was great as it was not much fun in my motel, without a car, during the evenings and Rita always provided wonderful food.

One day whilst the two of us were revising for our written exams at Meacham, in a room on our own, Ed suddenly divulged his 'demons'. He informed me that he had been flying his Apache helicopter gunship with his observer/co-pilot in the front seat in Vietnam. He was passing over a trail of refugees proceeding along a narrow track. They were fleeing the Vietcong, which Ed and his co-pilot had just identified in a position to the side of the track. They engaged the enemy that they feared were about to ambush the refugees.

The Apache helicopter then sported revolutionary features with its helmet mounted display. One of the capabilities of this new system was that the pilots could make the gun track head movements to point the weapons where they were looking. It was explained to me by Ed that in other words that whilst engaging a target with the 30 mm automatic gun if this system was connected wherever the gunner looked the gun would fire at that point.

Ed noticed that the refugees were being machine gunned by what he thought was the Vietcong. 'Bodies were flying everywhere amongst the dust'.

He asked his observer what he could see and where the firing was coming from.

'That's you, the helmet mounted eye sight has been enabled and you are firing the gun,' replied the co pilot tersely.

With that Ed burst into tears in front of me, stating that he felt that he had misused the system thereby killing all those innocent people including children. He then went on to inform me that Rita and he had gone out to the area in Vietnam after the war. They had spoken to some survivors of this incident and adopted their little girl Jasmine who had been orphaned in this massacre. It appeared that nobody knew who was responsible for it.

Whether or not this story should be believed, as it is so horrific, was at the time and still is, beyond me. To me this is an example of how modern weaponry if misused could be so unmercifully destructive.

Ed and I both completed our licence conversions within two weeks and we went our separate ways. Ed was hoping to fly 'the big stuff'. We kept in contact with Christmas cards etc. for about three years so what happened after that I do not know. I hope that Ed's 'demons' did not get the better of him.

Elizabeth suddenly made an appearance at this stage and I was thrilled to see her. Claire was looking after the business and Alona for four weeks. Our priority now was to purchase a car so that we could see a bit of Texas and Mexico. Most importantly we needed this vehicle to drive across the United States to Pennsylvania where I would be completing the agricultural flying course.

I found a ten-year-old red Volkswagen Beetle. It was in good condition and I was amazed to note that there was not any rust to be found. This apparently is common in areas such as this as the humidity level is so low. I purchased the car at a bargain price as the vendor, an Iraqi, was in a hurry to get home.

However I soon found that there was a problem in as much as that the car did not have any brakes. Fortunately I had taken another flying friend, Randy, who was a mechanic, on a check drive, having paid my cash to the vendor; Randy was calm and responded to the blaring of horns and wild gesticulations being made by the other road users who I was trying to miss. Eventually I got a clear run onto an upward slope and by using the gears I managed to stop the vehicle on the side of the highway.

Randy was great getting recovery organized and repaired the problem that was a broken and leaking brake pipe. It was obvious that the vendor should have known about this. It was only a matter of days before we were back on the road.

Having cruised Texas and a bit of Mexico Elizabeth and I then set course for Gettysburg via Colorado in our little red Beetle. The roads were amazing with little traffic, being smooth and straight, (apart from when nearing the cities). The speed limit was 40 mph which I always adhered to (with petrol at £0.44

pence per *gallon* it was an economic trip). However whenever my co driver, Elizabeth, took over this was increased to 60 mph as she wanted to get there!

Elizabeth and I eventually departed Texas in our VW Beetle planning on the drive across America taking some seven days with some sight-seeing stops en route. We had been advised to stop over at Colarado for a day or two which we did. It was a fascinating trip experiencing all weathers from the hot dusty prairies with tumbleweed blowing across the road, to the cold snow-covered mountains. We found the Americans all very friendly and hospitable, especially in the country.

We arrived in Gettysburg, a historical town. Our accommodation was the upper floor of a house belonging to an elderly couple, who charged us the equivalent of £20 a week for the rooms. It was quiet, clean and comfortable. We would drive some twenty minutes to 'Ag-rotors' based the other side of Gettysburg every day. Elizabeth then took the car on and would have a good time exploring the local area!

I enjoyed my agricultural flying course flying over the extensive hills and colourful woodlands of the area. It was the start of the hunting season and the brightly coloured baseball caps of the hunters could be easily seen amongst the golden trees below. We were warned to fly well above 2000 feet whilst transiting these areas as it was not uncommon to find shotgun pellets embedded in your aircraft. It was well known that some hunters would fire at anything that moved, including low flying aircraft.

I successfully completed the agricultural flying course by the end of November and Elizabeth and I returned home having sold our VW Beetle for more than we paid for it due to the immaculate condition and the Texas number plate.

Claire had done a wonderful job keeping the business on track and above all looking after Alona, now aged four. I had grown a beard in America and this was a shock for my little girl. Whilst she recognized my voice she could not recognize me for a while and hid behind the sofa or any other part of furniture that would offer refuge! Eventually after encouragement from Elizabeth and Claire, Alona hesitantly gave me a hug and that was it, I was accepted once again as Daddy.

I spent December working on the farm and business catching up on the jobs that needed doing with the intention of returning to the Cotswolds in February of the following year. I would now be flying as well as carrying out ground support duties.

However, the 'Environmental Noose' was tightening around Jake's neck with particular reference to the aerial spraying of chemicals. Jake was concerned about this and warned me accordingly.

Chapter 41
Microlight Flying - 1982-1988

I returned to help Jake with the helicopter agricultural business in February 1982. Things were not going too well with restrictions being placed on him in connection with chemical spraying. However, there was plenty of aerial fertilizing, known as 'top dressing' to be getting on with. I also spent some time refuelling and ferrying his two helicopters to varying positions so that he and another experienced agricultural pilot, who had recently joined him, could get on with the job.

Eventually by the end of March, Jake decided that he really could not afford to pay me. Another problem he was now facing was a tremendous increase in insurance premiums. There had been an unusual number of flying accidents with other companies the previous year and this had a knock-on effect.

I was beginning to miss my family and farm so this came as a relief although my farewells came with a certain amount of sadness. I had enjoyed this adventure, which had presented opportunities that both Elizabeth and I took advantage of. Jake and Biddy were great to work for and there was no doubt in my mind that Jake would survive. He was currently working on a new system of spraying.

On return to the home farm and business I started to expand on the marketing with a good response. Claire had done a great job managing it all in our absence proving how capable she was. Easter was busy with the riding and we purchased some Hereford cattle to keep the grazing right.

We had a good summer and in the autumn Elizabeth and I went on a three day break touring Cornwall with Claire once again at the helm. Whilst driving around the north coast I noticed a small fabric covered aircraft flying some 2000 ft above me. This was fascinating so I informed Elizabeth that I was going to track it as it was not travelling very fast.

My tracking took me to Davidstow where there is a disused airfield. My quarry landed and taxied over to some dilapidated Nissan Huts. I followed the unsuspecting pilot and was surprised to find him entering a warm office. It was then I introduced myself as a 'stalker' and started asking some questions to the amusement of those present.

Fortunately my approach was accepted. Over a cup of tea, the chief instructor having introduced himself as Ian, then went on to present the pilot who I had tracked. He flew for one of the well known airlines based down here and enjoyed flying of this nature. It was explained to me that these aircraft are microlights that are easy to fly, maintain and store. Whilst a flying licence is required it would only need to be a variation of the Private Pilot's Licence as my commercial helicopter licence would not be acceptable.

Much to my surprise Ian suddenly suggested that his assistant instructor,

Graham, could take me up for a quick 'flip' around the airfield.

'What, now?' I asked thinking about Elizabeth in the car.

'We could give you some twenty minutes absolutely free. There she is ready to go,' Graham responded pointing to the twin seated aircraft, a 'Quicksilver' that I had just been tracking.

I checked Elizabeth and she was sleeping in the car. This was just too good to be true and brought back memories of Blackbushe Airport all those years ago.

A thermal flying suit was produced for me to wear along with some gloves and having been strapped in off we went.

It was entirely different to any type of flying I had experienced, being totally exposed to the elements. I was given the controls once airborne and managed to land her without problem. I was sold and decided there and then that I was going to take this up.

I approached the CAA and they directed that I should do a minimum number of hours along with a qualifying cross country flight. Actually I did have a problem with this qualifying flight. Following takeoff, as I was about to leave the circuit to start the cross country phase, my engine on my hired aeroplane stopped. However I was in a suitable position to make an emergency landing on the airfield without problem.

Ian and Graham were soon there with their toolkit and the reason for the engine failure was discovered to be fuel starvation. This was easily rectified and whilst I had lost an hour I was now concerned as the weather seemed to be deteriorating with visibility decreasing due to a low cloud base. I spoke to Ian about this and he reckoned that if I got going and did not get lost there would be no problem.

There was no compass attached to this aircraft so without some form of horizontal reference it was difficult to judge in which direction one was flying. I had not actually experienced this before and it was not long before I was lost. I could see the ground and had about a 2 mile visual window so I was trying to place points on the ground onto my map. This did not work!

Suddenly I came across a 'town' with a large church and then I could momentarily see the north and south coast. It was Truro and I was flying in a westerly direction when it should have been east. After this reference I started to return to Davidstow following what I recognized as a main road that was leading to Bodmin and then the cloud base became lower. It forced me into landing on a large field that had just been cut for silage.

It was a successful incident-free landing. I had to find some form of civilization so that I could make a telephone call back to the airfield. I followed the track from the field back to the farm and knocked on the door of the house.

The door was opened by a swarthy lad who was eating cake and drinking tea.

'Good afternoon I have just been forced to land my aircraft in one of your fields and I was wondering if I could use your telephone?'

'Yes of course, come in, would you like some tea and the phone is over there in the corner.'

'Thank you tea would be great and the call will be local I hope.'

I noticed another older man enter the room.

'So you have been caught by the weather as well, we had to stop silage making it was just getting too wet, which field have you landed in?'.

His son explained to his father that he had seen me land in the 'big 60'. I suddenly realized that I had no idea where I was. 'Oh by the way where are we?'

Bugle was the response.

I telephoned the CFI, Ian, who was relieved to hear that I was safe and warmly congratulated me for deciding on and in managing a successful forced landing. He informed me that Bugle was not far away and that he would collect me within the next forty minutes. He would then ensure that the aircraft was secure etc.

He arrived shortly after and could see no problem in recovering the aircraft, which he would probably do the next day as the forecast was good. I returned home a little later than usual, but I had let Elizabeth know what was happening so supper was waiting for me. It was good to be home. I completed my cross country shortly after with an orienteering compass strapped to my wrist. This was followed by a General Flying Test which I passed and was rewarded with a renewed PPL.

Chapter 42
My 'Goldwing' and Adventures

Whilst I was happy hiring and flying the Davidstow flying club microlights I noticed a new fibre glass plane packed away in one of the buildings. I discovered that it had just been built and it was for sale.

The builder of this aircraft was experienced in constructing this type of microlight that was known as a 'Goldwing'. It had a strange configuration with a small aerofoil in the front attached to the nose with swept back wings centrally positioned complete with a pusher propeller driven by a 330cc motor bike engine. It had a strong undercarriage, was built of fibre glass and a single seat enjoyed a cockpit with a wind shield. From below it gave the appearance that the plane was flying back to front as the local community were always quick to inform me.

I soon discovered that the wings were easy to bolt on, especially with help, and once assembled the time came to fly it. I nervously started the motor and strapped myself in when suddenly a man named Brian ran up to me waving his arms.

He was the builder of this aircraft and insisted that he should carry out the first flight which seemed fair enough. I extricated myself and he took over asking about what weight I had strapped into the nose. He explained that if the centre of gravity was not correct this aircraft would enter a flat spin that could prove fatal. With that he took out all my lead and carefully weighed some more. It was just as well Brian had arrived when he did as I, and others, were oblivious to these calculations.

Brian eventually took off and the aeroplane seemed to fly beautifully landing gently in front of us. Brian was thrilled and I then asked if it was aerobatic.

It was confirmed that it could roll and loop and Ian suddenly announced that he would give an aerobatic demonstration.

It seemed quite mad but we stood back whilst Ian strapped in. It was confirmed that there was plenty of weight up front and sufficient fuel for the loops and rolls that were about to be performed.

Ian climbed to a decent height and then started looping. These loops appeared to be tight, almost flicks, but he just carried on with this manoeuvre obviously enjoying the flying. Then just to make the point he carried out a number of barrel rolls, some of which seemed a little low.

The point had been made and Ian landed my aerobatic aeroplane looking exhilarated. So now it was my turn and I also enjoyed the flight. I asked Brian if he would accept a cheque, which he did, and I purchased my first aircraft for £2000.

The next challenge was to get it home and to find a field nearby that I could use. I was tempted to try our long field by our local pub in Widecombe, the Rugglestone Inn, but the Landlady, Audrey, was nervous that I would fly into the pub. The locals found this conversation amusing with one suggesting that it would be alright if she kept both the front and back door open whenever I was flying as if anything happened I would just pass through.

I calculated that I could transport my new acquisition in our Bedford TK horse box as there was sufficient space to fit the fuselage in the back and to hang the wings, that would be padded either side. Thankfully this worked well and I soon had my pride and joy back on the farm in a secure part of a barn.

Then I had to find a suitable site to fly from and I quickly found a neighbour's field some 2 miles away. It was 'tight' but had enough of a run for an accurate landing and takeoff and also had adequate access from the road. I was set up ready to go.

In the autumn of 1983 I started flying trips around the West Country. I soon discovered that this was a low flying area for the RAF particularly popular with Hawk fighter jets out of RAF Chivenor and RAF Valley. I got the impression that at times I would be used as a target or a dummy. On one occasion I had one fly over me inverted and the other close below me in a 'mirror' or more like it a 'sandwich' formation. This was deafening and left me breathing in the fumes from their jet engines. It was quite exhilarating!

An unforeseen problem with my field soon occurred. I had flown down to Lands End and back. When I made the final evening approach into my field I was shocked to see that the field was full of cattle. Attempts were made to fly low over them to try and drive them to one side but this had no effect as they were intent on the new sweet grass.

On the third attempt to move them, with relief I noticed that the owner of the field, Ian, and his partner, Claire, had appeared and were driving the bullocks into another field. I made a successful landing and was grateful as I was considering diverting to another field which would have been really inconvenient.

Ian and Claire were pleased to have assisted me and were very apologetic for letting them in. They thought that I had landed and gone. I used this opportunity to introduce them to my aeroplane and they were fascinated. However Claire pointed out that my pride and joy was now covered in cow dung that had been thrown up during my landing.

Ian insisted that they would assist me in scrubbing the aircraft clean with buckets of water taken from the nearby stream and after half an hour it was pristine white once again. They then helped me to unbolt the wings and to load it up into the lorry. I was late returning home but Elizabeth was used to this and my supper was waiting for me.

The lorry transport system was unwieldy so I designed a trailer that I could tow behind our farm vehicle, a Subaru. To my surprise I found this a straightforward task and soon learnt to weld and keep things straight and upright in construction. This enabled me to assemble and dissemble the aircraft on my own with the support of two log trestles upon which I would place the wings.

Whenever the weather was suitable, even for short periods of time, I would be flying. However on one flight whilst flying over the moor near home at some 2000 ft there was a resounding crack and the engine revved up into the red. I had lost my propeller so I throttled back, closed the engine down and started a steady glide. I could see my airfield in the distance and I calculated that with the present glide rate I could possibly land back there.

I began to relax, wiping the sweat from my eyes, and concentrated on flying at the optimum speed for the glide angle and was surprised on how well the aircraft was performing without a propeller.

I made a good landing into my field closely followed by a friend, Vince, who also flew a Goldwing who had appeared from nowhere. He taxied up next to me and asked why I was not getting ready for take off as we had planned to fly together to Eaglescott Airfield in North Devon.

I pointed out that I did not actually have a propeller so for me the flying day was over. He helped me dissemble and load up onto my new trailer which he admired and then departed for North Devon.

I spent the next five days searching over the moor on horse back for my propeller to no avail. It was a particularly remote area so I was confident that no damage had been done on the ground. I sought advice from my CAA aeronautical engineer who informed me of what specification I would need to replace the sheered prop shaft. He reckoned that the incorrect standard of stainless steel shaft had been used in the existing propeller reduction gear. I soon had it repaired with a new propeller and was ready to go.

***

The new propeller worked well and many flights were successfully completed without incident throughout the South West. Having joined the Territorial Army (TA) in 1982 (see following chapter), I had a chance to fly 'recce missions' over Dartmoor at times. I also wrote 'a paper' that was sent up to the Ministry of Defence (MOD); This was done through my commanding officer titled 'The benefits of the tactical use of an unmanned aerial vehicle' (UAV).

Whilst UAVs have been in existence from the 1800s they had been normally used as a weapon delivery system or as a target. I was promoting the fact that these devices could be used for reconnaissance and recovery.

Surprisingly in response I received a congratulatory letter from the MOD and my commanding officer on this paper that had been noted and was to be acted upon. I heard nothing further, but was I instrumental to the birth of the 'drone' as we know it today?

Taking all reasonable care I always filed my flight plan with the RAF when flying over Dartmoor, as this area was and is a low flying designated area. I also met up with two other Goldwing owners, Vince and Brian, and at times we would fly around in formation landing at various local airfields.

On one occasion on a Sunday I decided to fly to Bodmin airfield, Davidstow and stopping at another disused RAF field, St Merryn, all in Cornwall; I had arranged to meet a microlight pilot down there who I had not met before and he had promised me a picnic lunch of coffee and sandwiches.

I was so enthusiastic to get started from my field in the early morning that somehow I had forgotten to strap myself into my aircraft. I discovered this when after takeoff I had came across turbulence that nearly threw me out of the cockpit. Somehow I managed to hook my knees under the instrument panel keeping me in the cockpit. I returned to my field and on the ground strapped myself in.

Once secured into my cockpit, I enjoyed a direct flight to St Merryn. Having landed on one of the disused runways I waited for my new friend to appear with the picnic lunch. Sure enough a car appeared and parked in front of me. A rather official looking character introduced himself as Customs and Excise and started asking questions about my activity.

I thought that this was a joke as obviously my new friend had a rather odd sense of humour. I noticed a flask of coffee and a box of sandwiches on the back seat of the car. I thanked him, and whilst stressing the fact that I was pushed for time, started on the sandwiches and coffee.

There was a definite look of shock upon the face of my new friend who then produced proof of identity (as they do in the films), stating that he was a Customs and Excise officer and that I was to return what was left of his lunch and to stand next to my cockpit as he was going to search my aircraft.

Suddenly the cheese and ham sandwich that I was eating took on a different taste. Whilst no weapons were involved that proof of identity wallet was as good as a pistol being pointed at me. Should I swallow that mouthful of sandwich or spit it out. I decided to swallow it and was as apologetic as I could be. I then noticed another car approaching and the driver got out speaking to my 'apprehending Customs officer'.

They appeared to know each other and eventually my 'questioner' burst into laughter. It was negotiated that he should have my lunch and I could complete his. We then discussed the reason for this inspection in as much as that smuggling was apparently rife in this area. Customs and Excise were being active and smuggling by aircraft was not unheard of. We then discussed various areas of my aircraft where packets of contraband could be hidden or carried.

After lunch and searching I managed to find a phone box and telephoned the RAF to ask if I could amend my flight plan. I wanted to fly south west over St Mawgan, then being used by the US Airforce. I realized that this was a prohibited air space, but it would reduce my flight time by some fifteen minutes. Much to my surprise the operative cleared me over St Mawgan at a specific time on a given bearing and height as it was a Sunday afternoon. It all seemed a bit odd but it would save me time.

I took off as soon as possible and followed my instructions. It was fascinating to fly over this large airfield at two thousand feet and I noticed a lot of activity on the ground. I was sure that missiles and guns were being trained on me and could clearly see figures running on the ground along with vehicles speeding about.

I thought nothing further about all this and landed at my destination field to meet more friends. Following this I then flew back to Davidstow late afternoon.

On arrival I was interrogated by the CFI, Ian, who had been waiting for me. He asked if I had flown over St Mawgan and I confirmed that I had according to the instructions issued. I had written these down in note form along with a reference number that had been issued.

Apparently the CAA had telephoned Ian to inform him that a microlight, similar to mine, had violated prohibited airspace and that a full enquiry was in progress. It was thought that nuclear weapons were stored on this site and it was touch and go whether the infringing aircraft (that was me), should be destroyed as it could be a possible terrorist attack.

Weapons had been trained on me, not for practice purposes, but for real. An instant decision had to be made on whether this threat should be eliminated or not. Fortunately the weapons tight order was given and I have survived to tell this tale.

Ian telephoned the CAA and informed them about what had happened. After a brief delay Ian was informed that I was free to go. I heard nothing further over this incident.

I now had to fly home and time was pushing on. It was a lovely evening and having reached my cruising height I could clearly see banks of fog covering the western fringes of Dartmoor. I continued my flight confident that the fog would be clear over my part of the moor which was towards the east.

However this was not to be and once over Princetown I could see nothing but fog. The ground was not visible apart from the top section of the Princetown communications mast that was protruding through the fog.

After flying around the mast for some thirty minutes I noticed that the fog if anything was getting thicker and less of the mast was showing. I had to do something so I started a slow descent through the murk over where I thought my field was.

This was a foolish thing to do and I was fearful of flying into the ground or an obstruction such as a large rock. I had no instrumentation for this type of flying. Heart in mouth I slowly descended when suddenly I saw something white running away in front of me. It was a sheep and everything was brown so I was flying over the moor somewhere. I could not see more than fifty metres ahead of me and the ground was not suitable for landing as there were a number of rocks around.

Without hesitation I climbed back to two thousand feet and once again settled above the fog with just the top of Princetown tower now showing. I calculated that I had about an hour's worth of fuel left. Once I had used this I was committed to a 'blind landing'. Whilst contemplating my fate and trying to calculate where to descend a hole suddenly appeared just east of Tavistock, by what I later discovered was Pork Hill. I descended as rapidly as I could. Unbelievably I could see a suitable field by the side of a road so without hesitation I landed, narrowly missing a telephone cable.

I just could not believe that I had pulled this miraculous forced landing off without incident. Once on the ground I saw the fog close in again. I knew this area and that there was a telephone box not far away. I telephoned home and Elizabeth was away but Tracey took the call. I instructed her to collect the Subaru and trailer from my field and asked if she could collect me giving her a grid reference of the access gate to the field. This was no problem for Tracey and by midnight my plane and I were home. It was a day to remember and one that I survived!

***

I was once again getting the yearning for aerobatics in a conventional aircraft so I converted my licence to fly a Slingsby T67 and a Cessna 152 from Dunkeswell.

At the same time I put my Goldwing on the market, and on one of the demonstration flights to a possible purchaser, suffered from an odd problem on my final approach to land at my field.

The visor of my helmet suddenly and without warning ripped free of it's holding in the slipstream. This meant that the visor was now fully exposed producing a tremendous drag in a sideways direction on my helmet.

In other words my head was suddenly jammed over to the right and try as I might I just could not turn my head to the left so I could not see ahead of me.

I overshot the landing and applied maximum revs to gain height referring to the horizon over my right wing so at least I could remain in a steady climbing attitude.

When I thought that I had reached a safe height I started to try and fix the problem. I ducked my head down as far as I could beneath the windscreen to try and move it. This did not have any effect. I attempted in vain to rip the visor off and then I managed to lower it and this worked. Once again I could see ahead of me.

I carried out a normal landing in front of my interested purchaser with a rather stiff neck. When I explained what had happened this mishap seemed to have had a positive reaction. I sold my Goldwing for the asking price in 1988.

I was later informed that the new owner had crashed it through what was thought to be pilot error. Fortunately there were no injuries although the aircraft was totally destroyed.

Chapter 43

Territorial Army and the Mess Boots Saga - 1982-1995

I decided in 1982 to join the Territorial Army by being able to re-establish my officer's commission. I became a Lieutenant in 'E' Company, 1 Wessex based in Exeter, having shown my commitment to the Commanding Officer by participating in a weekend defence exercise being held on Salisbury Plain.

The weather was the usual with driving rain most of the time and I was amazed at the enthusiasm shown by the TA soldiers throughout this time. There were only two cases of exposure amongst the thirty soldiers taking part and I learnt a lot about what to expect.

I was impressed with the set up in Exeter. The company commander, Chris, a Major, was a TA soldier who was a landlord of a pub in Buckfastleigh with his wife. We immediately bonded and he confided in me that the MOD was actively recruiting to strengthen the TA which was to become an integral part of the Regular Army.

To support Chris, there was a Permanent Staff Admin Officer, a retired Quartermaster Major with years of military experience. On the ground there was a serving Company Sergeant Major along with a couple of Regular Army Sergeants. They were known as Permanent Staff Instructors, PSIs. This worked well and it was not long before another ex regular Royal Marine Lieutenant, Nigel, joined the company, like me as a Platoon Commander.

Our numbers steadily grew and we soon had enough soldiers to make up two platoons. My platoon was made up mainly from soldiers who lived in the Plymouth area and Nigel had those from Exeter.

We had to parade every Wednesday evening and there was a weekend activity every other week. We normally gathered for the weekend on the Friday evening. More often than not some sort of alcohol was involved here, normally in the form of a bar that was carefully controlled.

On top of the weekends and evenings, an annual two week camp had to be attended. This meant that some twenty-four days had to be completed, all of which was paid for on the British Army pay scale and expenses.

Efforts were made by the Permanent Staff and indeed the commanders to make the training as interesting as possible. The new recruit had to undergo a selection process and if successful underwent a two week recruit training course before becoming a Territorial Army soldier.

Training was varied and I attended a number of two-week camps abroad such as is in Denmark, Germany, Cyprus, and a number of home camps in Thetford, Salisbury Plain and on one occasion a national home defence exercise within the West Country. I also took advantage of undergoing training for sailing qualifications such as Coastal Skipper and Yacht Master at Gosport. I was hoping that with these credentials I could skipper the Army yachts whenever possible. It was hard work but great fun with many laughs to be had. One early morning another yacht master candidate, a Colonel named Freddie, and I decided that to save time we would use the ladies showers and toilets as there were no ladies on the course. Whilst we were sitting on the toilet the door of the block suddenly swung open and some eight ladies came in to carry out their morning toiletries. They were on a large naval yacht that had just come alongside.

We sat there silently wondering what to do next. Suddenly a roll of toilet paper rolled from the next toilet under the partition wall in front of me. I was asked to pass it back by the lady next door so I tried to do this without showing my hands. However my position was compromised. Freddie and I apologetically beat a hasty retreat accompanied by wolf whistles and two ladies we had to pass gave us a 'frothy flash'. I have never been so embarrassed.

I was also fortunate enough to enjoy a 'flight experience' sortie as a Military Liaison Officer with 63 Squadron then based at RAF Chivenor, flying in the fast jet fighter, the Hawk. The RAF had the routine for accommodating 'guests' well organized. First a medical had to be passed and then the flying gear fitted, which included the 'G' suit. Following this the 'guest' was well briefed on the flight. Most importantly strict instructions on how and where to be sick were given and that any 'mess' would have to be cleared up by the perpetrator. There was also a stern warning that the flight would not be cut short even if the passenger was suffering.

My instructor, a young Flight Lieutenant named Mark, was introduced to me and he supervised me being strapped into the front seat. He would be sitting behind me and we would communicate through the intercom. I was informed where the ejector seat mechanism was and was instructed on how to eject from the cockpit if I was commanded to do so.

Having started the engine and completed his interior checks Mark, instructed me to remove two pins from my ejector seat and to stow them in a particular place. This I did and having done so he then informed me with a chuckle that I was now sitting on an explosive device!

We were soon airborne travelling at some 550 knots at low level which was around 500 to 250 feet above ground level. We flew east, covering about nine miles a minute, to 'enjoy' the Exmoor low flying area, then skimmed across the Bristol Channel to find some 'targets' within the Welsh hills that were photographed. After forty-five minutes a demonstration on how this aircraft could climb 5000 feet straight up within seconds, was given by Mark who leveled off at 6000 feet.

He handed the fighter over to me to fly which was a great thrill. I realized that we were over the North of Dartmoor and was cleared to fly over our farm at low level. I knew the terrain from the air well around here and managed an 'attack' on the farm skidding around the prominent hill, Hameldown, at low level pulling 5 'g' in the turn, grunting as we completed the manoeuvre. I saw our manager, Annette, in the yard with her hands over her ears as I flashed past, but none of the horses seemed disturbed.

It was a great privilege to have been able to do this and certainly gave an insight into the precision and pressure these fighter pilots undergo. As a token of appreciation I painted 'HELLO 63' on the roof of one of our barns. I did wonder how many photos were taken of that.

My promotion to Captain shortly followed and then it was decided that 'E' company 1 Wessex would become the base for the conception of another TA battalion which would be known as the 4th Battalion The Devonshire and Dorset Regiment. This would be supported by the MOD who launched an active recruiting drive accordingly.

A new company was to be formed in the Plymouth area along with another in Exeter. I was selected to be the Company Commander of the Plymouth company and had to attend a two week course at Warminster followed by exams and tests. Having completed all this I was promoted to a Major, or Company Commander of 'A' company in Plymouth.

It was hard work to start and I was not used to dealing with female soldiers. This was made all the more difficult as these girls were of a high standard and many were particularly good rifle shots, leaving the lads struggling.

Our first test exercise was a two week national defence one and my company had the task of defending the Royal Naval fuel tank compound on the River Tamar. We were billeted in a concrete bunker and had to keep the area secure against marauding students, employed from Exeter University and special forces who were intent on infiltration. Security seemed an impossible task on the face of it as it was such a large area only protected by a wire fence.

I soon got to know the manager of the site and whilst being briefed by him I noticed where he kept the exercise programme (the pink) in his desk. This paper would detail every movement during the exercise which was important for him as there was a possibility that a real enemy could slide in under the auspices of the exercise and destroy the fuel depot.

I spoke to my second in command, Dermot, over this and he reminded me that we did have a soldier who was a locksmith and perhaps it would be no challenge for him to pick the lock of the manager's door and then we could take sight of and maybe copy the exercise instructions.

During this covert operation we just happened to inadvertently bump into what we considered, by their uniform, to be three members of the Special Boat Service (SBS). They were not aware that we were watching them and it became obvious that perhaps they had the same idea. However they gave up as they felt that the depot manager might take exception to having his office door broken into and left the area.

I was left wondering how they had managed to get into the compound undetected and then it was our turn. We did not have to break the door down with our specialist doing the work. It was all so simple and we achieved our aim.

It was an interesting exercise and we managed to cope with everything that was thrown at us as we had plenty of warning. We discovered where special forces were infiltrating the area. One of my soldiers was just having a quiet surreptitious cigarette in the early hours when he saw three canoes approach from the river. He rushed back to the command centre in the bunker and reported this. We then captured six SBS members and they were not amused. This was not in 'the pink'.

So it went on and I noticed that we seemed to be collecting more umpires who just could not understand how and why we had this ability to preempt any planned moves against us. The exercise was completed by a dawn attack from a Regular Army company and as usual we were lying in wait having set up an ambush. Again they were not happy and my company came out of it all rather well.

There were also many social occasions and there was one such event, a ladies night being held at Exeter. This is where the various ladies connected with the brigade are invited to dinner by the Officers' Mess and entertained accordingly.

This was a good evening with plenty of alcohol. The bar was on a second floor with the drill hall below being used as the dining area. All officers were in mess kit and ladies were in long dresses.

Somehow these lads always got things well sorted and the drill hall looked good with the tables laid out in a rectangle with the respective regimental silver laid out sparkling in the candlelight. The dinner was cooked by our chefs, who always produced excellent food, whether at dinners such as this or in the middle of nowhere in a howling gale and rain. The chief chef was actually a long distance lorry driver but he certainly knew how to cook.

After dinner whilst in the bar, a lady somehow managed to drop her silk scarf out of the window. It got hung up half way down on a protrusion in the wall. Without hesitation I offered my assistance to rescue the stricken scarf and briefed Nigel accordingly. The plan was for him to hang me out of the window, upside down, by my legs. Once I had retrieved the scarf Nigel and maybe others would haul me back in.

Nigel lowered me gently down from the window. I could not quite reach so I asked him to lower me a bit more. I retrieved the scarf and then I felt myself slipping out of my mess boots, which Nigel should have had hold of. I somehow managed to land on my back in a thick bush just below the window.

It was uncomfortable as I was just wearing a shirt on my upper body and I heard Nigel shouting for me as I seemed to have disappeared and some of the ladies were screaming. Someone shouted in a male voice, 'Oh My God he's gone.'

I had sunk low into this bush and was supported just above the ground. The foliage above me had fallen back into place thus concealing my whereabouts. It was then that I realized how lucky I had been and a mischievous thought came to mind. I could quickly run away and watch the chaos from a distance. This I did and my problem was now suppressing my laughter that would have given my position away.

First on the scene was Nigel: 'Where in the fuck is he?'

Then Chris: 'He must be hung up somewhere.'

Followed by Jack: 'We must inform the police, Rod has probably landed on his head and may well be out there raping and pillaging.'

Nigel reckoned that I was about somewhere and started to search the bushes. It was time to leave so I escaped unnoticed back into the drill hall and then to the bar to present the lady with her scarf, swearing all present to silence. I put my boots and mess jacket back on and noticed the chaotic search going on below amongst the bushes.

Nigel looked up and saw me and casually remarked: 'OK Rod, I thought that you might be up there, we will be up shortly.'

We reassembled in the bar, with the scarf reunited with its owner and the evening continued as if nothing had happened. No questions were asked until the next morning. It was one of those memorable evenings in the TA.

Training and soldiering were undertaken with all due sincerity and enthusiasm that can only be found in the Territorial Army. Many TA soldiers carry out tours in active theatres supporting the Regular Army being awarded medals for their service and are much respected by their Regular counterparts.

I was medically discharged from the TA following an accident I had on the farm as described in the next chapter. They were happy days with much camaraderie.

Chapter 44

Farm Accident - Fall From a Roof - 1995

As always much work needed doing on the farm, mainly with the fences and hedges. However one job that did need doing was to repair an old barn roof that consisted of corrugated iron on one side and old slate and pitch on the other, which was leaking. We had planned to replace this roof under a grant scheme the following year.

I had borrowed a roofing ladder for the job and started the repair at around midday. I had an important meeting that evening and had to finish the job by no later than 16.30 hrs that afternoon.

All went well and I had completed the job by 16.00 hrs and on the way down the roof ladder, on my final trip, I noticed the corrugated iron roof starting to bend inwards with my weight.

This resulted in the top of the ladder tilting upwards thereby disengaging the top lugs that protrude over the other side of the ridge of the roof. I felt the ladder sliding down the roof and realised that I was in for a fall from a considerable height onto a road below.

I realised that it was essential that I should somehow land on my feet to survive and as the ladder gathered speed as it went over the edge I managed to push myself out away from the wall of the barn and did land on both my feet.

My left ankle shattered under the impact of landing but strangely to start with there was no pain, just numbness. I got up and stupidly tried to put weight on my injured ankle. There was a searing pain that was so severe that I pitched forward onto my face on the road, knocking myself out.

Consciousness was regained shortly after and I had been moved to the side of the road, by our young farrier, who had just completed a first aid course. Much to my horror I then felt and saw him trying to straighten my fractured ankle, strapping it to a broom handle. The pain was unbearable and I let him know this fact in no uncertain way.

Elizabeth and Tracey, who had now arrived on the scene, instructed him to leave me alone. Tracey went into the house to phone for an ambulance and Liz was trying to comfort me. A blanket was placed over me and I asked for a stick or something to chew on to help with the pain as I was shivering uncontrollably and slipping in and out consciousness. Tracey slipped two hot water bottles under the blanket and this was a great comfort.

The road ambulance arrived first after some fifteen minutes and the medics gave me morphine to ease the pain. The air ambulance arrived shortly after landing close by in one of our fields. It was decided that I should be flown to

Torbay Hospital and this took seven minutes. Once in Accident and Emergency I was assessed and informed that I would receive surgery immediately although it was stressed that the main operation to repair my fracture would take place at a later date. This operation was to stabilize me.

I recovered from the anaesthetic at about 02.00 hrs in a large ward. My leg was in an open cast up to the thigh and I had a stainless steel rod through my knee. It was only now that I realised how badly I had been injured and this was confirmed by a nursing sister as I was asking when I could leave hospital in a confused state.

I was moved shortly after to a smaller ward consisting of four of us: a builder who had fallen from a ladder and broken his back, a lorry driver who had fallen from the back of his lorry and broken both legs and a gardener who had slipped over and broken a leg and of course me. We were all bound to our beds and had individual nurses to care for us. My nurse, Kay, was great and kept me going when things got a bit tough using her dry mature sense of humour. We all realized that we were in for a long stay and might as well make the most of being served upon.

The next day I was visited by my consultant surgeon, Ian Winstone (now Lord Winstone), who inspected my injury. My ankle did look a mess although there was no bone visible. However, I was surprised to see blisters that had appeared around the fracture. It was explained to me that these were 'fracture blisters', which could go gangrenous. If this happened it would result in an amputation of my leg below the knee, but that after ten days the danger should be over.

If I was clear after ten days the situation would be reassessed and if all went well my ankle would be operated on. This operation, if successful, would give me a limited mobility but I had to wait the ten days.

This wait was a horrible time with the wound being treated twice a day. Elizabeth and Tracey visited me every day and this was a great relief and support. They prayed with me asking for healing and sure enough on the tenth day I was given the go ahead by my surgeon who was to operate immediately.

The operation was a success although I was now immobilized for at least six weeks. I was assured that I would be able to use my ankle eventually although it may be a little stiff on uneven ground.

After six weeks the plaster was removed and that was a great relief as all the old dead skin, that had been driving me crazy through itching, was removed. Another lighter plaster was placed below the knee and whilst I was still non weight bearing on this leg a pair of crutches was produced by a physiotherapist.

Things were looking up, as once I had mastered the challenge of using the crutches at least I would have some mobility. I could escape the ward and visit Bay View Restaurant and buy my ward mates egg and bacon sandwiches along with cake.

Of course it did not quite work out that way and first I had to learn to walk on crutches. This was soon done although there was one embarrassing incident when my attractive physiotherapist and I fell down a flight of stairs together whilst practising 'stair drills'. Fortunately, there were no injuries sustained although I was about to be discharged from hospital. It was decided that perhaps I should stay another week.

Elizabeth did not seem too upset with this decision as she reminded me that I was receiving one hundred pounds a day whilst in hospital from my accident insurance. I was also about to receive one hundred pounds a day for a six week recovery period once discharged from hospital so it only made sense to be sensible and not push things.

I was eventually discharged from Torbay Hospital in February 1995 after nine weeks. I was still in a plaster but after another twelve weeks that was removed and was replaced by a special boot and I was now 'weight bearing'. I had to be mobile now as with two friends, Robert and Jo, Liz and I had just purchased in partnership a 28-foot yacht named *Wild Oat*. Our partners Robert and Jo had been a great help and support getting everything sorted for the launch in April 1995.

It had been a difficult time, but I made a recovery. Elizabeth and Tracey visited me nearly every day I was in hospital and this was a tremendous support. I was partly mobile although two years later I had to have this ankle operated on again to have it arthredised, or strapped by bone to reduce movement that would cause pain.

My life had to be adjusted now that I was disabled and, sadly, I had to leave the TA as I was unable to walk let alone run any distance. However, I did have a distraction in the form of our yacht and with support from Elizabeth, Robert and Jo we sailed to the Channel Islands and the Isles of Scilly in that summer of 1995. I discovered that you do not need legs to sail with a good crew!

One particular sailing trip I remember was when I was sailing *Wild Oat* back from Falmouth single handed on a pleasant sunny afternoon in September 2001. The wind was favourable and the sea was reasonably calm and I was averaging 5 knots over the ground. It was good and I was listening to *Steve Wright In The Afternoon* on Radio 2. It was suddenly announced that there had been reports of a plane crashing into one of the twin towers in New York.

Following this it was then reported that another aircraft had crashed into the other twin tower and that it was beginning to look as if this was a serious terrorist attack on New York and that as soon as any further information was available it would be transmitted.

Slowly it became apparent that something serious was happening out there. It was as we now know it '9/11'. Later I dropped anchor in Plymouth at Cawsand Bay feeling confused and depressed. It was a sad and strange experience on one's own at sea during this time.

Chapter 45
Cut Wrist Artery and Hand - 2001

Readjusting my life was no problem and I soon learnt what I could do and delegated those farm jobs, which were now a struggle, to contractors. This actually made life a whole lot easier and gave me more time to pursue my love for the sea and sailing.

Jo was now running the riding business with Elizabeth and I and it was going well. I was 'managing the estate' as best as I could making the most of the agricultural capital grants for the farm buildings and land management that were available at that time.

One of the jobs on the farm that I was able to achieve was to carry and saw the house firewood that fed the three wood burning stoves that were our main source of heating.

Whilst sawing a load of wood for the house I stupidly decided to operate the chain saw with my right hand whilst holding the wood I was sawing with my left hand. I had attended a chain saw course and was well experienced in handling these machines. Whilst I was wearing the correct protective clothing I was fully aware this very action was dangerous but it saved time and energy and I had the strength to do it.

The result was that at full revs the chain saw (which had a new sharp chain on), inadvertently came down on my left hand rather than the wood I was holding. It cut through my protective glove, my left wrist and half my hand leaving a horrific gory mess.

The pain was outrageous, as this was a ripping wound rather than a cut and I saw blood spurting from my wrist onto a nearby wall. (This area is now known as 'bloody corner'.) My hand was hanging down being held onto my wrist by what appeared to be sinews and it was obvious that I had cut my artery due to the pressure of the blood that was throbbing out of me.

I realised that I was seriously injured and that every minute counted. It was essential that I should remain calm but the problem was should I dial 999 and hope that medics would arrive within the next fifteen minutes in this remote area, or try and get to hospital myself with Liz driving. I walked calmly over to the house and found Elizabeth and Tracey in the kitchen.

I opened the door and shouted for somebody to phone for an ambulance as I was suffering from an arterial cut to the wrist. I stayed outside as I did not wish to cover the house in blood and asked Liz to find a form of tourniquet and some old towels and rags so that I could try and staunch the flow of blood from my wrist. Elizabeth came out with some towels and a bandage that she was going to try and use as a tourniquet.

I noticed that whilst this was going on it had been fifteen minutes since the time of my accident and I seemed to remember from one of the first aid courses that I had attended, that with an arterial cut such as this it would take forty-five to sixty minutes before the loss of blood could cause complications. Tracey was trying to call an ambulance from the local hospitals but unbelievably despite emphasizing that she had a casualty with an arterial wound who was bleeding to death she was informed that as it was five 'o' clock the hospital was closed and that she should dial 999. I was already running out of time and I felt that my life was spurting away before me.

Elizabeth got me into the car with my bloodied arm sticking out of the passenger side window and drove me with all speed to Torbay Hospital. The traffic was at the normal rush hours, density but most drivers seemed to realize the seriousness of the situation making way for us. We somehow got to the hospital in forty minutes with Elizabeth keeping her cool and driving brilliantly with horn blaring and hazard lights on. Tracey had telephoned through to warn Accident and Emergency that I was about to arrive.

On arrival Elizabeth ran into A & E and two nurses came running out, one with a wheel chair, another with a tourniquet that she applied to my injured arm. I was now feeling quite dizzy and weak and as I left the car I noticed that the passenger's side of the car was completely covered in my blood. It was quite a sight.

I was rushed into a cubicle by the nurses where three doctors were waiting dressed in aprons and all were wearing protective glasses. One doctor released the tourniquet to test the fact that this was an arterial cut. It was confirmed that it was and the tourniquet reapplied. One of the doctors informed me that he was going to get a surgeon who was still in the hospital to look at my wound as he felt that she might operate immediately this evening.

It was not long before an attractive middle aged woman introduced herself to me as the surgeon and was assessing my injury. She was positive in what she had to do and would operate immediately. I recovered from my general anaesthetic at two 'o' clock the next morning feeling hungry. My injured hand was bandaged and held up beside me in a cradle.

A nursing sister asked how I felt and I told her that I was starving. Much to my surprise a plateful of sandwiches and a mug of tea was produced after which I felt good. In fact I went to sleep and awoke the next morning at breakfast time. The curtains were drawn around my bed and I heard a familiar female voice. It was that of my former nurse, Kay, when I was previously in this hospital with a broken ankle. She must have known that I had awoken as she assured me behind the curtain that it was not a nightmare and that once again she was to be my nurse.

With that she drew the curtains serving me my breakfast. As usual she was her normal cheerful self stating that this time it would only be a short stay of probably around five days, rather than months, depending on how my injury healed. She then produced a waterproof arm glove stating that she remembered that I enjoyed my morning shower and if I felt like it after breakfast she would prepare me for a shower to start the day right.

I completed that challenge without problem with Kay pleading with me not to slip or fall over. Shortly after I was visited by my surgeon who was pleased with what she had achieved. She informed me that the artery repair was no problem but stitching my left hand back together was an intricate operation. It had taken over two hours but she was confident that given time I would not notice the difference. She was correct and I am so grateful for this surgeon's effort and indeed her positive attitude that nothing was going to defeat her, and didn't.

After five days on my discharge from hospital I said farewell to Kay who had cared for me in her usual happy and positive way. My left lower arm was in a plaster for eight weeks and once that was removed I underwent physiotherapy. I made a full recovery and just about have full use of my left hand with only a scar to show for my adventure.

Following this accident I decided, much to the amusement of my friends, to study for a Health & Safety certificate and diploma. To everyone's surprise I attained the NEBOSH Health & Safety certificate with credit along with a NVQ level 6 diploma. I then went on to become a part time Health & Safety practitioner mainly instructing the subject.

Chapter 46

Tamar Bridge Collision - 2008

It was a lovely day so I slipped away early in the morning to my boat *Wild Oat* on her mooring at Hole's Hole, on the River Tamar with the intention of either turning left or right when I got to the Plymouth Breakwater depending on the wind and weather. I proceeded to motor the 8 miles down the river on a full spring ebb tide towards Plymouth. The weather was clear and sunny and having passed Weir Quay Boat Yard I raised my main sail as there was a gentle easterly breeze. I was doing about 5 knots plus the speed of the downriver current (the ebb tide).

I have owned this boat since 1995 (see Chapter 44), and have always kept her on this mooring so I knew the river and this area well. I was single handed on this trip and have proceeded up and down this river countless times as such. In fact I have many thousands of hours logged as a single handed skipper.

A course was steered on my auto helm to take me well clear to starboard of the main obstruction, being the central pillar of the Brunel Railway Bridge, (that was built in 1859). As I drew closer to the bridge I recall that I noticed a semi submerged obstruction (possibly a section of a tree trunk and it looked similar to a body), to my front so I altered course to port (left), to avoid this obstacle as I thought that I was well clear of the central pillar of the Brunel Bridge.

I was momentarily distracted by this semi-submerged object that I was watching now passing close to my starboard side, and in so doing it would appear that I had altered course towards the bridge pillar. The strong ebb tide, that I believe can run up to 3 knots in this location, must have carried me onto the bridge. I do not remember the point of impact and my next recollection was that I found myself sitting on the floor in the front of the cockpit looking towards the stern. The back of my head and my left side were painful and I was shocked and dazed but I could move. I noticed that the mast, the rigging and mainsail were above me in the cockpit, with the boom resting on the starboard, lifeline and the lower part of the mainsail was covering the majority of the cockpit. The motor was running and was still in gear, so I put it into neutral.

At this stage I did not know what I had hit so I cleared a space so that I could see outside the cockpit. It was obvious that I had struck the central pillar of the Brunel Railway Bridge and was now drifting downstream, mid river, clear of any immediate obstacles so had a bit of time to recover the situation. There were no other persons or property involved.

I next cleared the tiller of rigging so that I had full and free movement and then checked there were no loose lines in the water that could snag the prop. The mast was lying on the coach roof and the port pushpit with the top section, complete with sails in the water over the stern. The boom was resting on the starboard lifeline. It appeared that all lines were still secured to the mast.

Having put the motor in gear I turned into the current and found that I had normal control of the boat under motor. I then slowly proceeded upstream and as I passed close to the offending pillar (that is built of massive granite blocks at this level), I had a good look to see if there was any damage done to the stonework and was surprised to note that I could not see any marks.

Not far away I noted a free mooring buoy on the western (Cornish), side of the river and successfully picked this mooring up. I was now temporarily secured, so I checked the bilges to see if I was taking on water, which I was not, and then carried out a self assessment of my personal injuries, that were a swollen back of the head and painful ribs on my left hand side. I concluded that this was probably just bruising, possibly broken ribs.

I then checked the rest of the boat externally from the bows to the stern. From the damage I noticed, in my opinion, the boat had suffered a glancing blow with the central bridge pillar on the forward port hand side of the bow, thus removing the bow stem head, including the forestay plate hence the reason for the rearward collapse of the rig. However it appeared that the hull was undamaged and was not taking in water. I also checked the engine mounts and propeller shaft and all seemed O.K.

At this stage I contacted insurers to notify them and to ask for instructions as I wished to know whether to use any particular agencies. The response was a reply phone call from James Howe of the insurers who instructed me to seek assistance wherever I thought fit as they did not know this area. James was more concerned over my physical well being and I much appreciated this call that I found reassuring.

The next problem was to lift the mast and rig out of the water onto the coach roof. As I was considering this another single handed yachtsman on a 45 yacht on the next door mooring invited me alongside his yacht, pointing out that he had rigged up his spinnaker pole and fenders ready. He went on to state that it would be a 'pleasure to assist another single handed yachtsman'. I accepted this offer and prepared the boat, started the motor, slipped the mooring and went alongside as invited.

I attached some lines to the mast and we started to hoist the mast on the spinnaker pole. A Royal Naval RIB with two crew on board, which apparently was passing asked if they could be of any assistance suggesting that perhaps they could lift the section of the mast in the water and I accepted this offer. In a matter of minutes the mast, rigging and mainsail had been lifted out of the water and placed on the coach roof where it was secured and the mainsail removed. I thanked the Royal Navy for their assistance and they departed.

After some consideration I decided that I should approach the riggers I normally use, as I knew and trusted them, for the start of the recovery and repair. I discussed this with my friend who had assisted me thus far and appeared to be a very experienced yachtsman. He confirmed my decision stating that he also used these riggers, based at a marina in Plymouth known as Queen Anne's Battery (QAB). This would also solve the mooring problem as I had no stem head fittings required for a mooring.

The riggers were telephoned and I informed them of my predicament. They offered to send a recovery team to me which I declined stating that I could make my own way to QAB. I was informed that they would organize a birth at QAB for me and would meet me there on the pontoon if I could phone them some fifteen minutes prior to entering the marina.

Having informed my friend of what was planned I thanked him for his assistance and company. I offered some compensation which he refused stating that it was his pleasure to have helped me. I then slipped and motored down the river without incident to QAB where I was met by two riggers on the pontoon who assisted me in mooring up. With my consent they then removed my mast and rigging from the boat.

I confirmed the berth with the marina office and was informed that it would cost £26.40 a day. I was then collected by my brother who drove me home. I later discovered that I was concussed and had broken three ribs. It was very painful and it was confirmed through a bone scan that I had indeed broken three ribs on my left hand side following the diagnosis of prostate cancer. (See next chapter.)

Chapter 47

Late Diagnosis of Prostate Cancer - 2010-2013

Come 2010 I really was not feeling too good, being persistently fatigued and I seemed to be urinating many more times at night. This did not assist with my daily work within our partnership business and with the farming activities due to sleep deprivation. I thought that this was all part of growing old, but Elizabeth made me go and see the doctor.

I had a number of blood tests taken including a prostate specific antigen (PSA) check. On checking the results I was informed that all was well, which was surprising so I confirmed with Elizabeth that it was me just getting old.

The following year, 2011, my daughter Alona married Tom in May. The fourth (we have five girls) home wedding with around 150 guests invited resulting in elaborate planning mainly by Alona. A marquee was erected in the field next to the house and we were blessed with favourable weather. It was a great success and the following day was spent with the newly weds opening some of their wedding presents in the marquee before they departed for their honeymoon.

In 2012 I really was feeling very tired and I had lost weight, not to mention the fact that I was having problems urinating, especially at night, when I could be up anything up to ten times within an eight hour period. It got to such a degree that Elizabeth insisted that I should visit my doctor again, making the appointment accordingly.

My doctor this time not only took another PSA test, but examined me as he informed me that I was suffering classic prostatism symptoms. He found that I had an enlarged prostate but in his opinion he thought that this was a benign enlargement typical in a man of my age (sixty-four). The result of the PSA test would confirm any diagnosis.

I tried to discover what the result of the test was, but there appeared to be some confusion. I was told that if there was any problem I would be contacted. Also I had been informed by my doctor that in his opinion my enlarged prostate was benign so I thought nothing further of the matter and a drug was prescribed to improve the urinary symptoms.

At the beginning of 2013 I felt as if I was on my last legs. However, our first greatgrandchild, Thomas, was born to Jesse and Kelly, followed shortly after by our youngest grandchild, Jack, who was born to Tom and Alona. There was plenty of incentive to survive.

My doctor was away so I did actually see Elizabeth's doctor, upon her insistence. Having examined my records he seemed a little concerned and took another PSA test. If the results were found to be elevated it could indicate that there may be a possibility of prostate cancer.

That evening I received a telephone call from this doctor who informed me that there was a problem with the PSA test, which was elevated, and urgently required immediate further investigation. He had therefore, booked me in to see the local urologist consultant at Torbay Hospital, asking if I could telephone to confirm the appointment which I did.

Strangely I felt calm over this, taking the attitude that I had survived other life threatening incidents and this would be another survival. Not only that but 'what would be would be' and there is nothing to be gained by panicking as all action was being taken and I was impressed with that

Prostate biopsies were taken shortly after and I was told that I had a Gleason Score of 9 out of 10. This meant that I had an aggressive cancer and it was immediately recognized the prostate cancer was beyond the confines of local treatment as it was probable that it had spread.

The urinary consultant mentioned the fact that it appeared that I had two previous PSA tests taken in 2010 and 2012 and that they had been abnormal. He was asking whether or not any action had been taken as it seemed strange that there was nothing in the file over this. I responded by stating that I was not aware of this and asked for further details. I was shown my file with the details of the PSA tests that clearly showed the results that were 5.26 ng/ml in 2010 and 21 ng/ml in 2012. My consultant stated that these readings should have resulted in a referral.

Elizabeth and I felt sickened as we now began to realize that it was probable that a chance to fight this cancer back in 2010 had been missed. At that time there could be a possibility, with simple treatment, to expunge the disease and there was a chance that I would have been cured as confirmed by expert opinion. However, as I see it, due to what appeared to be admitted negligence by my GP of the time, the opportunity may have been missed.

I explained to Elizabeth there was nothing to be gained by feeling bitter and blaming others in this situation. I had to move forward positively and go for the treatment that would be available. She was supportive although understandably very upset over the matter.

I seemed to spend July 2013 in Torbay Hospital having tests carried out. One of them, a bone scan, made me radio active through a substance that was injected into my system. I was instructed to wear a yellow wrist band and I had to use a special toilet within the hospital. I was also warned that I should not try to go through airport security! However I soon discovered that I would also set off shop security systems and had to present my yellow wrist band to avoid being detained. I found this entertaining and I tested every shop within The Willows, the shopping complex next to Torbay Hospital. It soon became apparent that the store managers seemed quite conversant over this. I later learnt that my bone test was negative. However it was pointed out that I had broken three ribs on my left side recently and this of course was the Tamar Bridge yacht collision. (Chapter 46.)

I was immediately started on hormone therapy and I soon discovered that this did produce side effects such as fatigue, lack of sexual drive, hot flushes and feeling that doing anything required effort. It was depressing to start so I employed self denial and adopted a positive attitude. I had plenty to live for with such a wonderful family.

My PSA reading started to go down and in February 2014 I commenced a course of radiotherapy treatment consisting of 37 visits to Torbay Hospital. It was a tremendous service although again I did suffer side effects of loose stools, an increase in urinary tract symptoms, some lymph oedema and fatigue. It was not a pleasant experience.

However following this I was rewarded with very low PSA readings. Every three months I was to have a hormone injection and I have been placed on a PSA tracker system, whereby a PSA test is made at the same time as the hormone injection. At time of writing my PSA is below 0.14ng/ml which is proof that my cancer is now well suppressed.

I am grateful for all that has been done for me during this difficult time. It started with the immediate and honest action of the GP that noticed the problem. It was followed by the prompt action of the Torbay consultant and all those tests that came under the wing of the National Health Service. I could not have asked for a better service from the NHS practitioners and nurses who were always friendly and cheerful.

This is not to mention the support I received during those difficult early days. On diagnosis at the hospital I was approached by two prostate cancer support nurses who explained everything to Elizabeth and me. I was presented with my 'Patient Held Record Book', that I had seen the cancer support nurse presenting to another man before me. As I stated to her it was rather like being approached by 'The Grim Reaper' and being awarded your contract. She light-heartedly informed me that actually a well-known consultant within the hospital had stated exactly the same thing not long ago.

My family was also a great assistance remaining cheerful and supportive throughout the difficult time of accepting reality. My brother Simon introduced me to a judge who had suffered this cancer and after treatment was recovering. The girls remained cheerful and I stressed the fact that my PSA level was at a very low reading so I was now in full remission.

I also made use of Prostate UK making a number of telephone calls on their help line, that were always received with patience and understanding. In fact on one occasion I was actually phoned by a 'survivor' of prostate cancer who was a marathon runner. He was exuberant because not only was he managing to continue his running, but he had just started a 'hormone holiday' after three years. This was really reassuring for me and I looked forward to the time when I could reassure other men, which I could do after two years of recovery.

There was also 'The Lodge' that was a cancer support and information centre annexed to Torbay Hospital. Elizabeth and I visited when I was undergoing the radiotherapy and were surprised at everything that was offered there, including the complementary therapy. It was truly a wonderful experience that we both enjoyed and are so grateful to those wonderful volunteers.

It is supported by Macmillan, which is also very much there if required.

Overall it seemed a wonderful world of others who were out there caring about you. I certainly was not on my own and this gave me an inner strength. Thank you to all. However I was troubled over what I considered the reason why I was in this situation and that was because of, what I am under the impression is, a late diagnosis of cancer by my doctor of the time.

Consequently I wrote to him and asked why he had somehow managed to apparently overlook two of my abnormal PSA blood tests. Regretfully I did not hear back so I chased for a reply that eventually came, after eight months, in 2014. It was apologetic but no exact reason could be given. I decided after much thought that I would consider taking legal action against this doctor and the surgery. My main reason for this was to try and protect other men in the future and even in the past. Maybe a clinical negligence claim for a late or overlooked diagnosis, with the resulting consequence of the cancer progressing and spreading thus shortening the prognosis, could have an affect on GPs, some of whom may take more care. However it all looked as if this would be a non starter due to the expense and worry of carrying this action out.

I received excellent free legal advice from my local solicitor who explained that to proceed with a clinical negligence claim is not simple or cheap. Many obstacles have to be crossed before the claim can be lodged. She suggested that some household insurances would cover claims of this nature normally up a limit of £50,000.

It was emphasized that to succeed I would have to show, with the use of medical evidence, that the standard of care received fell below that of a reasonable body of practitioners and that as a consequence I suffered an injury.

I checked with my insurers and sure enough I was covered for this event by DAS Insurance. I was asked if I wished to take legal action and this I confirmed. Shortly after I was contacted by a firm of solicitors based in Cardiff who sent me various forms to complete and sign. This was followed by an opinion from an expert witness who was a consultant urological surgeon in London. He had studied my medical records and the evidence connected to my case. I was amazed at how much detail he obviously had at his disposal about me. It did not make good reading in connection with the prognosis. This was actually the first time any form of prognosis had been offered.

Strangely having instructed my lawyers in June 2014 the media suddenly started reporting that the Health Secretary, Jeremy Hunt, wanted to expose doctors whose failure to spot the initial signs of cancer may delay sending patients for life saving treatment. Following this I soon learnt, from what was being reported, that there were many cases similar to mine.

The expert witness was supportive of my claim from the start and following a Liability and Causation medical report I had to travel to London in February 2015 to have a Condition and Prognosis medical report drawn up on me by him. It was an interesting trip and the first time that I had travelled by train for a number of years. Ironically I was suffering from a lower urinary tract infection that spoilt it as I was not feeling too bright.

The conclusion of my expert witness was that if I had been referred in a timely fashion in 2010, my treatment would have been less and I would probably have been a candidate for radical surgery and I would certainly not now be on hormonal therapy and all its consequent side effects.

The claim against my former GP and the surgery was lodged in July 2015. I was informed by my solicitor that the other side, the defendants, had four months to respond. That response would either be admission of liability or denial. An admission response was entered and settlement for damages was made at the end of December 2016.

Chapter 48

Severe Heart Failure and Atrial Fibrillation - 2015

The summer of 2015 came and went. I was not feeling good and above all in July I started to loose the mobility in my left ankle. I could not walk on that side and had to revert to crutches to get anywhere. I was fortunate in as much as that I had spent two years on crutches when I had last broken my left ankle following the fall from the barn roof in 1995. I was, therefore, physically enabled with upper body strength to cope with everyday life, just about, and I was determined that it was not going to drag me down.

I was offered an ankle replacement operation on the NHS in November so things were looking up and I met Barry, a marine engineer, who had recently undergone this operation. He was encouraging, informing me that he could now do things that he could not before and the pain had been alleviated. He was once again walking on his bad ankle.

However in September I really was not feeling well. Fatigue and lethargy were my main complaints, along with a pain in my right side that was similar to a broken rib. I began to fear that the cancer was now beginning to kick in. I also started to suffer breathlessness similar to pneumonia or bronchitis and it got to a stage when I could not bear it any longer when I started to suffer another pain in my left side.

I made an immediate appointment with my surgery to see a doctor. An hour later I was seen by a nursing practitioner who examined me, concluding with an ECG. From this it was apparently obvious that I was suffering from atrial fibrillation but concern was expressed about the pain in my sides, that I thought was muscular skeletal caused by bronchitis. It was explained that these pains could well be clots, as there was a possibility of further heart complications that the surgery could not diagnose.

The surgery asked if I was on my own, could I get somebody to drive me into Torbay Hospital or else they could organise an ambulance. Strangely I did not understand the urgency of the situation until it was explained by one of the doctors. The pains in my sides could well be blood clots and if these found their way to my brain would probably be fatal. In other words, as I now understood it, I was a stroke waiting to happen.

Contact with the farm was eventually made and I asked for a lift into Torbay but time was pushing on. One of the doctors decided to phone for an ambulance and then my lift appeared and I was taken into hospital by Elizabeth and Alona. I had immediate blood tests, another ECG, x-rays and blood pressures taken under a cheerful junior doctor and a lovely Fijian nurse.

It was not long before I was told by a consultant that I was suffering atrial fibrillation and indeed further heart complications that could only be confirmed tomorrow by an echo cardiogram. I would have to stay in hospital and medication was started to prevent blood clotting and to settle my condition.

This caused a problem as Elizabeth and Alona were about to travel to the National Exhibition Centre, Birmingham. The Horse of the Year Show was taking place there and two Dartmoor ponies, that Elizabeth had bred, were competing. This was a great achievement for Elizabeth and it was important that she should attend this competition.

Elizabeth and Alona had every intention of staying back, but with encouragement from me and, indeed, my consultant, who had somehow got involved in the conversation, she was convinced to go. The consultant stated that I would be very well looked after and that there was nothing to worry about.

With that she decided to go and they departed. I suddenly felt rather lonely and unsupported but soon pulled myself together with the help of the doctor, Christian, who was very cheerful.

I was then admitted to the Emergency Assessment Unit number 3, (EAU 3), and was amazed at the activity within this ward with beds being wheeled in and out. I was the youngest in the ward at sixty-seven and my neighbour, a retired music teacher, had a bowel problem. He insisted on walking about the ward, without trousers on, and coming over to talk to me whilst I was lying on my bed. I noticed that he was constantly dribbling and it was concerning when two nurses having wheeled him out on his bed to an isolation room, then started to disinfect the general area within the ward including my bed and bed space.

I had started my medication including an unpleasant anticoagulant injection under the skin of the stomach in the evening. It was an uncomfortable night as I was not feeling too good and was breathless despite the efforts made by the nurses. There was constant movement and the lights were on most of the time. The nursing staff were great always asking if they could do anything and I was having constant blood pressure readings. As I had missed the evening meal this was organized by one of the nurses and I had a good meal.

It was good to see the dawn and daylight. I decided to get up at daybreak as it was so uncomfortable in bed. I hobbled around the ward on my crutches and had a shower making me feel a lot better. After breakfast I went for another wander around the hospital on my crutches, having signed out first.

On return I decided to sit by my bed and read the newspaper that I had purchased on my wanders. This was a good decision and I was actually asked to stay within my bed space by one of the nurses, as I was due some visitors. The visitations started with the ward's general consultant who informed me that I would shortly be undergoing an echo cardiogram and this would be followed up by various visits from the heart specialist team.

Following this a registrar appeared with the echo cardiogram equipment along with another junior doctor, who had not seen this done before. It was fascinating watching and listening to what they were saying about this scan. I could quite clearly see my heart pumping away on the screen. I asked if they could let me know if they found anything untoward or good and he replied by informing me that he would not be able to notice anything until the information gathered by this procedure had been placed on a computer. He would then be able to interpret the readings accordingly and this would take the best part of the morning.

Shortly after this, a cardiac practitioner appeared and explained to me what atrial fibrillation and heart failure was. I was beginning to feel a bit overloaded with information and even started to get concerned now. This apprehension was indeed answered, as my next visit was from the ward consultant who informed me of the results of the echo cardiogram. It was not good in as much as that I was actually suffering a severe heart failure with my heart producing from 15% to 20% of output when it should be around 50% to 80% for a man of my age. I was therefore diagnosed with two heart issues, a severe heart failure and atrial fibrillation. However, I was informed that with medication and possibly an external electrical cardioversion my condition could improve along with my prognosis.

My head was now spinning as it was becoming apparent that I was suffering heart problems. Would I be able to drive let alone walk about on the farm again?

My questions were soon answered by a cardiac consultant who explained everything and even produced some literature on the two conditions I was suffering from. Whilst it all sounded awful, it was not as bad as it could be, especially if I could sustain the proposed medication. Part of this treatment was the cardioversion electrocution defibrillation process that was explained to me, and actually from the way it was actually presented, things did not seem too bad. I was grateful for that consultation.

The night started to draw in. I was beginning to dread the nights as this was the time I suffered with breathlessness, fatigue and worry. I was on my own as Elizabeth and Alona were still in Birmingham at the NEC enjoying the Horse of the Year Show. However on my rambles around the ward I had found a small warm secluded room, titled the Relative's Room in which there were some arm chairs and a sofa. I made this my base away from that ward as it was so peaceful.

At about 19.30 a nurse stuck her head around the door and announced that my brother Simon had arrived to visit me. I was thrilled and it really was great to see him. He came bearing gifts of reading material, a radio and some chocolate. We went for a walk around the now quiet hospital discussing matters. He left at around ten O'clock and once again that veil of darkness started to close in on me.

I desperately wanted to sleep but just could not lie down. The nurses tried sitting me up in my bed but this did not work. I was actually visited by a young doctor, at 03.30 hrs who explained that I was suffering from paroxysmal nocturnal dyspneo or PND for short. This was all part of what I was suffering from and that nothing could be done about it apart from, perhaps, activity such as getting up and walking about. I explained that I really was suffering from sleep deprivation and she just held my hand to try and comfort me. It was hard and I then burst into tears. However I was resolute not to let this affect me and after the young doctor had left I got a grip and actually managed to get an hour of sleep before the morning ward activity.

That dawn was very welcome and again I got up, had my shower and hobbled about the ward. I was determined to fight this challenge and knew that I could defeat it. I was now working on the medical team for me to leave hospital as my brother was waiting to take me home. I was assured that further tests were needed and maybe after these I could go home but it would not be until after 17.00 hrs that day.

This sounded good to me so I telephoned my brother Simon to inform him and he stated that he would be coming in at around 16.00 hrs whatever happened and hopefully he would be taking me home that evening and cooking me dinner as Elizabeth would not be back until the following day. He would go to Waitrose to buy the food on the way.

Despite the fact I was feeling awful my spirits were now high. I visited my prostate support nurse, based at another location within the hospital. She was actually about to perform in a Macmillan nurse film shoot but found time to stop and talk to me which was great.

Later that afternoon I was told by the ward consultant that my pressures and tests were acceptable. He was prepared to let me go home with my brother, who was going to care for me and instructed a junior doctor, to organize my medication and visits.

I now began to understand why there had been hesitation in letting me out of hospital.

For a start I had to have an injection once a day in my stomach or thighs and a blood test every other day not to mention the administration of the copious drugs that I had to take. It was complicated and the young doctor spent over an hour working it all out.

Whilst I could self-administer the drugs, she was not sure whether I would be prepared to inject myself. If I was not, I would have to travel into Torbay Hospital once a day. The answer was obvious so I received tuition from my nurse on how to carry this task out. A week's worth of medication was prescribed along with appointments for me to visit the hospital for a number of blood tests. It was complicated but I was determined not to spend another night in that ward.

She responded by informing me that she understood how important it was for me to get away. She was amazed that I was prepared to inject myself as it was an unpleasant procedure. I was so grateful to this young doctor who did spend some time organizing everything for me. Above all there were no hitches and it all went well.

At 18.00 hrs I was cleared to leave the hospital. Simon had arrived at 16.00 hrs and we had killed time in The Bay View restaurant and walking about the hospital. We also read newspapers in the 'quiet room'.

As I departed I realized how grateful I was for the treatment I had received. Overall, throughout the three days I had spent in hospital with this disorder, I had been visited by 22 practitioners and the nursing was wonderful. Nothing was too much and all those that worked there seemed so cheerful despite the pressure of the present hospital life. I discovered one particular radiographer had been on shift for seventeen hours. When I asked how she coped she responded that she just loved her job. I was also informed by one of the junior doctors that they were doing shifts from 08.00hrs to 22.00hrs, (fourteen hours). This apparently was all part of the course but they did find it hard. It was obvious to me that there was pressure on those that worked in this profession and that caring for others was their prime objective. I could not recommend this ward, hospital and those that work there more highly.

Simon drove me home in his comfortable BMW series three X type and then cooked me supper. Elizabeth and Alona were not due back from Birmingham until the following evening and I was looking forward to seeing them again. It was during this evening that I decided that I was going to give up alcohol which meant that Simon could have the bottle of wine. He organized a pill box with the daily routine written out that I still use to take my nine pills a day, morning, mid day and in the evening. I also had to inject myself in the stomach once a day. I had been warned that it was essential to keep this dosage correct.

I decided that I would sleep on the sitting room sofa beside the fire sitting up in front of TV. I normally slept in that position before going to bed anyway. Simon was concerned about me as I snuggled down, to hopefully, a quiet night. It was as before with that breathlessness verging on gasping for breath at stages, However there were times when I could relax in the peace and quiet and sleep came and went.

I slept like this for the next five nights with my condition gradually improving as the medication started to relieve the situation. Simon left me the following day at about tea time having painted the view we have of the moor from the house. He is a good artist who is beginning to succeed in the Cornwall area selling a number of paintings and gaining commissions.

It was thrilling to see Elizabeth and Alona when they returned in the evening. They had a good trip and Elizabeth's ponies, now belonging to new owners who had purchased them, had done well in the competition which was satisfying. After supper I settled down on the sofa and slept reasonably well now Elizabeth was back.

After five days I had an afternoon rest on a bed and slept well following a physical morning. I decided that I would now try sleeping the night on a bed again. I built the head side of the mattress up with blankets and placed blocks of wood under the feet of the bed so that I was lying with my head and chest raised. I was rewarded with some eight hours sleep. Above all, when I got out of bed in the morning the pain in my left ankle was not there. I could walk again without the aid of crutches.

This was thrilling and I tried walking the 100 metres out to the yard without crutches or stick. There was no problem and I even started thinking about walking up our hill. This was nothing short of a miracle and I thanked the good Lord. I also noticed that my nocturia (getting up at night to urinate), had reduced from around eight visits to the toilet to just two calls. I was now sleeping well and whilst I still had the shadow of prostate cancer and heart failure over me, regaining my mobility and being able to sleep again overrode everything.

The medics informed me that I could carry out physical tasks as long as I did not overdo it. In fact I should not just lie in bed or sit in a chair. I had to exercise my heart and remember that it was a muscle.

It was soon apparent that I could enjoy gardening and digging ditches. I could walk small distances and got to the bottom of our hill without feeling breathless or limp. Life had improved and the next challenge was to ensure that the anti coagulant tablets I was taking (Warfarin) were producing the correct International Normalised Ratio (INR) in my blood to prevent blood clots. This was done through blood testing at regular weekly intervals in my surgery.

It was not long before this correct INR was established over four weeks which could mean that I would be eligible for external cardioversion, subject to further pre procedure tests. I telephoned the right department at Torbay Hospital and informed them of my readings. Much to my surprise they knew who I was and booked me in for the cardioversion in two weeks time. The day before this procedure various tests and an ECG had to be taken and I was reassured that it would be a 'nurse led' process. The procedure is for a brief general anesthetic and if all went well with the defibrillation the patient would be able to walk out of the hospital with a normally beating heart later that day probably in the afternoon if not sooner.

Time was fast approaching and I was looking forward to returning to the normal world of proper heart beats. I was warned that there could be a possibility that I may not get my heart efficiency back again but time would tell.

The two arrhythmic nurse specialists that I saw, were great. I was soon put at ease and filled me with confidence. Their positive and cheerful attitude dispelled any anxiety over the procedure as with the other patients. I left almost looking forward to this 'electrocution'!

Chapter 49
The Cardioversion - 2015

Elizabeth, Alona and I arrived at the correct section of Torbay Hospital at 08.45 hrs. We found that there were four other patients with their supporters also waiting for their cardioversion. Not unnaturally there was a tense atmosphere and there were no chairs left. One lady stood up offering her seat to me as 'a patient' with a smile and a man offered his to Elizabeth. Alona had to stand. The twelve of us then sat in silence for the next fifteen minutes waiting for the next move. This came in the form of a cheerful arrhythmia specialist nurse, who asked the only lady in first as she was a 'lady'.

I suggested that Alona and Elizabeth could go shopping now as we were about to be called in. There was nothing further for them to do and that I would meet them sometime around lunchtime. They hesitantly left having bid me farewell and I suddenly felt rather lonely.

We continued to wait and then the specialist nurse reappeared after some thirty minutes carrying a mug of tea and a plate of toast for the first lady. We had been told that we would get that if we wanted it after the procedure. I blurted out that at least the lady had survived and then we were asked in one by one. There was another male patient, before me.

I was met by a nurse practitioner, who was going to 'do' me and once again following her briefing yesterday, I felt relaxed and confident. I was introduced to my friendly anaesthetists, David, and a tall Russian doctor who gave me a firm handshake.

After more questions and correct answers the electrodes were stuck onto my upper body by my nurse. I had visions of my body heaving away under the electric shock as you see in the films when defibrillation is undergone. I was then anaesthetized and slipped gently away with, as the nurse described, too many gin and tonics with the ceiling starting to spin! Apparently I took my time to become fully sedated as I was singing what was described as 'a sea shanty', which they all enjoyed. I was unaware that I was doing this and do not know any 'sea shanties' so no doubt it was something else.

I was woken shortly after and was informed that I had been defibrillated without problem first time. It all looked good although after the procedure I did feel a little groggy. I was asked if I would like my tea and toast and this appeared some five minutes later.

The other patient and I got up after some thirty minutes and dressed. The other patient was informed that he had used up a lot of electricity as he had to be shocked twice but everything was fine now. We were asked to wait outside where we compared notes. We discovered through one of the specialist nurses that a heart ECG monitor (that could be attached to a smart phone), was available for purchase on Amazon.

She then produced one and we played around with it. Following that we were discharged having had needles removed from us and being issued with the paperwork. We walked out of hospital at 11.00 hrs feeling a little groggy but fine. We were instructed to rest for twenty-four hours and not drive, do anything strenuous or make any legal decisions. I do not know how the others did but my friend and I once again had a proper heart beat.

I wish to thank the arrhythmia team at Torbay Hospital. I did not have to wait long for my cardioversion that I hope and think will make all the difference. The treatment was, in my opinion, superb and above all, as a patient, I felt confident in the doctors and nurses supported by the ever present cheerfulness. What could be thought as a frightening procedure was confidently turned into what I consider an almost enjoyable experience where the patient was fully informed. In my opinion in this case 'knowledge does dispel fear'.

During the next two days I began to feel really fatigued and rather strange. I checked my blood pressure, on a device that Elizabeth had purchased from the chemist, and noticed that not only was my blood pressure low but so was my pulse, that was around forty beats per minute at rest.

I telephoned my 'heart specialist' nurse, and she asked me into hospital for a check up. It was confirmed that my cardioversion had relapsed and once again I was in atrial fibrillation (AF). I was informed that I could have another cardioversion but it was decided by the cardiac consultant that medication should be increased, as it may be the condition of my heart that was causing the problem.

The following week I had an appointment with the arrhythmia team who had carried out the cardioversion. They also confirmed that my cardioversion had relapsed but the good news was that my AF was not as bad as before. This was followed up with two more appointments with my heart consultant and another echocardiogram, which showed that my condition had not improved, which was disappointing although functional improvement was noted.

Chapter 50
Dealing with Cancer and my Heart Problems - 2016

With the settlement of the clinical negligence claim (see Chapter 47), I felt that time had come to write this my final chapter. With the summer oncoming and life continuing the question soon arrived over whether I should go on sailing my 28ft yacht, especially single handed. Would I be fit enough and capable to carry out the normal sailing tasks such as rowing out to the mooring, climbing aboard, setting the sails, dropping and raising the anchor and so on. I decided to try it out and if it was too much obviously I would have to think again.

My family was not too keen and my brother Simon, whose mooring I was using with my boat, promised me support with getting the inflatable dinghy to the water so all I would have to do would be to row out to the boat. He and his wife, Sarah, always kept an eye on me until I had slipped the mooring and was out of sight.

My medical heart support team were surprised at what I was attempting both on the water and on the farm and to my pleasant surprise seemed to understand. Whilst they did not approve of this it was appreciated that this was my life which they did not wish to interfere with, although I was warned over what could happen if I overdid it.

To start with my condition was not too bad and I could deal with the breathlessness that those with heart failure often suffer. It was a case of resting when you had to and then continuing which was no particular problem. I found that I had no difficulty to row out, get on the boat, prepare for sailing and then slip the mooring. In the right conditions I could sail out of the River Tamar and out to sea. It was great. To start with I managed to sail to my old haunts around the South coast some distance away despite my tiredness, managing to cat nap on the way!

It was not long before my condition started to deteriorate with any physical task being met with breathlessness and sometimes dizziness. I was also suffering fatigue and sleep loss, worse than that experienced by my cancer hormone treatment, which I thought was bad enough. This brought on depression and I was determined not to offload onto family or friends as I did not wish to upset them. I decided to speak to my support nurse about my depression and she informed me that this was part of heart failure. Also amongst other things it was suggested 'that I was my own worst enemy' and was encouraged to talk to someone other than her and this made sense, or did it?

The 'children' (the youngest aged thirty-nine), still look upon me as the patriarch of the family and my wife has been recently diagnosed with Parkinson's disease so I was at this time very much needed! I felt that I could not approach them, as after all, I was not really 'a nice person' with my morbid life-threatening problems, despite recent good test results. I left it under the impression that I had recovered, as I was informed by my heart support nurse that my tests showed that I was 'clinically sound' and stable.

However I did heed the advice that was being offered and informed one of my daughters of my plight. She was visibly shocked as she had no idea and I felt so guilty. Following this I knew that I had to keep things to myself and the practitioners for the time being.

My heart failure support nurse has listened, supported and cared for me. She explained the various situations and did not seem to object when I offloaded. However she continued to emphasize the fact that she would not be able to do this on her own and encouraged me to find other supporters, such as my GP.

The cardiac consultant encouraged me to seek information and to be proactive. This information I found invaluable although at times it made dismal reading. In fact by doing this I discovered that my cardiac support nurse had recently written a case study in a medical publication, which I found interesting!

One aspect of this support that occurred to me was that of the personal relationship that should be between patient and the specialist nurse. Whilst psychological assistance is available how close can the patient get to the practitioner? Is there a mutual respect? Does the nurse really care? Are you the patient, just a number? How many other patients are being cared for? How far can the patient go in offloading? Can you really trust your support nurse and will they keep the information you give them confidential? These were some questions that I asked myself as a former Samaritan.

In my opinion, these specialist nurse practitioners are exceptionally professional individuals who seem to enjoy a clinical autonomy and could be seen as taking on the role of the junior doctor. As I see it their patients are on a one way ticket, duration unknown, with little hope of recovery, so how these specialists deal with that is beyond me. I am very grateful to my support nurses, complete with their teams. I think that I have now reached the stage of acceptance in my three life threatening disorders and I am enjoying life.

I have experienced a wonderful service from my heart support nurse through a number of hospital appointments and telephone calls and it would seem that at present, despite everything, I appear to be improving in my cancer and I am determined not to die of atrial fibrillation or heart failure.

Life has continued on the farm and at home. I was beginning to find the fatigue that I was suffering, an obstacle as I seemed to spend a lot of my time sleeping and resting and those little jobs that I should be doing were ignored. However there were two big events that really kept Elizabeth and me going. Alona our youngest daughter was due to give birth at the end of May or beginning of June and at the same time number two daughter, Claire and her husband Ross, who are farmers in New Zealand, were visiting us. It was actually all quite exciting.

At the beginning of June we became grandparents to number ten grandchild, a granddaughter, along with Claire and Ross arriving. It was almost too much and I realized how fortunate I was to have such a wonderful family and to be living in an exceptionally beautiful environment on Dartmoor.

It was a happy summer and Claire insisted that we should take a take a holiday cottage for a week in Cornwall. It was a good week which included a family gathering on Alona's birthday. I now felt strong enough to start facing the medical negligence claim (see Chapter 47), and started pushing through my solicitor for a reaction from the defendant, my former GP, as it seemed to be some time since there had been any action.

To my surprise medical negligence was admitted by this GP but his insurers contested causation. I received an expert opinion from the defendant's lawyers which seemed to argue the fact that my cancer was so aggressive nothing at any stage of this affliction would have altered the outcome. In other words from the start there was no cure to this grade of cancer. Furthermore the opinion went on to give me an estimated 'cancer specific survival' expectancy of up to 2020 - 2022 accordingly.

In addition at this time I found a headline on the British Heart Foundation heart failure web site. It read *'For patients diagnosed with severe heart failure the chances of surviving more than five years are worse than most forms of cancer.'*

All this really did make depressing reading and I confess to offloading onto my heart support nurse who responded in her normal level sensible way pleading with me to also consult with my GP, which I did. This filled me with the fighting feeling and I responded to my lawyer claiming that this expert opinion was nothing but supposition, statistics and that every patient is different.

Shortly after this I received an e-mail from my lawyer stating that he had just taken a phone call from lawyers representing insurers in this medical negligence case making a non negotiable offer of settlement in full and final settlement of my claim.

This was a relief as I was expecting this claim to go on for at least another year and really it had all started in 2013 and it was now the end of 2016. I conferred with my family who were keen to settle and I asked my solicitor if he could advise over the quantum. After some research he advised that it could be possible to gain more than was being offered but it could end up in Court. This in his opinion was fraught with risk not to mention the delay.

The decision seemed straightforward and much to the relief of Elizabeth and the family I accepted the offer as it stood. I was pleased to hear that my solicitor also agreed with the decision. This was confirmed in a pleasant letter from my solicitor that also stated that I had been one of his favourite clients over the last twenty-nine years of his career. This made pleasant reading!

I am fully aware of my prognosis and cannot emphasis the value of the nurse specialists more. The support teams have enabled me to live an almost normal life at present even with the diagnosis of the three life threatening medical disorders that I currently suffer. Time will tell and life is uncertain but that is the same for all of us. One thing for sure, I will always live for the day and I am grateful for all that has been done so far and I am a fighter and survivor.

Conclusion - 2016

In this biography I have written about the challenging parts of my life. It does not include all incidents or the happy periods that I have also enjoyed in abundance throughout and there lies another story. As my brother Simon has stated it is quite likely that there will be further chapters to add, but I wish to take time now to relax and reflect. It is obvious that for me to have survived thus far is a noteworthy act of achievement.

There were times which I experienced that I would not wish on any individual but as things evolved my life has worked out well. Without doubt in my mind the most important part was meeting my wife, Elizabeth and her four daughters, Nikki, Claire, Tracey and Jo. (Chapter 37.)

I feel that from this moment my life changed course. Together we succeeded being able to hand over the main responsibilities of the business and farm to our youngest daughter Alona and her husband Tom. This to me is an achievement as a success is empty without successors. It is also rewarding to watch the girls thrive and to see their children mature not to mention the great grand children!

The winter of my life has now passed and I look forward to the spring and summer to watch things develop in the future. It is wonderful to observe Alona and Tom striving effectively forward with the business and farm that Elizabeth and I have successfully worked and loved for a great number of years.

I also believe in the power of prayer. I have been informed a number of times from varying friends 'you reap what you speak and think'. I am fortunate in that I will never give up and when I believe in something I do so with passion. My mother and also my wife have often informed me that I am obstinate. However I believe that used in the correct way this can be a great strength.

A lesson that I soon learnt in life was that dishonesty will always be detected. It may be an immediate discovery or take a number of years perhaps even surfacing after death. Invariably, in my opinion, this will bring about sadness and destruction and should be avoided at all costs.

Well, time 'To get a move on', as many have heard me say, and to finish this manuscript. My message in life would be to never give up and to adhere to one's capabilities. Remember there is no such word as 'can't' and that if you remove that last letter you will get the correct word!

Rod Newbolt-Young
December 2016.